Migration, Minorities and Citizenship

General Editors: **Zig Layton-Henry**, Professor of Politics, University of Warwick; and **Danièle Joly**, Director, Centre for Research in Ethnic Relations, University of Warwick

Titles include:

Muhammad Anwar, Patrick Roach and Ranjit Sondhi (*editors*)
FROM LEGISLATION TO INTEGRATION?
Race Relations in Britain

Sophie Body-Gendrot and Marco Martiniello (*editors*)
MINORITIES IN EUROPEAN CITIES
The Dynamics of Social Integration and Social Exclusion at the
Neighbourhood Level

Naomi Carmon (*editor*)
IMMIGRATION AND INTEGRATION IN POST-INDUSTRIAL SOCIETIES
Theoretical Analysis and Policy-Related Research

Adrian Favell
PHILOSOPHIES OF INTEGRATION
Immigration and the Idea of Citizenship in France and Britain

Simon Holdaway and Anne-Marie Barron
RESIGNERS? THE EXPERIENCE OF BLACK AND ASIAN POLICE OFFICERS

Danièle Joly
HAVEN OR HELL?
Asylum Policies and Refugees in Europe
SCAPEGOATS AND SOCIAL ACTORS
The Exclusion and Integration of Minorities in Western and Eastern Europe

Jørgen S. Nielsen
TOWARDS A EUROPEAN ISLAM

Jan Rath (*editor*)
IMMIGRANT BUSINESSES
The Economic, Political and Social Environment

John Rex
ETHNIC MINORITIES IN THE MODERN NATION STATE
Working Papers in the Theory of Multiculturalism and Political Integration

Carl-Ulrik Schierup (*editor*)
SCRAMBLE FOR THE BALKANS
Nationalism, Globalism and the Political Economy of Reconstruction

Steven Vertovec and Ceri Peach (*editors*)
ISLAM IN EUROPE
The Politics of Religion and Community

Östen Wahlbeck
KURDISH DIASPORAS
A Comparative Study of Kurdish Refugee Communities

John Wrench, Andrea Rea and Nouria Ouali (*editors*)
MIGRANTS, ETHNIC MINORITIES AND THE LABOUR MARKET
Integration and Exclusion in Europe

Migration, Minorities and Citizenship
Series Standing Order ISBN 0–333–71047–9
(*outside North America only*)

You can receive future titles in this series as they are published by placing a standing order. Please contact your bookseller or, in case of difficulty, write to us at the address below with your name and address, the title of the series and the ISBN quoted above.

Customer Services Department, Macmillan Distribution Ltd, Houndmills, Basingstoke, Hampshire RG21 6XS, England

Immigrant Businesses

The Economic, Political and Social Environment

Edited by

Jan Rath
Senior Researcher and Programme Manager
Institute for Migration and Ethnic Studies
University of Amsterdam
The Netherlands

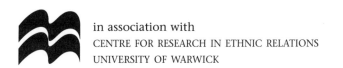

in association with
CENTRE FOR RESEARCH IN ETHNIC RELATIONS
UNIVERSITY OF WARWICK

First published in Great Britain 2000 by
MACMILLAN PRESS LTD
Houndmills, Basingstoke, Hampshire RG21 6XS and London
Companies and representatives throughout the world

A catalogue record for this book is available from the British Library.

ISBN 0–333–68314–5

 First published in the United States of America 2000 by
ST. MARTIN'S PRESS, INC.,
Scholarly and Reference Division,
175 Fifth Avenue, New York, N.Y. 10010

ISBN 0–312–22775–2

Library of Congress Cataloging-in-Publication Data
Immigrant businesses : the economic, political and social environment /
edited by Jan Rath.
  p.   cm. — (Migration, minorities and citizenship)
Selected papers from a workshop, held in Sept. 1995 at the
University of Amsterdam...complemented with a number of papers by
other authors who were invited to contribute. (Preface)
"[Published] in association with Centre for Research in Ethnic
Relations, University of Warwick."
Includes bibliographical references and index.
ISBN 0–312–22775–2 (cloth)
1. Minority business enterprises Congresses.   2. Immigrants–
–Employment Congresses.   3. Informal sector (Economics) Congresses.
4. Minority business enterprises—Finance Congresses.   5. Ethnic
groups—Economic aspects Congresses.   6. Entrepreneurship
Congresses.   I. Rath, Jan, 1956–   . II. Centre for Research in
Ethnic Relations (Economic and Social Research Council)
III. Series.
HD2344.I46   1999
338.6'422—dc21   99–41120
                                                                CIP

Selection, editorial matter and Introduction © Jan Rath 2000
Chapters 1 – 10 © Macmillan Press Ltd 2000

This book is printed on paper suitable for recycling and made from fully managed and sustained
forest sources.

10   9   8   7   6   5   4   3   2   1
09   08   07   06   05   04   03   02   01   00

Printed and bound in Great Britain by Antony Rowe Ltd, Chippenham, Wiltshire

For Marlein and Wies

Contents

Preface

This book emerged from a research programme at the Institute for Migration and Ethnic Studies (IMES), University of Amsterdam, the Netherlands. The objective of this programme is to describe, analyse and explain the social and economic transformations that cities in advanced economies are currently undergoing and their impact on the socioeconomic incorporation of immigrants, in particular their self-employment. One project in this programme focuses on immigrant businesses in manufacturing. The central research covers such topics as changes in the international division of labour and their impact on the location of production sites, the institutional framework and its political environment, the management strategies of entrepreneurs, labour relations and so on. As these topics indicate, the programme crosses disciplinary boundaries as it combines the insights of economics, sociology, cultural anthropology, political science, geography and law.

Since its establishment in 1994 the IMES has endeavoured to carry out interdisciplinary research, since it believes that such research is most rewarding. A seemingly simple topic such as immigrant businesses can be examined more fruitfully by employing numerous angles, leading to more meaningful results when combined with deliberation. This admittedly is a truism, but one cannot find many instances of broad interdisciplinary research. It is obvious that many academic practitioners find it extremely difficult to step beyond their disciplinary boundaries. In order to promote the crossing of disciplinary boundaries and explore the possibility of a broad and theoretically grounded research programme of immigrant businesses, an international workshop was held in September 1995 at the University of Amsterdam. Experts from Europe and the United States, each representing different scientific disciplines, took part in this scientific journey to bridge the gap between the various disciplinary boundaries.

This book evolved out of this undertaking. It contains a selection of the papers presented at the workshop and a number of papers by other authors who were invited to contribute. The contributors have backgrounds in economics, sociology, cultural anthropology, political science, geography and history. Their contributions serve two aims: to present a pronounced theoretical position on the topic of immigrant businesses, and to contribute to an interdisciplinary research programme. Of course, since it is neither possible nor desirable to straitjacket the authors or to ignore theoretical debates, the book as a whole does not represent a single theoretical view. The authors do, however, show an interest in the advancement of theory and interdisciplinary research.

It goes without saying that this book is not the product of a single person, even though there is only one name on the cover. My deep appreciation goes to the organisations that supported our work on immigrant businesses and helped make this book possible: the Committee for Social Oriented Research (CMO), the Netherlands Organisation for Scientific Research (NWO/ISW), the Amsterdam Municipality, the Royal Dutch Academy of Sciences (KNAW) and the Institute for Migration and Ethnic Studies (IMES) at the University of Amsterdam. I owe a special debt to those academic colleagues who have given me help and support, in particular Marja Dreef, Robert Kloosterman, Adem Kumcu, Ivan Light, Rinus Penninx, Stephan Raes and Flavia Reil. My thanks also go to Frans Lelie, Cathelijne Pool, Sanna Ravestein-Willis and Heleen Ronden, who provided technical support in the editing process.

Amsterdam/Rotterdam JAN RATH

Notes on the Contributors

Mae Baker is Lecturer in Accounting and Finance at the Leeds University Business School. She obtained her PhD from the University of Leeds in 1994 and is currently engaged in researching and publishing on issues relating to accounting and the history of education, the relationships between the financial markets and institutional investors and employment relations in the contract clothing industry. She has extensive teaching experience, both in Europe and the Far East.

Giles Barrett is Lecturer in Human Geography and Urban Studies at Liverpool John Moores University, England. He is a graduate of the former Liverpool Polytechnic and has previously worked at Liverpool University. With David McEvoy and Trevor Jones, he is coauthor of a number of published papers on ethnic minority business, including a recent review of theoretical discourses on ethnic minority enterprise for the journal *Urban Studies*. He has recently completed his doctoral thesis, which focuses on various aspects of African-Caribbean and South Asian small businesses in England, such as the political economy of black enterprise, sources of start-up finance for the new firm and black women in business.

Bert Bulder is Assistant Professor of Sociology at the Department of Sociology, Utrecht University, the Netherlands. He studied sociology at the University of Groningen and is currently writing a PhD dissertation on the effects of public-sector reforms in the Netherlands.

Henk Flap is Associate Professor of Sociology at the Department of Sociology and fellow of the ICS-Research school, Utrecht University, the Netherlands. He studied sociology at the University of Groningen and received his PhD from Utrecht University. Previously, he was a fellow of the Netherlands Institute of Advanced Studies at Wassenaar, the Netherlands, and visiting professor of sociology at Columbia University, New York. He is coauthor of a textbook on sociology, *Sociology: Questions, Propositions, Findings* (1996). His research interests include networks studies, labour market research and organisational sociology. His articles have appeared in *Kölner Zeitschrift für Soziologie und Sozialpsychologie, Social Forces, Social Networks, Social Science and Medicine, Revue Française de Sociologie,* and *L'Année de Sociologie*.

Gary P. Freeman is Professor of Government at the University of Texas and Director of the Public Policy Clinic. Among his recent publications are 'Modes of immigration politics in liberal democratic states', (*International Migration Review*, 1995); 'Mass politics and the immigration agenda in liberal democracies' (*International Political Science Review*, forthcoming); 'Mexico and world-wide US immigration policy', in Frank Bean *et al.* (eds), *At the Crossroads: Mexico and US Immigration Policy*, and 'The quest for skill: A comparative analysis', in Myron Weiner and Ann Bernstein (eds), *Migration and Refugee Policies: The International Experience and its Relevance to South Africa* (forthcoming).

Trevor P. Jones is Reader in Social Geography at Liverpool John Moores University. He studied at the London School of Economics and worked previously at Huddersfield Polytechnic. His collaboration with David McEvoy and others on ethnic minority business and ethnic segregation has produced papers in *Area, Annals of the Association of American Geographers, New Community, New Society, Social Forces, Sociological Review, Revue Européenne des Migrations Internationales, New Economy* and *Urban Studies*. His essays have also been included in numerous books. He was senior author of *Geographical Issues in Western Europe* (1988) and *Social Geography* (1989).

Kevin Keasey is Director of the Financial Services Research Centre and the Leeds Permanent Building Society, and Professor of Financial Services at the University of Leeds. He has studied at the universities of Durham (BA) and Newcastle (MA and PhD) and held academic posts at Newcastle, Nottingham and Warwick prior to going to Leeds in 1990. He has published widely in a variety of prestigious academic journals on economic and financial accounting issues, particularly in the areas of decision making under uncertainty, the financing of small and medium-sized enterprises and corporate governance.

Ronald van Kempen is Associate Professor of Urban Geography at the Urban Research Centre, Faculty of Geographical Sciences, Utrecht University, the Netherlands. He obtained his PhD in 1992. His research activities are mainly focused on social exclusion, housing for low-income groups, neighbourhood developments and the segregation of ethnic minorities. He is coeditor of *Turks in European Cities: Housing and Urban Segregation* (1997), and of two volumes about high-rise housing in Europe and spatial segregation in post-Fordist cities all over the world. He is one of the coordinators of a European Network for Housing working group on immigrant housing and is currently chairperson of the editorial board of the *Netherlands Journal of Housing and the Built Environment*.

Robert Kloosterman is Senior Researcher at the OTB Research Institute for Housing, Urban and Mobility Studies, Delft University of Technology. His main areas of research interest are urban economies and urban labour markets, welfare states, entrepreneurship and popular music. He has published in *Popular Music, Urban Studies, West European Politics, Regional Studies, Area* and *New Community*. He is coeditor of a book on immigrant entrepreneurship in the Netherlands (1998). He and Jan Rath are cofounders of an International Network on Immigrant Entrepreneurship.

Adam Kumcu studied sociology at Utrecht University and is currently writing his PhD thesis at the University of Amsterdam. His subject is management strategies of Turkish contractors in Amsterdam. He is also involved in the Centrum voor Expertise over het Ondernemerschap (CEO) to provide training and advice to immigrant entrepreneurs.

Ivan Light earned a bachelor's degree in history from Harvard University and a PhD in sociology from the University of California, Berkeley. He is Professor of Sociology at the University of California, Los Angeles. He pioneered the sociological study of entrepreneurship, especially the entrepreneurship of immigrants and ethnic minorities. His first book on this subject was *Ethnic Enterprise in America* (1972). *Immigrant Entrepreneurs* (1988) is a case study of Korean immigrant entrepreneurs in Los Angeles from 1965–1982. His *Immigration and Entrepreneurship* (1993) is an edited book with contributed articles on this topic from France, Britain, Israel and the United States. His most recent book is *Race, Ethnicity, and Entrepreneurship in Urban America* (1995). This book uses census data to examine the entrepreneurship of whites, blacks, Asians and Hispanics in 272 metropolitan areas of the United States.

David McEvoy is Director of the School of Social Science and Professor of Urban Geography at Liverpool John Moores University. He is a graduate of Manchester University and previously worked at Sheffield University, Durham University and North East London Polytechnic. His research on ethnic minority residence and ethnic minority business in Britain and Canada stretches over 20 years. His collaboration with

Trevor P. Jones and others, including Giles A. Barrett, has been funded by the Social Science Research Council (SSRC) (UK), the Economic and Social Research Council (UK), the Commission for Racial Equality (UK) and the Canadian High Commission in London. He was awarded the TIEM Canada prize for best paper at the 32nd World Conference of the International Council for Small Businesses.

Nedim Ögelman holds an MALD from the Fletcher School and is pursuing a doctorate in political science at the University of Texas, Austin. His previous publications include 'Recent developments in East-West migration. Turkey and the petty traders' (*International Migration*, with Cengiz Aktar, 1994), and 'Ethnicity, demography and migration in the evolution of the Polish nation-state' (*The Polish Review*, 1995). He received a Fullbright Fellowship in 1991 to study Turkish immigrant politics in Berlin. A German Federal Chancellor's Scholarship through the Alexander Von Humboldt Foundation in 1996–97 enabled him to research political and organisational developments in the Turkish community of the Federal Republic of Germany.

Stephan Raes read European Studies at the University of Amsterdam, the Netherlands. He undertook field research in Egypt on the development of Egyptian textiles and the Egyptian clothing industry. He taught the political economy of the Mediterranean and the Middle East at the Catholic University of Nijmegen. He was also involved in studies at the Department of Political Science and the Institute of Migration and Ethnic Studies, both at the University of Amsterdam, on the position of immigrant sweatshops in Amsterdam in the changing international division of labour in the clothing industry. He is now at the Dutch Ministry of Economic Affairs.

Jan Rath received his MA degree in cultural anthropology and urban studies and a PhD from Utrecht University, and has also been active in political science, the sociology of law, economics and economic sociology. He previously held academic posts at the University of Leiden, Utrecht University and the Catholic University of Nijmegen, and is now Senior Researcher and Project Manager at the interfaculty Institute for Migration and Ethnic Studies (IMES) at the University of Amsterdam. He is the founding and managing editor of the Dutch quarterly journal *Migrantenstudies*. He is the author of numerous articles, book chapters and reports on the sociology, politics and economics of postmigratory processes, including *Minorisation: The Social Construction of 'Ethnic*

Minorities' (1991), and coeditor of a book on immigrant entrepreneurship in the Netherlands (1998). He and Robert Kloosterman are cofounders of an International Network on Immigrant Entrepreneurship.

Ans Rekers received a MA degree in human geography from the University of Amsterdam. She was involved in a research project on ethnic entrepreneurship conducted by the University of Utrecht in cooperation with the University of Amsterdam, and has published several articles on this subject. At the moment she is working at the Career Center at the University of Amsterdam.

Richard Staring obtained a MA degree in cultural anthropology and is currently writing his PhD thesis at Erasmus University Rotterdam. He conducted fieldwork in a small village in Central Anatolia, Turkey, on the subject of returned guest workers, and did research among imprisoned commercial bank robbers. His present research focuses on the daily lives of undocumented Turkish immigrants in the Netherlands, with special emphasis on the nature of their relationships with conationals. He is also coeditor of the anthropological journal *Focaal. Tijdschrift voor Antropologie.*

Roger Waldinger is Professor of Sociology and Director of the Lewis Center for regional Policy Studies at the University of California, Los Angeles. He received his BA from Brown University and a PhD from Harvard University. He is the author of more than fifty articles and book chapters on immigration, ethnic entrepreneurship and urban change, as well as four books, the most recent ones being *Still the Promised City? New Immigrants and African-Americans in Post-Industrial New York* (1996) and *Ethnic Los Angeles* (edited with Mehdi Bozorgmehr, 1996), winner of the 1997 Thomas and Znaniecki award for the best book in the field of international migration.

Robert Watson is Professor of Finance and Accounting at the Leeds University Business School. He has studied at the Universities of Hull (BA) and Manchester (PhD). Prior to going to Leeds in 1995 he held academic posts at the University of Newcastle and the University of Manchester Institute of Science and Technology (UMIST). His main research interests include small and medium-sized enterprise development, labour market and remuneration systems and issues of corporate governance.

Introduction: Immigrant Businesses and their Economic, Politico-Institutional and Social Environment

Jan Rath[1]

Introduction

'The West is best again', featured in *The Economist* (9 August 1997), describes the remarkable recovery of California's economy in the mid 1990s. 'After its worst recession in half a century, California's economy is once again outshining the rest of the country.' Contrary to the previous boom in the 1980s, which was led by the Los Angeles aerospace industry and nurtured by federal dollars for the build-up of the defence industry, today's economy is much more diversified. A 'surprisingly wide range of industries' are doing well, from computers and software, to films, furniture and tourism, as well as clothing and toys (see also *The Economist*, 31 May 1997). The clothing industry of Los Angeles is now the largest in the country, easily surpassing New York, and it is still growing. The city's producers of clothing – often Korean immigrants who hire Latino workers – are part of a system of flexible production in which firms respond quickly to subtle changes in fashion. The close connections between these producers and trend-setting Californian designers constitute another asset of the industry as a whole.

A more or less similar mushrooming of relatively small businesses can be observed in the toy industry (*The Economist*, 6 September 1997). The bulk of companies in the Los Angeles toy district are run by ethnic Chinese immigrants, along with a handful of Mexicans and Koreans. They are well connected to cheap industries in the toy capital of the world, Hong Kong; and by cooperating with a cluster of competitor neighbours they are able to share infrastructure such as shipping, and thus save costs. Growth in the diversity of industries has not only reduced California's dependence on public finance but also its dependence on large companies, since more than half of the businesses have

1

only a handful of employees per company. Together they have contributed to the creation of virtually countless jobs to the advantage of, among others, many newcomers. To be sure, the present economic boom coincides with a peak in immigration from Third World countries, a process that took off in the mid 1960s and has resulted in Los Angeles becoming the United States' number one city of immigration.

This development is not unique to Southern California – one can witness similar economic and demographic developments in other North American and European metropolitan areas such as Miami, New York, Amsterdam, Berlin, London, Birmingham and Paris. First in the United States and Britain, and later in other advanced countries in Europe, the number of small-scale entrepreneurs has greatly increased (OECD, 1993), and so has the share of immigrants in the population. Quite a number of them have entered self-employment, making it obvious that immigrants play an important role in these advanced urban economies (cf. Barrett *et al.*, 1996; Body-Gendrot and Ma Mung, 1992; Häussermann and Oswald, 1997; Light and Rosenstein, 1995b; Portes and Stepick, 1993; Rath and Kloosterman, 1998; Waldinger, 1996a).

The emergence of a 'bourgeois class' of immigrant entrepreneurs is, at least ostensibly, at odds with the bleak picture painted by many researchers and other observers. According to the latter view, even in times of economic boom immigrants find it difficult to obtain work due to insufficient education, their one-sided networks and discriminatory recruitment procedures. As immigrants are often – or seem to be – subjected to permanent social exclusion, many have concluded that they constitute 'a new urban underclass' (cf. Clark, 1998). This conclusion, however, is misleading in relation to the entrepreneurial immigrant. It is a fact that numerous immigrants – making use of their own capital and favourable economic conditions – successfully make the transition to self-sufficiency via entrepreneurship and achieve a high degree of economic success. In so doing they show that these rather gloomy conclusions fall short of describing what is really happening in many advanced cities (cf. Srinavasan, 1995; Waldinger and Bozorgmehr, 1996; Werbner, 1980).

Having said this, it should be admitted that all that glisters is not gold. For many immigrant entrepreneurs economic success is not assured: more often than not their entrepreneurship involves low-level activities that take place on the fringe of the urban economy. They operate at the lower end of the market where obstacles to admission are weakest, but even here they lead a difficult existence economically. Although immigrant entrepreneurs work long hours – often assisted by family, coethnics or other immigrants – profits are often minimal, and – judged by the standards of established businesses – their corporate management leaves much to be desired, with substandard labour conditions (Ram, 1993). In addition they often resort to illegal practices, ranging from tax fraud to the employment of undocumented or illegal immigrants. This in turn leads to actions by the government or other authorities that may threaten the continuation of the enterprise (Kloosterman *et al.*, 1998, 1999; Rath, 1998; Chapters 1 and 4 of this volume). The findings of various researchers point to the fact that the post-industrial economy also has a shadowy side in which marginal social groups in particular reside. For the latter, the prospect of the 'Lumpenbourgeois' looms large. Whatever the outcome, it is clear that the fate of advanced cities and that of immigrants have become closely intertwined. The extent and measure of economic development is partially determined by the economic activities of immigrant entrepreneurs, while the success of their activities is influenced by their relations with and the dynamics of the environment. The question is: how to understand these processes.

Research on immigrant businesses

Immigrant entrepreneurship in conjunction with informal practices has been the subject of a number of studies, particularly in Britain and the United States, but more recently also in other European countries. In a number of these studies it is suggested that immigrants have particular advantages that foster their entry into (and success in) business. Portes and Sassen-Koob (1987, p. 48), for instance, when referring to entrepreneurial activities in the informal economy, argue that 'immigrant communities have provided much of the labour for these activities, have frequently supplied sites for their development, and have furnished the entrepreneurial drive to initiate them'. Waldinger (1996a) draws attention to the remarkable willingness of immigrants to carry out tasks that nationals turn down and links this to normative expectations and preferences that are strongly related to the conditions in the land of origin.

The explanations of ethnic entrepreneurship are diverse. The initial research tended to focus exclusively on immigrant *ethnic* minorities, thereby implying that some ethnic minorities display a greater proclivity for self-employment because of their (allegedly) specific cultural heritage. This would be especially true for so-called middleman minorities and immigrants involved in so-called ethnic enclaves (see

Bonacich, 1973; Bovenkerk, 1982; Metcalf *et al.*, n.d. Werbner, 1980). These studies emphasise the ethno-cultural practices and preferences of ethnic entrepreneurs such as ethnic ideologies, social networks and ethnic institutions, and have produced fruitful insights into the cultural practices and preferences of immigrant ethnic entrepreneurs and their strategies. However, as Light and Rosenstein (1995a, p. 19; see also Chapter 7 of this volume) argue, cultural explanations may fit 'classic middleman minorities, whose histories betoken a prolonged tradition of entrepreneurship' but 'are not universally satisfactory'. These authors cite the example of Cubans and Koreans in the United States as immigrants who did not have a prior history of entrepreneurship elsewhere in the world but nevertheless built up an impressive record of entrepreneurship. The very fact that immigrant self-employment normally exceeds non-immigrant self-employment in situations where entrepreneurship is legally permissible for immigrants and non-immigrants alike compels one to go beyond unique cultural traditions for an explanation.

Other studies have done so and focus on the effects of disadvantage in the labour market or on racism in society in general, arguing that the exclusion of immigrants from the economic mainstream pushes them towards self-employment (Light, 1979; Phizacklea, 1990). In the latter cases it is the structural lack of economic alternatives that provides immigrants with the motivation to set up shop.

Waldinger *et al.* (1990b) have argued in favour of a more integrative approach, that is, an approach that not only takes account of sociocultural features but also of the economic and institutional environment in which these entrepreneurs operate. In their *interactive model* they distinguish between group characteristics and the opportunity structure. In their view, the latter consists of a combination of market conditions (namely consumer markets) and access to ownership (business vacancies, competition for vacancies and government policies). In doing so they identify economic and institutional factors as crucial for the strategies of entrepreneurs. This interactive model – perhaps more of a classification than an explanatory model – has been used by many authors as an instrument to understand ethnic strategies and as such has been influential. This is not without justification since the model represented an important step towards a more comprehensive theoretical approach and programme of research. This of course is to the credit of Waldinger and his associates.

However there has been criticism of the model, for example by Morokvasic (1993), who feels that too little attention is paid to gender;

by Bonacich (1993), for whom the political and economic context is undervalued; and by Light and Rosenstein (1995a), who raise objections about methodology. Some criticisms – some possibly too harsh – are not unfounded. Waldinger and associates too easily make the assertion that immigrants constitute ethnic groups and as entrepreneurs act accordingly – on the premise that immigrants can be equated with ethnic groups. Moreover they are rather dismissive of economic and politico-institutional factors: in their model market conditions are mainly related to the ethnicisation or de-ethnicisation of consumer markets, while the politico-institutional factors only seem to constitute a short list of those laws and regulations that apply specifically to immigrants. Let us examine these criticisms more closely.

As already stated, Waldinger *et al.* assume that immigrants constitute ethnic groups and that their economic activities are mainly ethnic by nature. This may well be the case, although there will be strong variations in terms of the extent to and the way in which this takes place. Still, to treat the 'ethnic nature' of their activities as a fact and to regard it as point of departure for research is going too far (Light and Rosenstein, 1995a; Panayiotopoulos, 1996; Rath and Kloosterman, forthcoming). What principally distinguishes ethnic entrepreneurship from other forms of entrepreneurship – the origin of the entrepreneur, business strategies, personnel, clientele, the products or product combinations – is neither worked out theoretically nor shown empirically. They assume that there are essential differences, simply because one is dealing with immigrants.[2] Subsequently they concentrate on ethnic traditions, ethnic moral frameworks and behavioural patterns, ethnic loyalties and ethnic markets. Thus they tend to reduce immigrant entrepreneurship to an ethnic phenomenon within an economic and institutional vacuum.

Waldinger *et al.* do distance themselves from absolutist viewpoints on ethnicity, opting for a more situational approach to the phenomenon. They detach themselves from the idea of ethnicity as a primordial phenomenon or as imported from the land of origin and focus on the social structures in which ethnic identification and ethnic group solidarity develop (cf. Cassarino, 1997; Koot and Rath, 1987). Despite this, their argument reveals a tautological line of reasoning. In their words:

> ethnicity is a *possible* outcome of the patterns by which inter- and intergroup interactions are structured. Our central contention is that ethnicity is acquired when the social connections among *ethnic group members* [emphasis added] help establish distinct occupational,

industrial or spatial concentrations. Once established, these concentrations promote frequent and intensive face-to-face interactions that breed a sense of commonality and identification with members of the same ethnic group. Ethnic concentrations may also give rise to common ethnic interests, reinforcing a sense of identity.

(Waldinger *et al.*, 1990b, p. 34)

In other words ethnic concentration can strengthen common ethnic interests and promote a feeling of identity among those who, according to Waldinger *et al.*, are already members of an ethnic group. Apparently there was already mention of ethnic identification among the immigrants.

Such ethnic identification can contribute to the strengthening of social capital. In this regard the interactive model emphasises the importance for ethnic entrepreneurs of embeddedness in social networks as well as the possibility of using or manipulating these networks for economic ends. The link with economic developments, the material and immaterial costs entailed in using these social networks and the meaning of limited or one-sided information exchange within such networks has not been worked out theoretically. The impression is given that ethnic groups, once formed, constitute one happy family, a community without conflicts of interest, without gender-specific resource allocation and that all members are immediately and without reserve ready and willing to help one another. Bonacich (1993, p. 686) rightly reproaches Waldinger *et al.* for painting a very favourable portrait of ethnic entrepreneurship, for example their suggestion that ethnic loyalties can soften class distinctions. The opposite situation has been overlooked by them, namely ethnic loyalties being manipulated in order to disguise class-based loyalties, thus freeing the way for the exploitation of labour (Anthias, 1992).

Let us now turn to the political economy of immigrant businesses. The economic structure of a country or town, the specific features of various markets, developments in time and their determinants, and the impact on opportunities for immigrant entrepreneurs have received little systematic attention from Waldinger *et al.* In their book a number of circumstances that influence the entry of immigrants into consumer markets, such as 'underserved or abandoned markets', 'low economies of scale', 'instability and uncertainty and ethnic good', are mentioned but not really discussed. Hardly any attention is paid to structural developments in the economy, such as internationalisation or the tendency towards the vertical disintegration of businesses. Some students of political economy claim that such processes have had an enormous impact in recent years, especially in the so-called 'global cities'. Sassen (1991a), for example, has analysed the effects of the globalisation of the economy on the opportunity structure of small (immigrant) businesses. She argues that the headquarters of international businesses tend to locate in areas with good support facilities, that is, financial services, real estate firms, marketing bureaux, legal consultancies, cultural agencies and so on, and that the concentration of these types of business promotes the development of a high-quality service industry. Meanwhile the 'old' labour-intensive manufacturing industry is moving into computerised manufacturing and subcontracting to firms in low-wage countries or to domestic subcontractors, particularly if greater flexibility and a quick response are required. This creates an increasing demand for relatively low-quality activities at the lower end of the market where entrepreneurs show a high degree of flexibility, production is labour-intensive and added-value relatively low.

According to Sassen, this demand is generated directly by contracting out specific tasks such as cleaning, catering, security and transport, as well as indirectly by the extension of personal services, for example when highly qualified, highly paid white-collar workers hire personnel for cleaning and child care. Sassen asserts that entrepreneurial immigrants can profit from this new demand for services. That immigrants are mainly concentrated in relatively small businesses is, then, not without significance. The interactive model, however, does not really deal with such processes. Perhaps Waldinger *et al.* attach little value to such assertions because for them the empirical foundation is weak (cf. Waldinger and Lapp, 1993; Waldinger, 1996a; see also Hamnett, 1996) or because the application to cities other than New York can be problematical (Kloosterman, 1994; Rath, 1998). Whatever the reason, no attempt is made to discuss these issues.

Bonacich (1993), in her critique of *Ethnic Entrepreneurs*, asserts that large firms in the Californian clothing industry use small and powerless immigrant firms as a buffer to exploit labour and generate extreme profit levels, and she reproaches Waldinger *et al.* for ignoring this. Waldinger (1993) refutes her criticism as an exaggeration, which may be the case, but the problem remains that the interactive model does not provide adequate guidelines for empirically researching the economic embeddedness of immigrant entrepreneurship. After all it is not unreasonable to assume that the economic structure, its operating principles and balance of power influence the chances and behaviour of small (immigrant) businesses.

Comparatively unsatisfactory is the discussion on the politico-institutional framework. The chances open to small immigrant firms are not only determined by the extent to which foreign entrepreneurs are legally permitted to set up business, as suggested by, Waldinger *et al.*, but by a mixture of general – that is, not only applicable to foreigners – laws and regulations on education, taxes, labour relations, residency status, job quality, safety, health, the environment and so on. Not only the actual laws and regulations themselves, but also their enforcement and any political conflict on these issues are relevant. This is *a fortiori* the case where the informalisation and formalisation of business activities are concerned. Thus the opportunity for immigrants to set up business in the Amsterdam clothing industry has diminished drastically since a task force of law enforcement agencies – the alien police, the FIOD (the Internal Revenue Service) and the GAK (the Industrial Insurance Administration Office) – have systematically hunted down illegal practices. It took until the beginning of the 1990s to set up this task force because for a number of reasons (including the political decision taken by the municipal authorities to safeguard the employment of lower-class immigrants rather than combat illegal practices) the local authorities had turned a blind eye to these illegal practices. It was only after pressure from established firms, their interest groups, trade unions and the national government for a 'hard line' to be taken that control measures were tightened. Partly due to this, the number of small immigrant firms in this sector decreased (see Chapter 1 of this book and Rath, 1998).

Finally, central and local governments have been allocated a central role in the enactment and enforcement of laws and regulations, especially in advanced welfare states such as the Netherlands and Germany. Those wishing to gain an insight into the embeddedness of immigrant business would do well to research their embeddedness in the politico-institutional framework, with special regard to the role of government. Bonacich (1993), in her critique of Waldinger *et al.* (1990b), does just this but takes the bend just a little too sharply in suggesting that government has become the accomplice of capital – thus reflecting a rather stereotypical and economist viewpoint.[3] Nonetheless it is true that local and central government frequently take on the role of protector or regulator of certain interests (which is not automatically the same as the interests of 'capital', should such a body exist). In this capacity the government is responsible for the regulation of immigration, harmonious social relations, the welfare state and the labour market. These all influence immigrant entrepreneurship, but they are not afforded the recognition and attention they deserve in the interactive model.

A number of those who contributed to the interactive model have since revised their views. Light and Rosenstein (1995a, 1995b) are the most radical in this respect. In their recent critical review of the model they rejected it as theoretically and methodologically inadequate. According to Light and Rosenstein the causal relationships between the different factors and immigrant entrepreneurship are uncertain, while the location of ethnic group resources are treated as invariant. In their opinion the explanation for immigrant self-employment must first be sought in specific combinations of class and ethnic resources and local economic characteristics. In other words they suggest much more complex and open configurations contingent on the intricate interaction between concrete 'groups' and 'spaces'.

More recently Waldinger (1995, 1996a; Waldinger and Bozorgmehr, 1996) has emphasised the role of social networks and the process of ethnic succession. According to him the opportunities open to immigrants are less the result of economic changes than of already established groups climbing up the social ladder, thereby creating vacancies for newcomers below. The 'game of ethnic musical chairs', as Waldinger has labelled this process, is driven by the mobilisation of network resources. The social networks are to a large extent formed by processes of group categorisation and by ranking these groups in a hierarchy of desirability, thereby positioning members of the in-group at the top of the imaginary social ladder and all others on lower rungs. These ideological processes have practical relevance since they give direction and legitimacy to the privileged treatment of in-group members. The combination of preferential treatment to in-group members and the manipulation of social networks can, under certain conditions, be used as a business resource. The mobilisation of network resources and the arrival of newcomers in specific economic positions leads to ethnic concentrations and the possible development of ethnic niches. As members of these niches move up the social ladder, new vacancies open that can be filled by the most recent immigrants, and so on. This model, extensively presented in a magnificent book on New York, can be viewed as a logical elaboration of one aspect of the interactive model (Waldinger, 1996). Here Waldinger, this time in more detail and using the force of empirical argument, puts his finger on the meaning of social embeddedness (cf. Rath, 1999).

This much is clear: the interactive model contains a valid and interesting basis for theoretical consideration and empirical investigation of entrepreneurial immigration, but it is not the theoretical authority that some researchers consider it to be. The various processes relevant to entrepreneurship, especially the economic and politico-institutional ones, have not as yet been adequately elaborated upon, and these aspects should be examined before developing a more comprehensive theoretical model.

Exploring the economic, politico-institutional and social environments

In this book we submit a number of these processes and their interrelationship to more detailed theoretical study. A first point of departure is that the opportunities and strategies of entrepreneurs are closely linked to their embeddedness in the economic, politico-institutional and social environments. In practice they will depend on the precise mix of these various types of embeddedness. A second point of departure is that this exploration can only be optimally carried out if insights from complementary disciplines are used.[4] It is evident that the study of small-scale ethnic entrepreneurship can only be fruitful if it is not limited to economic sociology but widens its field of vision to include, for example, disciplines such as business economics and international political economics.

Which economic factors in the global economy play a role in immigrant businesses, the structural elements which flow from this, the role played by similar factors at the local level and how all these influence the entrepreneurship of immigrants – as well as what relates to the internal business operation and its position in the market place – are some of the central questions explored by Raes, Jones *et al.*, Rekers and van Kempen, and Watson *et al.* in Chapters 1–4 respectively.

Raes (Chapter 1) gives special attention to the spatial organisation of production in an economic sector that is highly relevant for immigrants, namely clothing manufacturing. In different writings on the entrepreneurship of immigrants in this sector the significance of the globalisation process is quite evident. Raes recognises the central importance of the globalisation process for the emergence of immigrant businesses, but considers the term too coarse and therefore misleading. After all the internationalisation of production is not taking place in all economic sectors and does not cover the entire globe, rather it is restricted to certain regions. This means that the process of globalisation is taking place in a specific way in certain localities and sectors (cf. Persky and Wievel, 1994). This process is influenced by the economic initiatives of immigrants, while their business perspectives are partially determined by their degree of embeddedness in the local and international economies.

Jones, Barrett and McEvoy (Chapter 2) are especially concerned with the belief that social changes and economic restructuring in the so-called post-Fordist era have created the essential conditions for ethnic entrepreneurship to flourish. Due attention should therefore be paid to the way in which the restructuring of market demand sets strict boundaries within which such firms live or die, survive or thrive. Not only does it affect the number, size and earning capacity of firms, it also helps to determine the kinds of business activity for which minority entrepreneurs are eligible. Jones *et al.* argue in favour of a sense of spatial market hierarchy. Some authors have implied that all markets in which immigrant entrepreneurs are active are local, whereas in reality they can be city-wide, regional or even international. Jones *et al.* conclude their chapter with a typology of four hypothetical market spaces, based on consumer ethnicity and customer proximity.

Rekers and van Kempen (Chapter 3) point to the relevance of space, a factor that is notably absent from many studies. They demonstrate that the urban context can affect the opportunities of immigrant entrepreneurs. They argue that the globalisation and internationalisation of the economy, the growing importance of information and services, sociocultural developments and migration are affecting most large cities in the Western world. Internal factors such as the structure of the local economy, the quality of neighbourhoods and the environment, the population structure of the city or its neighbourhoods, and more abstract features such as ideology, history and tradition interact with broad international developments to give each city its own character and position in the (national and international) urban system.

It goes without saying that the chances offered to and the demands made upon entrepreneurs differ according to market type, and that the types of entrepreneur attracted to the various market types will also differ. Entrepreneurs from communities with relatively poor (formal) labour market opportunities appear to be willing and able to enter highly volatile and competitive sectors such as clothing manufacturing, even though such sectors are characterised by high failure rates and low returns. The interaction between market opportunities and the characteristics of entrepreneurs can be studied from a myriad of perspectives, not only from a macroeconomic or sociological one. In Chapter 4 Watson, Keasey and Baker argue from a financial-economic point of view that, irrespective of the ethnic origins of the owner-manager, many small firms can be expected to find it difficult to obtain financial capital from the formal capital markets, simply because the legally enforceable contracting (governance) mechanisms available are often inadequate to protect the financial interests of these institutions due to the high and difficult to quantify risks involved. The perception that banks and other financial institutions discriminate against ethnic minority businesses and/or are simply unfamiliar with the *modus operandi* of such enterprises, further reduces the formal capital market's contribution to this sector of the economy. Watson *et al.* suggest that these entrepreneurs have been able significantly to reduce their cost base and exposure to business risks by virtue of their access to the relatively cheap and highly flexible coethnic labour that is commonly available in many urban locations. They may also have established themselves within a viable network of embedded business relationships, which engenders trust despite the high degree of contractual incompleteness involved. Watson *et al.* argue that by engendering mutual trust, resource sharing and innovation, such embedded ties create a viable and less costly alternative to formal governance systems based on contracts.

Immigrants, most of whom lack the social capital considered appropriate by the standards of the receiving country and are only marginally embedded in the social networks of potential native clients and suppliers, are usually only able to set up firms at the lower end of the market, where new firms require small outlays of capital and labour is the most important production input. As competition in most of these sectors is focused on price, many small entrepreneurs resort to the infringement of rules and regulations as a feasible strategy to cut costs (Kloosterman *et al.*, 1998, 1999; Rath, 1998). Some authors suggest that this behaviour is related to the preindustrial background of immigrants from Third World countries. Bovenkerk (1982; Bovenkerk *et al.*, 1983), for instance, claims that immigrant entrepreneurs originate from predominantly agricultural societies in which they have familiarised themselves with informal practices. Portes and Sassen-Koob (1987), however, argue against the opinion that informal activities are 'essentially transitory, being a consequence of the imperfect penetration of modern capitalism into the less developed regions'. Likewise they refute the idea that the informal economy is 'primarily a feature of peripheral economies such as those of Latin America, Africa, and most of Asia' or a feature of immigrants from those areas. Informal practices are in fact part and parcel of post-industrial economies.

This begs an exploration of the politico-institutional framework and its impact on immigrant entrepreneurship. Kloosterman (Chapter 5) and Freeman and Ögelman (Chapter 6) take important steps in this direction. Freeman and Ögelman, guided by the 'new institutional economics', argue that the institutional structure of societies has an independent role in shaping economic outcomes as it affects the transaction costs of economic exchange. Institutions are conceived as sets of rules – both formal and informal – that govern behaviour, whereby various sets of institutions constitute regulatory regimes. These regulatory regimes involve laws, regulations and policies governing, for instance, immigration, the market and welfare. Each welfare state has a regime regarding the right to enter and remain in a country, the (re-)distribution of social resources and the procedures for economic transactions. The space for economic activities is, for instance, determined by laws, regulations and policy incentives concerning the minimum wage, taxes, social contributions, working hours, health and security, immigration and so on. A liberal immigration policy can foster the settlement of entrepreneurial immigrants. A restrictive immigration policy, on the other hand, can impede entrepreneurship by limiting the flow of new (legal) workers. This, of course, is not to say that besides these institutional barriers there are no socioeconomic ones, such as the saturation of markets (see Chapter 9). Very stringent rules can, however, lead to an increase in illegal immigration which, as Staring argues in Chapter 10, in turn leads to economic transactions becoming partially informal. Besides the rules and regulations themselves, their implementation is also of importance (Kloosterman *et al.*, 1998, 1999). Both aspects of regulatory regimes are not 'natural' situations but have to be understood as particular outcomes of contingent historical processes. As a consequence neither regulation nor enforcement are fixed or clear-cut, and therefore neither is the boundary between the formal and informal economies.

At the national level there is a certain relationship between laws, regulations and policy and the organisation of the welfare state. Here the institutional framework refers to the make-up of the welfare state. A relatively high level of social welfare, such as that in corporatist and social-democratic welfare states on the European continent, guarantees a relatively high minimum level of public purchasing power. On the one hand this helps to maintain or create an internal market for products produced by (immigrant) firms, while on the other hand it reduces the necessity of entering the labour market. The fewer incentives there are to generate an income, the less likely it is that individual immigrants or natives will start a business. The opposite argument is also possible, as Kloosterman shows in Chapter 5. While the neo-American model of welfare states has a low labour-security level but a high level of labour participation, the Rhineland model has a strongly decommodified and protected labour market. The level of labour participation is low in the latter, due, among other things, to the fact that a section of the potential working population has been manoeuvred out of the labour market – more or less permanently – by unemployment and disablement benefits. These different regulatory regimes have important implications for entrepreneurship. The low level of labour-market flexibility in European continental welfare states forces immigrants searching for work and an income to investigate the possibility of self-employed entrepreneurship. Nevertheless new entrepreneurs meet high entry barriers in the form of laws, regulations and protective measures. Entrepreneurs in the more liberal welfare states seem, according to Kloosterman, to have more freedom of choice and economic space.

However these regulatory regimes do not solely operate at the level of national government *per se*. In more corporatist societies some government tasks have been taken over by or delegated to private institutions or quasi non-governmental organisations (quangos). Moreover certain tasks have been delegated to lower local government levels, thus creating local differentiation. On the other hand a number of supranational institutions have come to the fore, such as the European Union and the World Trade Organization, which increasingly influence economic transactions (Appelbaum and Gereffi, 1994; see also Chapter 1 of this volume). This influence varies according to economic sector.

No matter what the economic or politico-institutional influences may be, they alone do not determine the establishment and success of small businesses. A great deal depends on the ambition and abilities of the entrepreneurs, and the extent to and ways in which they are embedded in the social and economic environment. In this respect Bonacich's 'middleman minority theory' has been very influential. The theory seeks to explain the development and persistence of a particular configuration or form: ethnic minorities concentrating in intermediate positions where they engage in trade, commerce or other activities with outgroup members. Initially Bonacich (1973) argued that middleman minorities begin as sojourners, enduring short-term deprivation for the long-term goal of return, and choosing specialisations that are easily transferable to other societies or convertible for return home.

The characteristics and behaviour of middleman minorities – including in-group solidarity and distance from the host society – induce hostility from host society groups, especially business and labour, who find themselves in competition with price-cutting middleman minorities. Later Bonacich and Modell (1980) argued that the essence of middleman minorities lies in the way they organise their economic activities.

In Chapter 7 Waldinger presents a critique of this theory and argues that it suffers from a competitive and culturalist fallacy. According to Waldinger, Bonacich wrongly assumes that competition characterises the underlying economic reality that middleman minority groups encounter at the time of their incorporation into capitalist societies. Instead he argues for an alternative that emphasises structural processes designating middleman minority groups into non-competing economic segments. Furthermore he refutes Bonacich's explanation that the behaviour of entrepreneurs is a consequence of prior cultural differences that are resistant to economic change.

However Waldinger agrees with Bonacich's argument that social relations are of utmost importance for entrepreneurship. In this, both authors are in line with general economic and sociological viewpoints. The importance of social networks has also been highlighted by Granovetter, Portes and others in response to the under- and oversocialising arguments of neoclassical economists and sociologists (Granovetter, 1992; Portes, 1995b; Portes and Sensenbrenner, 1993). In their work they conceive embeddedness in social networks as being grounded in social phenomena such as bounded solidarity and enforceable trust, and as such it is potentially a kind of social capital. Although their critique is aimed at economic sociology in general, they consider that their approach is especially applicable to the economic actions of immigrants. According to Portes and Sensenbrenner (1993, pp. 1325–7), bounded solidarity and enforceable trust depend on

> a heightened sense of community and hence have the greatest affinity to the experience of immigrant groups ... It is the particular circumstance of 'foreignness' that often best explains the rise of these types of social capital among immigrants.[5]

'Foreignness' may exist when a group is distinct from the rest of the society – or rather is considered to be distinct and becomes the object of prejudice. This, according to Portes and Sensenbrenner, is the case when a group has distinct phenotypical or cultural characteristics.[6] When there is a low probability of exit, strong sentiments of in-group solidarity among its members may emerge, especially when they can activate a cultural repertoire that allows them to construct an autonomous portrayal of their situation and to reenact past practices and a common cultural memory. This type of situational solidarity constitutes an important source of social capital that can be used in the creation and consolidation of small enterprises. Next to this, there is enforceable trust, which is a stronger source of social capital as the level of outside discrimination is higher and the economic opportunities in the society at large are proportionally lower. This means that blocked economic opportunities and pressure placed on the groups concerned enhance the potential for realising this economic action. In this respect it is important to underline that the flourishing of networks as social capital is related to the political, economic and ideological conditions in which these networks are used. If this theoretical position is correct, this might help to explain why some groups of immigrants are involved in specific forms of economic action and others are not. As Light *et al.* (1993) have rightly argued, the use of social capital and the constitution of social networks can vary considerably from one immigrant group to another.

The positive effects of being embedded in social networks grounded in bounded solidarity and enforceable trust are significant. Portes and Sensenbrenner mention preference for coethnics in economic activities and altruistic support for community members and goals as two direct effects of bounded solidarity. They further suggest that enforceable trust has the positive effect of flexibility in economic transactions through the reduction of formal contracts, privileged access to economic resources and reliable expectations concerning effects of malfeasance. Roberts (1994), writing on the informal economy, identifies similar effects. He argues that the greatest advantage of informal economy enterprises lies in their flexibility, which is in part based on the importance of social relations. Trust, then, is of ultimate importance. This trust 'is mainly generated by kinship and community relationships, including ethnic ones', rather than by formal laws (cf. Epstein, 1994). It is evident that such networks are instrumental in the recruitment of labour and working capital, as well as in distributing information and acquiring knowledge.

However social capital has its price and may even induce counterproductive effects, as Flap, Kumcu and Bulder show in Chapter 8. Entrepreneurs can have too much or even the wrong kind of social capital. Receiving support in the form of information, capital or labour from other members of one's network requires new social investment and thus implies costs. A great deal of time and energy has to be spent on the maintenance of networks, which is an investment without direct rewards. Business people may experience pressure to hire relatives or friends of friends because of moral constraints or a social commitment to particular persons, but they are not necessarily the best people for the job. Status management or reciprocal obligations interfere and may negatively affect the efficient conduct of business. Furthermore the information available in networks can be one-sided and limited. What is often forgotten is that social capital is goal-specific.

The connection between social networks and the economic environment has been worked out in a provocative manner by Light. In Chapter 9 he presents a conceptual criticism of the globalisation theory based on the insights of network theory. Globalisation theory claims that global restructuring provides a complete explanation of phenomena such as immigration, immigrant employment, immigrant businesses and their informalisation. However, as Light shows, global restructuring cannot have caused all these phenomena even if, for the sake of argument, we assume that global restructuring works as its proponents claim. To a substantial extent, immigration causes itself and also causes the economic informalisation that is a condition of its self-production. This view explains immigration and informalisation by reference to the mature migration network's capacity to lower the economic, social and emotional costs and hardships of migration. This cost-cutting capacity expands informalisation in and migration to the developed countries by permitting the economic exploitation of unorganised and covert demand that would otherwise remain inaccessible. It completes this operation in two ways.

Firstly, the networks reduce the hardship and costs of low-wage work, thus permitting many more immigrants to find employment in the destination economy and many more informal firms to exist. Secondly, networks permit immigrant entrepreneurs to exploit ethnic social capital in the recruitment, training and retention of workers, thus lowering the costs of the immigrant-owned firm. Globalisation theory credits demand in the advanced countries with too much determinism and immigrants with too little agency. Light proposes the concept of 'spillover migration'. Spillover migration starts as demand-driven but in midstream it becomes network-driven. This shift occurs because migration networks reduce the costs and hardships of migration, expanding the supply of migrants and lowering their reservation wages. Informalisation also advances because immigrant entrepreneurs tap social capital in migration networks, thus permitting them to access hitherto inaccessible demand. The concept of 'spillover migration' links globalisation theory and migration network theory into a plausible but not necessarily inevitable sequence. Since states can regulate economic conditions and migration within their own borders, they can impede or possibly even disconnect this linkage.

Staring elaborates on this issue in Chapter 10. He argues that students of immigrant entrepreneurship – particularly those who are interested in the engagement of people in transnational social networks – have appreciated the relevance of personal networks but ignored the legal status of the immigrants involved. Especially in the labour market and within the immigrant economy, the legal status of immigrants is of importance for the entrepreneur as well as for the immigrants themselves. Staring identifies three different 'P-roles', as undocumented immigrants promote, produce and participate in immigrant business in a very specific way that sets them apart from their legal conationals. Immigrant entrepreneurs often depend on undocumented immigrants as they are loyal, hard working and cheap employees. By virtue of their number, undocumented immigrants also contribute to the demand for specific products provided by immigrant businesses. However they not only promote formal, legal coethnic businesses, but also constitute a market for criminal ventures such as forgery and trafficking. These activities by criminal entrepreneurs in turn encourage and facilitate further migration. Finally, undocumented immigrants are distinguished as producers of immigrant businesses as some start their own business, often small and to a large extent informal.

The various views presented in this volume do not of course constitute a coherent theoretical model for immigrant entrepreneurship. They do, however, offer insights into certain aspects and processes that must be included in any model. What is essential is that, whatever the model, the multifaceted nature of entrepreneurship and the context in which entrepreneurs operate must be given due attention.

Notes

1   The author wishes to express his gratitude to Robert C. Kloosterman for his comments on a previous version of this chapter.

2   This is not to suggest that ethno-cultural factors are fiction or that entrepreneurs – whether foreign or not – have no culture. Such factors are viewed, however, as inadequate *points of departure* for research on immigrant entrepreneurship.

3   Her comment reminds us of the literature on the role of government in the regulation of racial and ethnic relations. There too it is stated that

government is the accomplice of capital, for example by stirring up racism. For a criticism of this simplistic viewpoint see Bovenkerk *et al.* (1990).

4 Research on immigrant entrepreneurship has always been more or less inter-disciplinary in nature, with strong contributions from cultural anthropology and economic sociology.

5 It remains to be seen whether immigrants are really so unique in this respect. It can also be argued that this holds for city dwellers in general (cf. Hannerz, 1980).

6 Here Portes and Sensenbrenner present a rather essentialist view of social identities and relations, as they reify phenotypical and cultural characteristics.

1

Regionalisation in a Globalising World: The Emergence of Clothing Sweatshops in the European Union

Stephan Raes

Introduction

In many large cities of the Western world, the 1970s and 1980s witnessed an increase in the production of clothing in small-scale sweatshops, often run by immigrants. This development, which I shall discuss in the following section, was surprising in at least three ways. Firstly, it followed a period of decline in production and employment in the clothing industry in Western countries. Secondly, it seemed to be in contradiction to the new international division of labour, in which developing countries were increasing their participation in labour-intensive industrial production and trade. Finally, it unexpectedly led to upward mobility for immigrants in the form of entrepreneurship. For scholars of various backgrounds the question is how to understand this development. This will also be the central subject of this chapter.

In approaching this matter some writers have focused on the characteristics of immigrants that made them appropriate candidates for ethnic entrepreneurship, be it in terms of their presumed 'cultural capital' or their exclusion from other segments of the labour market. Others have connected the emergence of sweatshops to the development of 'global cities', from which the international economy is controlled. Finally, some see sweatshops as a break with the new international division of labour and a return of labour-intensive industry to Western countries. These theories are discussed in other chapters of this volume and will only be touched upon briefly in the third section of this chapter.

In this chapter the emergence of sweatshops will be approached from a different angle. In my opinion this development should be seen as part of the *globalisation process* that seems to have become the main trend in the international political economy since 1970. Barriers to flows of capital, information, trade and people have strongly diminished at the global level, subordinating domestic economies to the perceived exigencies of the global economy. This has enforced capital's position versus labour and the state. However this globalisation process did not necessarily lead to an actual shift of production around the globe in all sectors, nor to all locations: what becomes global is the *arena*, not necessarily the behaviour of the bulls or the bullfighters. For instance the global shift in clothing production in the 1960s and 1970s (mainly to Asia) was followed in the 1980s by what can be called a tendency towards *regionalisation*, encompassing a shift of production in some sectors to locations closer to the consumer. As such, regionalisation (the relocating of production closer to the consumer) constitutes the concrete spatial manifestation of the globalisation process in the clothing sector for the European Union (EU) in the 1980s. The emergence of sweatshops should be seen as part of this regionalisation and analysed as an element of a changing spatial organisation of production, with due attention to the sectoral specificity of clothing production.

In this chapter I shall develop a theoretical argument concerning the need for a sectoral and location-specific analysis of sweatshops. I shall present my argument from the perspective of the EU clothing market, with special reference to the Dutch situation. I start with an outline of the regionalisation tendency of which the emergence of sweatshops is a part.

Regionalisation of the clothing supply

From 1965 the clothing industry in the EU experienced a serious crisis, for which there were at least three main causes. Firstly, increases in productivity were not high enough to compensate for increasing wage costs in the industry. Secondly, international competition in the industry increased rapidly among the EU countries themselves and from low-wage countries, especially in East Asia. Thirdly, the consumption of clothing increased only moderately and even decreased at the beginning of the 1980s. These factors led to huge falls in employment and production in EU clothing. In the Netherlands for instance, where the decline set in relatively early, employment in clothing peaked in 1963 (77 000 jobs) but decreased thereafter, 71 per cent of jobs being lost between 1970 and 1980 (from 58 500 to 17 100). The index for production (in value terms, constant prices) fell from 181 in 1970 to 140 in

1975 and 100 in 1980 (Scheffer, 1992, pp. 91–9). The crisis was probably most strongly felt in the contract clothing industry, which concentrates on the (labour-intensive) assembly of clothing for retailers or other producers. Similar developments took place in other EU countries.[1]

However in the second half of the 1970s this pattern changed in two ways. On the one hand the clothing industry seemed to recover from the crisis. In the Netherlands, for instance, the fall in employment and production in the clothing industry became less pronounced during the 1980s. The production index decreased from 100 in 1980 to 77 in 1985 and 74 in 1989. Employment stabilised at approximately 10 000 in the second half of the 1980s (ibid.). Part of this was accounted for by the reemergence of contract clothing firms in Amsterdam. In 1981, 114 firms were registered at the Amsterdam Chamber of Commerce (of which 28 were run by Turks), but by 1986 this number had increased to 219 (of which were 157 run by Turks) (Bloeme and van Geuns, 1987, p. 99) and it reached its peak in 1992. Since many firms did not register officially, the actual number of firms probably exceeded the official number. Contract clothing firms concentrate on the production of small-batch, fashion-sensitive women's outerwear and work as subcontractors for Dutch producers and retailers. Sweatshops do not usually design clothing but concentrate on assembly. In major cities in other European countries immigrants also played an important role in the recovery of the clothing industry. As I have shown above, the recovery of the clothing sector was not limited to immigrant-run sweatshops but took place in the clothing sector as a whole.[2]

On the other hand there was also an increase in the importation of clothing from Asia by suppliers closer to the EU market (Mediterranean countries, Eastern Europe). An indication of the changes in the importation of clothing to the Dutch market in the 1980s can be obtained from data on the means of transportation by which clothing entered the Dutch market. Imports of clothing, knitwear and footwear increased from 267 000 tons in 1980 to 310 000 tons in 1992 (CBS, several years). The share of imports by land (mainly road transport)[3] increased in volume from 32 per cent in 1980 to 65 per cent in 1985 and 57 per cent in 1992. Imports by land from Mediterranean countries and Eastern Europe played an important role in this. These imports were often part of subcontracting arrangements in which a producer in the EU subcontracted the labour-intensive parts of the production process to these countries.

Both the reemergence of contract clothing manufacture and the shift in imports from Asia to Eastern Europe and the Mediterranean point in the same direction: a reduction in the distance over which clothing is supplied to the EU consumer. This process, of which the emergence of immigrant-run sweatshop production is a part, can be described as regionalisation of the clothing supply, in which the reduction of distance/delivery time is fundamental. Regionalisation is thus defined here as the relocation of production closer to the consumer. This is most evidently the case when production is moved from one country to another, closer to central consumer markets, or – within one country – from peripheral to more central areas. This process has also been analysed by Cheng and Gereffi (1994) for the US clothing market, which they describe as having concentric rings of supply:

> As one moves from the inner to the outer rings, the following changes are apparent: production costs and manufacturing sophistication decrease, while the lead time needed for deliveries increases. Therefore the high-quality, multiple season 'fashion' companies, as well as the more up-scale department stores, tend to source their production from the two inner rings, while price-conscious mass merchandisers and discount chains tolerate quality and longer lead times that characterize production in the two outer rings.
>
> (ibid., p. 66)

That sweatshop producers in the EU are also part of this inner ring can, for instance, be seen from the fact that in the Netherlands since 1992 the number of sweatshops has fallen sharply due to a police clamp-down on illegal practices and increased competition from Eastern Europe and Turkey. In some cases Turkish entrepreneurs in Amsterdam have moved their business to Turkey or switched to subcontracting in Poland.

Fordism and globalisation

The empirical overview provided in the previous section enables us to underline the limited explanatory power of approaches to immigrant entrepreneurship that focus either on the special cultural or ethnic traits of these immigrants (see for example Wong, 1987) or their exclusion from other jobs due to the segmented nature of the labour market (for instance Light, 1979).[4] Although both approaches provide useful insights into the position of immigrants in labour markets in Western countries, they cannot explain why the entrepreneurship is concentrated in specific sectors (especially clothing) and how it is connected to changes in the global division of labour.[5]

Here we shall concentrate on theories that do link the emergence of immigrant entrepreneurship to global developments. The main example of this is probably the work of Sassen (1988, 1991a, 1994). According to Sassen, the 1970s and 1980s witnessed a global decentralisation of manufacturing activity, an enormous increase in capital mobility and a strong centralisation of control of this globalisation process in so-called 'global cities'. These cities are home to the headquarters of financial and service firms that operate all around the globe. According to Sassen (1991a), it is striking that the concentration of white-collar, highly paid activities in global cities, has also contributed to an increased demand for marginalised, low-paid labour in small-scale services, cleaning, catering, laundry and so on. Lack of employment alternatives has forced immigrants into these kinds of activities. This line of reasoning allows us to understand the continuing demand for immigrant labour in deindustrialised cities and increasing immigrant entrepreneurship in this 'other side' of the global city. Such an analysis of course leads to the question of which cities can be considered 'global'.[6] Moreover, although it provides a useful explanation for entrepreneurship in service-related activities, it is doubtful whether it can explain manufacturing sweatshops.[7] In this case Sassen's suggestion that clothing sweatshops produce for both the urban 'yuppie' market and the marginalised 'underclass' market seems unsatisfactory, or at least in the case of Amsterdam (ibid., pp. 114–16).

Cohen (1987) has labelled Sassen's work as the other (and I would say 'service') side of the coin of the work of Fröbel *et al.* (1980, 1986) on the new international division of labour. Fröbel *et al.* analyse the 'runaway' of manufacturing production to developing countries as a consequence of the high wages in the West, the increasing possibilities for technology transfer and the improvements in communication and transportation technology. Following the logic of their argument, the reemergence of manufacturing production in the West in the 1980s was a 're-runaway' process that resulted from technological innovation and a reduction of labour costs due to labour market flexibility in the West (Cohen, 1987; Cohen and Henderson, 1982; Junne, 1985, 1987; Piore and Sabel, 1984). Although for some sectors this line of reasoning may provide a valid explanation, it is doubtful whether technological innovation in clothing sufficiently reduced the importance of labour costs to allow for increased production in Western countries. Moreover wages in EU sweatshops are still substantially above those in developing countries, making it unlikely that lower wages in the West are the main reason for renewed labour-intensive production. Furthermore the concept of 're-runaway' seems to suggest a return to a previous situation (instead of a new phenomenon), and is often limited to the return of production to Western countries (thus excluding other, related, changes in the spatial organisation of production).

Both approaches contain very useful elements. Sassen's insistence on the demand for immigrant activities complements in important ways the literature that concentrates on the supply of immigrant labour. The work on the new international division of labour leads us to take the dynamics of spatial organisation of production properly into account. On the basis of these approaches I shall endeavour to develop an understanding of the emergence of immigrant-run sweatshops and the regionalisation of the clothing supply, in which the emergence of sweatshops is placed in the context of more fundamental changes in capitalist societies since 1970. In doing so I shall follow a number of critical geographers who have analysed changes in the spatial pattern of production as a reflection of the social relations of production: that is, of the prevailing capital–labour relations (see for example Massey, 1984; Scott and Storper, 1986). At the macro level some broad patterns can be distinguished in these relations that provide an indication of the trend in the spatial configuration of production. However to understand the specific spatial outcome of social relations of production for a specific time, location and sector it is necessary to narrow the focus to the precise form that social relations of production take in this location and sector. In this section I shall concentrate on the broader macro level and its spatial implications; the sectoral and locational level will be dealt with in the subsequent sections.

The form taken by capital–labour relations from the Second World War until approximately the end of the 1960s has been labelled 'Fordism'.[8] Fordist mass production went hand in hand with the Keynesian welfare state, which through its macroeconomic policies maintained equilibrium by influencing aggregate demand, and through its labour and migration policies maintained production capacity while avoiding inflation. Fordism meant a change from craft-based production to mass production. Tasks in companies were fragmented to such a degree that each worker was responsible for only one small task in the production process instead of a wide range of artisanal activities. At the technological level this Taylorist organisation of labour was supported by machinery that was designed to perform one specific task. This mass production regime started in the automobile industry but came to encompass large parts of manufacturing. Fordism was made possible by a homogenisation of tastes and a mass market for consumer goods. In the search for economies of scale, vertical and horizontal integration became important company strategies. Multinational corporations increased their share of production and trade. Liberal immigration policies during the 1950s and 1960s ensured a sufficient supply of labour for mass production in industry. The liberalisation of international trade and fixed exchange rates under the Bretton Woods institutions (the IMF and the World Bank) led to an increase in the ratio of trade to GNP.

Fordism was first of all a national phenomenon. Schoenberger, for instance, notes that 'Fordism as a regime of accumulation is, in principle, internal to a given national social formation' (Schoenberger, 1988, p. 248). However it led to the spread of manufacturing over the globe. For example in the West, concessions to strong labour under Fordism provided a stimulus for capital to look for cheap labour elsewhere, so contributing to the new international division of labour.[9] I wish to emphasise that this new international division of labour did not mean that all sectors 'went international' or that all localities around the globe became attractive for manufacturing production. In some cases the development of manufacturing production in developing countries was not only directed towards exports, but also towards local markets in the developing countries themselves, leading to what Lipietz (1986, p. 32) calls 'peripheral Fordism'; in many cases however it was not, and entailed a 'bloody Taylorisation'. In this case the internationalisation of production did not lead to the internationalisation of consumption. Wages in developing countries remained low – thereby disturbing the Fordist balance between mass production and mass consumption – and increased capacity for mass production was not matched by a similar increase in mass consumption. The spread of manufacturing on an international scale was therefore both a product of Fordism and a factor in its decline.

This was one of the reasons for the crisis of Fordism at the end of the 1960s and the beginning of the 1970s.[10] The possibility of increasing productivity under a Fordist regime was reduced, which led to a fall in profitability and investment rates. The mass markets for durable consumption goods became saturated. The globalisation process that had contributed to the decline of Fordism increased enormously, especially in terms of the mobility of capital and services. This weakened the position of labour versus capital. Labour markets became more and more segmented between an established part and a more flexible marginal part, in which immigrant workers were overrepresented. Unemployment, especially amongst the more vulnerable segments of the labour market (women, immigrants), reached two-digit levels. Economies of scope replaced economies of scale and increased the importance of control over other firms instead of full vertical integration. Technology became directed towards the performance of different tasks by one machine. 'Just in time' delivery and the reduction of storage costs became important business strategies. This emphasis on rapid response made shorter lead times more important, which favoured production closer to the consumer. Immigration policies became more restrictive, which paradoxically contributed to the permanent settlement of immigrants in EU societies. The neoliberal break-up of the welfare state consensus between capital and labour was reflected in a downgrading of social policy. Internationally, the fixed exchange rate regime broke down and more and more non-tariff barriers to trade were introduced (see for example Harvey, 1989).

Spatially, the break-up of Fordism led to different responses by different actors. The tendency for vertical disintegration led, for instance, to a spread of production over territory (such as the spread of Fiat car production from Turin to the Italian countryside after 1969). The spread of manufacturing production also continued at the international level in some subsectors. On the other hand, rapidly changing consumer demand and 'just in time' production strategies put a premium on rapid and secure delivery, which (despite better and cheaper communication technology) is still inversely related to distance. Increasing protectionism also contributed to production taking place closer to consumers. According to Swyngedouw, this new phase led to 'spatial proximity of vertically quasi-integrated firms' (cited in Harvey, 1989, p. 178).

Schoenberger (1988, p. 257) maintains that 'production based on flexible technologies would tend to be reconcentrated in the core industrial countries'. The reason for this, according to Ross and Trachte (1990), is that the mere threat of shifting production to developing countries reinforced capital's position over labour and led to the degradation of labour standards in Western countries and the possibility of the return of labour-intensive activity.

The globalisation process that contributed to the erosion of the Fordist welfare state therefore brought about a number of different responses regarding the distribution of production around the globe. In some sectors and places it resulted in production spreading around the globe. In others – as in some segments of the clothing industry – it resulted in regionalisation, with production being located closer to the consumer instead of further away. Since in different sectors and locations Fordism took a specific spatial form, the impact of globalisation also had a different significance for these sectors and locations. To understand the spatial organisation of production it is necessary to look carefully at the precise relations between capital and labour in a specific sector (clothing) and location (EU/the Netherlands, Mediterranean countries and East Asia). It is to these specifics that I now turn.

The sectoral level

Whereas textiles can be considered as one of the crucial sectors in the industrial revolution, clothing cannot. Moreover until the end of the nineteenth century noncapitalist production relations remained predominant in the clothing sector. As in agriculture, in clothing production the costs of the reproduction of labour for capital were often reduced by the continuation of household production, generally by women. Another reason for the slow development of the industrialisation of clothing was that the structure of clothing production had changed little since medieval times. Clothing production by tailors was one of the sectors where the guild structure was strongest. Although guilds were abolished in many European countries during the Napoleonic era, resistance from organised tailors continued until well into the twentieth century. Not surprisingly perhaps, the industrial production of clothing, when it started at the end of the nineteenth century, was taken up by groups that had been excluded from the guild system, especially Jews. Jews had been active in the trading of second-hand clothing (which was not subject to guild organisation), but when Singer introduced the first efficient sewing machine to the market in 1851 they embarked on large-scale clothing production in both Europe and the United States. The lack of possibilities for economies of scale remained, however, which is one reason why household and sweatshop clothing production continued to exist and the manufacturing of clothing was mainly limited to the production of uniforms and other standardised wear. Even with the widespread growth of department stores in the second half of the nineteenth century, clothing was often sold 'tailored' and not ready-made, and when it was ready-made it was often not factory-made.

When we look at the relations between capital and labour in the emerging clothing industry the degree of heterogeneity is most striking, with large-scale clothing factories, the traditional tailor and household production existing side by side. However in the first half of the twentieth century tailors lost ground to factory production, whereas production by outworkers, both for own consumption and under sub-contracting arrangements with factories, persisted. Taylorism therefore existed alongside the individual tailor. The factories, which were mainly family-owned businesses, were engaged in a constant struggle with other factions of capital. For their supply of cloth they had to rely on the textile producers,[11] and for their sales they became increasingly dependent on retailers and jobbers. In general labour – mostly women – was only weakly organised and worked in deplorable conditions, in the factories as well as at home. 'It is a curious fact that the production of precisely those articles which serve the personal adornment of the ladies of the bourgeoisie involves the saddest consequences for the health of the workers' (Engels, cited in Wilson, 1985, p. 67).

Fordism can therefore hardly be seen as prevailing throughout the clothing industry. As Phizacklea (1992, p. 96) points out, Fordist methods in clothing production were only introduced after the Second World War and remained limited to certain items (men's tailored outerwear, shirts and underwear). Fashion wear (especially women's outerwear) underwent little change in production method.

What does all this mean for the international division of labour in the clothing industry? Very different trends took place in different segments of the clothing industry. Some production did take place under the Fordist compromise, usually in less volatile areas of clothing production where fashion did not play much of a role, making it possible to place orders long in advance. However because productivity increases in this section lagged compared with other industrial sectors, the linking of wage increases to overall productivity gains caused problems for clothing producers. In response factories started to subcontract more and more activities to low-wage countries and retailers started to import from abroad.[12]

This was reinforced by the low entry barriers to the industry, which made (international) competition very fierce, especially after the Second World War when communication and transportation technology improved. In Europe this was primarily due to the establishment of the European Community, which, for instance, enabled Italian, German and Belgian producers of clothing to export to the Dutch market. Since the 1960s developing countries, especially in East Asia, have managed to increase their exports of clothing to Europe. The clothing industry – particularly the less volatile parts of it that predominated until the end of the 1960s – was in a way one of the first global industries.

Only a few firms, mainly in Japan, have managed to use technology effectively to counter low labour costs in developing countries.

Technology in clothing production has changed slowly (the sewing machine is still the nucleus of clothing production).[13] Because investments in machinery (or fixed investments in general) constitute only a small percentage of total production costs (in which labour costs remain predominant), this makes the clothing industry – until this day – an industry with a low threshold.[14] Even now the return of clothing production to Western countries is unlikely to be facilitated by labour-saving technologies.

Other sectors of the clothing industry in Western countries continued to rely on outworkers to keep labour costs low. This kind of production was also touched by competition from abroad, but maintained its function in volatile, fashion-sensitive markets. Until the end of the 1960s, however, these sectors constituted a relatively small part of the market.

The internationalisation of production was also linked to the effectiveness with which capital and labour could use the state to protect their interests. Although clothing producers and labour managed to obtain protection from imports from developing countries, it took a long time for this protection to become effective (only under the second Multifibre Arrangement after 1979)[15] and differed from country to country. For instance the Netherlands was less restrictive in its interpretation and administration of the arrangement than other European countries. This may have been due to the generally open character of the Dutch economy and the strong position of retailers over producers. Producers, for their part, managed to achieve provisions – especially in agreements with nearby producing countries around the Mediterranean – that allowed for unlimited reimportation in the case of subcontracting. This contributed to a further weakening of labour's position versus capital.

This brings us to another important aspect of clothing production: fashion. The development of fashion in terms of changing clothing codes had been a feature of the development of capitalist production relations since the fourteenth century, but fashion increased enormously in importance during the second half of the nineteenth century. During the reign of Napoleon III, the *apogée* of nineteenth-century bourgeois Europe, Paris became the seat of numerous designers and producers of clothing. Although fashion at that time remained a privilege of the bourgeois and the aristocratic upper class and the diffusion of styles was not widespread, this was important because it meant that fashion became institutionalised, and perhaps more importantly the Janus head of fashion was revealed. As Frisby states, fashion combines 'the attraction of differentiation and change with that of similarity and conformity' (cited in Wilson, 1985, p. 98). This provided a major dilemma for the mass production of clothing. Mass production presupposes a standardisation of taste and behaviour (a mass market) that is part of the fashion message ('conformity'), while at the same time it is confronted with a wish for differentiation. It is again not surprising that the industrial production of clothing initially concentrated on market segments that were less sensitive to fashion change (for instance uniforms and men's clothing).[16]

Numerous theories have been proposed to explain fashion change (see for example Craig, 1994; Davis, 1992; Wilson, 1985). Some have described fashion as one of the ways in which dominant social classes try to distinguish themselves from the rest of society, but any innovation in design is picked up by others and imitated, leading the elite to look for new means of distinction. Others have focused on fashion as an expression of the *Zeitgeist*. In this view, numerous social developments are reflected in styles of dress. Some have analysed fashion as an instrument of female subordination to male dominance. Yet others view fashion as a sort of economic conspiracy in which producers and retailers of clothing try to manipulate demand. Fashion has also been studied along semiotic lines as a somewhat haphazard means of communication. Fashion is both a means of increasing clothing sales and a form of artistic creation and individual expression that cannot be understood in terms of class distinctions alone. As such it can be considered an institution that structures and in turn is structured by the behaviour of actors in the clothing sector.

Most analysts agree that fashion cycles have shortened during the twentieth century, and especially since the 1960s (see for example Wilson, 1985). This is partially a strategy by clothing producers and retailers to increase sales, especially when economic crises hamper consumption. However it is also part of a broader social and cultural change in terms of, for instance, individualisation. This process has made it necessary for retailers to change their collections more often and for stock to be delivered to them more quickly. According to Bull *et al.* (1993) the different clothing sectors in terms of quality and fashionableness that have come to the fore since the 1960s can all be connected to a particular location in the clothing supply. For example high-fashion, low-quality clothing can be expected to be produced near the consumer, in sweatshops or in nearby low-wage countries (ibid.).

In summary, we cannot explain the reemergence of contract clothing and the regionalisation of the clothing supply in the 1980s without a precise analysis of the sector itself. In this at least three characteristics of the clothing sector play a role. Firstly, Fordism and its mass-production-oriented technological innovations have never become the dominant trend in the clothing sector as a whole. Small-scale contract clothing sweatshops and outwork have always remained an integral part of the sector. Secondly, regionalisation is connected to the shortening of fashion cycles, putting a premium on quick delivery from locations close to the consumer. Thirdly, the more restrictive trade policy of the EU during the 1980s tried to counter clothing imports, particularly from East Asia, thereby contributing to the regionalisation process.

The locational level

'There is no single emerging pattern which characterises the integration of Third World countries into the international division of labour. It is possible to identify patterns both between and within branches and between and within countries' (Jenkins, 1984, p. 46). And this does not only count for the Third World, nor only for countries as a whole. So even if globalisation is the driving force behind contemporary changes in the spatial organisation of production, this can still have very different outcomes in different locations. In order to understand how globalisation in the clothing sector led to the spatial pattern of supply that I called regionalisation, it is necessary to analyse how capital–labour relations took a specific form under the impact of globalisation in the three localities that concern us here: clothing exporters in the Far East, nearby producers in the Mediterranean and Eastern Europe, and the importing countries of the EU.

Mediterranean countries, for instance, have been later to adopt a more export-led economic strategy than some East Asian countries. Although some Mediterranean countries had already adopted a more export-directed strategy in the 1970s (for instance Tunisia, Egypt and Portugal) it was mainly during the 1980s that these policies became more widespread. Some Arab countries along the Mediterranean had long been able to postpone painful structural adjustment measures because of direct as well as indirect (through migration, grants and, for example, Suez Canal revenues) moneys accruing to them from oil revenues (see for instance Beblawi and Luciani, 1987). Although Southern European countries had started a strategy of clothing exports earlier, changes occurred there too during the 1970s. In Italy, after the 1969 'hot autumn' of labour protests, the spread of clothing manufacturing to the countryside proved to be a successful exporting strategy. For Spain, and especially Greece and Portugal, the democratisation of the mid 1970s led to increased investment in clothing production and exports, especially when their barriers to export were taken away after accession to the EU (see for example Williams, 1984). In Eastern Europe, increased exports of clothing were in some countries linked to liberalisation during the 1980s (Poland and Hungary), but in others it took place after 1989. On the other hand, during the 1980s wages in some of the more successful East Asian countries rose (Hong Kong and South Korea), making clothing production in these countries less profitable. Other countries in the region (for instance China and Vietnam) succeeded in increasing their exports of mass-produced clothing, but not the more fashionable garments (Scheffer, 1992). My main point therefore is that in trying to explain the shift in the supply of clothing to the EU from East Asia to the Mediterranean and Eastern Europe, the relations between the capital, labour and institutions in these locations should be taken into account. The late transition to export-led policies in the Mediterranean and Eastern European countries has been crucial in this.

As an example, consider Turkey, which only became successful as an exporter of clothing to the European Union in the 1980s (whereas, as we have seen, some Asian countries became successful at an earlier date). The Turkish industrial structure is still strongly influenced by the legacy of Atatürk's state-led industrialisation of the 1920s and 1930s, despite the fact that the 1950s import-substitution programme provided more room for the private sector. This only changed in the 1980s. The vehement class struggle and political turmoil of the 1970s had led the army to seize power again in 1980, thereby clearing the way (through severe restrictions on union power) for Turgut Özal's structural adjustment drive of 1983. It is therefore not surprising that Turkish success in the export of clothing started in the 1980s.

But the analysis of relations between capital and labour should not be restricted to foreign supplying countries; we should also focus on the situation in Western countries. Much of what was said in the previous section also applies to the Netherlands during the 1970s and 1980s. During this period – particularly in the late 1980s – the social achievements under the postwar welfare state policies came under fire. The position of the unemployed deteriorated and the immigrant population suffered more than most. As such, the labour market became increasingly segmented in ethnic terms. As stated before, the reduced opportunity for immigrants to find regular jobs on the labour market

constituted a push towards ethnic entrepreneurship and, closely connected, contributed to the further marginalisation of immigrant labour.

This process occurred in most large cities in the Netherlands, and
can thus hardly provide an explanation for the concentration of clothing sweatshops in Amsterdam. We should therefore also analyse what
is specific in the relations between capital and labour in Amsterdam,
and the specific position that Amsterdam occupies in the Dutch
economy. This applies especially to the clothing sector, since firms
involved in clothing have their headquarters in Amsterdam, including
the World Fashion Centre, the wholesale centre for clothing in the
Netherlands. Rekers (1993; see also Chapter 3 of this volume) concludes that some more general characteristics in economic and urban
structure, lifestyle and the residential pattern of immigrants make
Amsterdam more attractive for specific immigrant entrepreneurial
activities than Rotterdam.

To understand the specific spatial expression of globalisation in the
clothing sector, it is therefore necessary to analyse carefully how
capital–labour relations develop in each location. Developments in
the 1980s in the three localities that concern us here all contributed to
a pattern of regionalisation. Rising wages made East Asia more expensive; structural adjustment made Eastern Europe and the Mediterranean
more attractive; and neoliberal policies marginalised immigrant workers in the Netherlands and stimulated their entrepreneurship.

Conclusion

In this chapter I have argued that the emergence of clothing sweatshops should be examined as part of a process of regionalisation of the
clothing supply to the EU. As such it is connected to the shift in
imports from the Far East to imports from Mediterranean and Eastern
European countries during the 1980s. The driving force behind this
regionalisation tendency is a process of globalisation in capital–labour
relations. Here, globalisation does not mean the development of a system that totally determines the spatial organisation of production. The
impact of globalisation in a sector – at a specific location – is determined by the specific sectoral and local relations between capital and
labour at that time. An analysis of the emergence of immigrant-run
sweatshops in the clothing industry in the EU should therefore be
directed to the global, local and sectoral dynamics of capital and labour.
In this the finalisation and internationalisation of Fordism, the specific
organisation of the production of clothing, rapid fashion changes,

selective restrictive trade policy and the timing and degree of the success of structural adjustment in the countries and cities involved in clothing production should all be the object of research.

Notes

1 This is not to underestimate the success of some European countries (especially Italy) in the export of clothing.

2 This is not to say that in some branches of the clothing industry the decline did not continue; we merely want to point out that immigrant entrepreneurship – as important as this may be in itself – is not the only constituent part of the partial recovery of the clothing industry in the EU.

3 Since imports by sea and air mainly come from East Asia, imports by land can be taken as an indication of imports from other European countries and the Mediterranean.

4 For other criticisms of these approaches see Chapter 5 of this volume.

5 The literature on the segmented character of labour markets points to the fact that immigrant enterprises often fill niches that have been abandoned by indigenous entrepreneurs. This could explain their focus on clothing. However, with regard to the Dutch situation, the Dutch entrepreneurs who withdrew from clothing after 1965 concentrated on different segments of the clothing market (producing mostly high-quality, low-fashion clothing such as raincoats, men's suits and ladies' coats) than the Turkish entrepreneurs in the 1980s, who concentrated on the more volatile segments of the market.

6 See for example Kloosterman (1996b) for a discussion of the global character of Amsterdam.

7 Although it could be argued that certain segments of the clothing market are being 'servicised', to the extent that customised, small-batch, quick-service production is becoming more important.

8 For further discussion of the concept of Fordism and post-Fordism see Harvey (1989).

9 At the same time, however, the strong position of unions under Fordism may also have *slowed* the closing down of factories and their moving to low-wage countries.

10 There has been considerable debate on the question of whether the post-Fordist period can be considered as a new period of stable relations between capital, labour and institutions. Some speak of a new period of flexible accumulation (Harvey, 1989; Piore and Sabel, 1984). Other authors suggest that the 'exhaustion of Fordism' (Noël, 1987, p. 317) is not complete (Brenner and Glick, 1991; Gordon, 1988).

11 Although some clothing producers developed out of the textile industry, and *vice versa*, some textile producers extended their activities to include the production of clothing.

12 This was especially the case in countries where retailers held a strong position *vis-à-vis* producers. In Holland nowadays for instance, the four largest retail chains account for over 40 per cent of clothing sales. Such a buyers' market reduced profit margins for Dutch producers, leading to their marginalisation and the internationalisation of production (see Scheffer, 1992).

13 Innovations did take place in cutting and design (CAD–CAM).
14 It was mainly directed to the development of new textile materials (rayon, nylon, polyester).
15 The Multifibre Arrangement is a treaty that enables developed countries to introduce restrictive measures (quotas) against imports of textiles and clothing from developing countries.
16 While fashion change in men's dress was more important than in women's clothing until the nineteenth century, this gradually changed.

2
Market Potential as a Decisive Influence on the Performance of Ethnic Minority Business

Trevor Jones, Giles Barrett and David McEvoy

> small firms live or die [according to] whether the economy is generating enough overall demand. Given the latter, other problems which receive fashionable attention as 'serious' problems for the small firm can be coped with or are put into perspective.
>
> (Curran *et al.*, 1991)

The issues

Since the dawn of the 1980s much scholarly energy has been devoted to understanding the remarkable against-the-tide rise of ethnic business. Throughout virtually the entire advanced capitalist realm, members of disadvantaged racialised minorities have been in the vanguard of the entrepreneurial explosion that has come to be seen as a hallmark feature of the age. An acutely paradoxical development defying easy explanation, the development of minority-owned business – 'development' here being understood as emergence, numerical growth, expansion and, above all, commercial performance and earning capacity – has been addressed in a voluminous, proliferating and somewhat confusing literature (Barrett *et al.*, 1996; Ram and Jones, forthcoming). At the extremes, explanations range from the entreprogenic properties of traditional religious beliefs imported by migrants into modern society as part of their cultural baggage (Werbner, 1984);[1] to self-employment as a last-ditch survival option in the face of what Parker (1994) calls 'the twin perils of racism and recession' (Jones, 1989).

Perhaps the most cogent and all-embracing framework of analysis is that offered by Aldrich and Waldinger (1990; see also Waldinger, 1995). Building on earlier guidelines suggested by Auster and Aldrich (1984),

Boissevain (1984) and Ward (1987a), they propose that ethnic business development be seen as resulting from an interplay between three sets of variables:

- *Opportunity structure*: the external commercial environment in which the ethnic group's entrepreneurs operate.
- *Group characteristics*: whether or not these entrepreneurs can mobilise informal resources from within the group on advantageous terms permitted by communal and familial solidarity.
- *Ethnic strategies*: essentially the manner in which group characteristics are brought to bear on the opportunity structure, the strategic deployment of ethnic resources to achieve an effective pay-off in the marketplace.

In this chapter we focus on one specific and arguably decisive component of opportunity structure, the *market*, the pattern of demand – or lack of it – for the kinds of goods and services in which ethnic firms choose to specialise (or upon which they are compelled to be dependent). To be completely accurate, the concept of opportunity structure ought to be interpreted as embracing a very wide range of elements (Jones *et al.*, 1992): a total commercial environment made up of numerous economic institutions (banking, finance, insurance, real estate), together with social elements and political actors such as the state itself, whose interventions can be crucial on all manner of levels, from national policies for enterprise promotion to local planning practices (Jones *et al.*, 1989). Nevertheless, in common with influential sources such as Aldrich and Waldinger (1990), we believe that the customer is the pivotal element in all this, the fountainhead from which all else flows. As indicated by Curran *et al.* (1991; see above), this is often overlooked in discussions on all kinds of small business development, whether general or ethnic minority-owned. While problems certainly are caused by scarce capital, management expertise and skills, the success or failure of small enterprises depends in the last instance on whether there is an effective demand for what they offer on the terms on which they offer it. All the capital, technology and managerial sophistication in the world is of little use if no one is prepared to buy the end product. This is one of many glaringly obvious truisms that nevertheless often go unacknowledged in this field.

In this chapter we are especially concerned with the belief that the social changes and economic restructuring of the so-called post-Fordist era have created the essential conditions for ethnic entrepreneurialism to flourish (Boissevain, 1984; Ward, 1987a). Due attention should also be paid to the way in which this restructuring of market demand sets strict boundaries within which such firms live or die, survive or thrive. Not only does it limit the number, size and earning capacity of firms, it also helps to determine the kinds of business activity for which minority entrepreneurs are eligible.

While it would be untrue to suggest that this question has been ignored, we nonetheless contend that the role of the market has been inadequately theorised. In some instances it has hardly been theorised at all, with writers continuing even now to highlight ethnic entrepreneurialism as a culturally determined, voluntaristic process and to pay minimal attention to the structural context in which it arises (see for example Basu, 1995). In this view, the social and cultural characteristics of certain immigrant-origin groups create entrepreneurs apparently irrespective of whether there is a market demand for them. Where the opportunity structure has been prioritised there is often a tendency to overemphasise the post-Fordist market as a positive source of opportunity almost custom-made for minority business, while downplaying its inherent constraints. Changes in consumption and production patterns have, it is argued, opened up advantageous 'niches' for immigrant-origin entrepreneurs (Boissevain, 1984; Ward, 1985, 1986, 1987a). Our contention is that many of these supposed market opportunities are in reality highly limiting, acting to inhibit performance and place unacceptably heavy costs on racialised entrepreneurs, a means of reproducing disadvantage rather than escaping from it – except in a small minority of individual cases. This situation is a product of restructuring on two fronts: the supply side and the demand side. On the *supply side*, labour market restructuring has had disproportionate consequences for racial minorities. Because of their historical role as replacement labour (Miles, 1982) and the prevailing racialised division of labour, migrant-origin workers have borne a disproportionate share of the calamitous job losses attendant upon deindustrialisation and similar processes (Brah, 1996; Kloosterman, 1994; Ohri and Faruqi, 1988; Sassen, 1991a). Consequently unemployment and blocked labour market entry have grossly swollen the ranks of potential recruits to self-employment (Jones *et al.*, 1989). Quite clearly, no account of market potential for ethnic businesses can take place without considering the possible oversupply of entrepreneurs crowding in to compete for this potential.

On the *demand side*, new market niches eminently well suited to ethnic enterprise have been created by a whole set of recent changes, including the switch to 'flexible' production and various changes in consumer taste. Given the flood of would-be entrants, however, these gold seams would need to be extremely rich to satisfy even a fraction of the prospectors. As we shall shortly see, they are not only far from expansive – one is reminded of the dictionary definition of 'niche' as a 'shallow recess' – but also spatially and sectorally uneven. In some instances, to continue the goldfield metaphor, they may actually be petering out. Furthermore escape from these constricted confines usually entails negotiating other blockages in the opportunity structure and mobilising the kinds of scarce resources that are customarily unavailable to such entrepreneurs.

What is the conventional view on the connection between economic restructuring/social change and the opportunity structure for ethnic enterprise? One of the first commentators to address the question directly was Boissevain (1984), who argued that the new socio-economic landscape of post-Fordism (though he did not use that precise term) was opening up new market space for small firms in general, with a consequent resurgence in the small-firm economy marking a reversal of decades of decline; and that many vital segments of this market space were potentially well suited to the special characteristics of immigrant-owned firms. Changing patterns of demand and supply were creating 'market niches' for ethnic enterprise. Expanding these arguments, Ward (1987a) specifies a fairly exhaustive set of niche markets for ethnic business. For clarity, we shall examine these under three headings: (1) the ethnic niche, (2) niches arising from changes in consumer demand patterns and (3) niches arising from manufacturing restructuring. We shall then propose an alternative method of classifying ethnic business market potential, designed in the simplest fashion to clarify several unresolved issues and provide an operational framework for research. This is derived from our own research (Jones and McEvoy, 1992; McEvoy and Jones, 1993) on South Asian-origin entrepreneurs (Indian, Pakistani, Bangladeshi and Sri Lankan) in Britain and Canada, and on African-Caribbean businesses in Britain (Barrett, 1997).

Ethnic niches: the pioneer stage

In North America and many countries of Western Europe one of the principal markets for ethnic entrepreneurs has always been their own community (Ward, 1987a). As Waldinger *et al.* (1990b, p. 108) remind us: 'Most newcomer groups have begun by clustering in distinctive areas ... opportunities for ethnic business first arise in such neighbour-hoods.' Somewhat ironically, this particular niche (arguably the most important in terms of the number of ethnic entrepreneurs it supports) usually has little directly to do with post-Fordist restructuring, since in most cases it decisively predates that period, certainly for many ethnic entrepreneurial communities in the United States and Britain. In the case of South Asians in Britain, one of the great contemporary exam-ples, the ethnic community consumer base resulted from the interna-tional migrations of the postwar boom period coupled with an acutely uneven and highly concentrated pattern of urban settlement (Cater and Jones, 1979; Robinson, 1986). This created dense spatial clusters of ethnic consumer potential. To be absolutely accurate here, we would have to say that this stage created a largely *latent* customer base, which was then activated by subsequent labour market restructuring that released thousands of Asian workers to search for self-employment in small shops and services.

Whatever its origins, the ethnic community market has been a major factor in ethnic enterprise development, notably in the early stages of emergence and consolidation. This was certainly the case for South Asians in Britain. To be historically precise, the first postwar Asian traders in Britain were pedlars hawking goods from door to door in all-white neighbourhoods (Hiro, 1971). However by the late 1960s these had become heavily outnumbered by settled shopkeepers based in urban areas with a high Asian presence. Early research on this Asian enterprise economy – roughly coinciding with its 'pioneer' phase – found a very high level of locational correlation between Asian retail outlets and Asian customers, the vast majority of firms being contained within the segregated residential enclaves of Asian immigrants (Aldrich *et al.*, 1981, 1984, 1986; Jones, 1981), thus indicating the degree to which the typical ethnic firm was dependent on a coethnic clientele.[2] This perfectly describes what Ward (1987a) means by the ethnic niche market, essentially a protected space in which entrepreneurs from a specific ethnic community enjoy virtual immunity from competitors outside that community. In the Asian case, this derives above all from the special culturally derived needs of the community: items of food, clothing, literature, leisure and so on that are culturally, linguistically or nationally specific. Only insiders have the knowledge, expertise, contacts and, above all, credibility to supply such goods and services. Consequently the ethnic market niche is effectively an ethnic suppliers' monopoly, a no-go area for outside competitors and as such the ulti-mate in 'nicheness'. Moreover Aldrich *et al.* (1981) found this monopoly to be further reinforced by *ethnic loyalty* (preferential patronage by members of the community) and by sheer *proximity*, a convenience factor which allows the ethnic entrepreneur to deal also in a range of non-culturally specific items such as cigarettes or general household goods.

Without doubt the availability of this captive market offered golden opportunities to the pioneering wave of Asian firms, some of which have built on their initial advantages to grow into substantial and high performance concerns.[3] At the same time, however, one of the inescapable properties of any 'shallow recess' is that it can be very quickly filled. Simply by virtue of its tempting prospects, it rapidly attracts additional entrant firms and so passes the point where the aggregate demand of its customer population is sufficient to support its population of firms at a satisfactory level of return. Almost by definition, the ethnic market is highly vulnerable to this saturation effect. As a general principle, there are clear limits on the number of its own members that any given population can support as retailers or service providers; or in the words of Hiro (1971), commenting on his own community, 'They could not *all* be grocers and restaurateurs', another obvious but often overlooked truism that precisely captures the contradictory nature of the ethnic niche relationship. The point is elucidated by Waldinger *et al.* (1990b, p. 112): 'the ethnic market can support only a limited number of firms, in part because it is quantitatively small and in part because the ethnic population often lacks sufficient buying power'. Such a view emphasises the 'minority' as well as the 'ethnic' in 'ethnic minority', a salutary reminder of the circumscribed nature of this market niche. Certainly for British Asian consumer outlets addressing little more than a neighbourhood Asian customer base, the saturation point was rapidly reached. When on top of this there is a huge influx of Asian labour market refugees seeking their salvation in the corner shop, entrepreneurial overcrowding becomes acute to the point of crisis (Jones *et al.*, 1989). Insulated though they may be from outside competition, ethnic niche firms are by no means protected from one another.

As if all this were not sufficiently problematic, there are further hazards connected with the location of the ethnic niche. Because of the typical patterns of racial residential segregation, this market base is more often than not located in old, run-down, inner city areas, where outdated, poor quality premises, security and crime hazards and generally blighted physical environments are now part of the fabric (Jones *et al.*, 1989; Patel, 1988; Waldinger *et al.*, 1990b). Hence, in addition to its own internal contradictions, the ethnic niche imposes the external costs attendant on operating in the most hostile commercial environments it is possible to imagine.

African-Caribbean underrepresentation in business ownership has, like the South Asian presence, been explained in terms of both cultural factors and the opportunity structure. The African-Caribbean propensity for commercial exploitation has been limited by a series of factors that include the availability of both class and ethnic resources and lowered expectations in life engendered by racism. In terms of market opportunity, African-Caribbeans in business are disadvantaged by few specialist consumer demands among the African-Caribbean community. This hinders the establishment of a local ethnic market (Soni *et al.*, 1987). Nevertheless some regard initial reliance on a coethnic market as essential:

> African-Caribbean business has to locate in a black area if it's to survive. It must find itself a niche amongst its own people before it reaches the white market... African-Caribbean business aiming initially at the white market will fail... here, we have a good location, we target the African-Caribbean market which are steps down the right road (Lewisham African-Caribbean hair and beauty specialist).
>
> (Soni *et al.*, 1987)

The specialism of this informant is consistent with the suggestions of earlier authors who identified hairdressing and beauty products as a potentially viable niche for African-Caribbean entrepreneurs (Creed and Ward, 1987; Reeves and Ward, 1984). There are a few parallel niches serving distinctive tastes in this ethnic community: music stores, West Indian and African foods, and the provision of relevant newspapers and magazines. Given the size, limited concentration and internal diversity of the African-Caribbean population however, few entrepreneurs can survive on the basis of the community market alone. Saturation of the market space for beauty services, for example, makes ownership in this sector highly competitive and frought with the potential for business closure. Consequently business performance, as measured by growth, expansion and number of employees, is characteristically disappointing (Barrett, 1997).

In sum, then, the local ethnic space provides lean pickings for the proliferation of tiny and often precarious firms within its stifling confines. Genuine entrepreneurial progress depends on breaking out into more expansive market space, where diversification into higher-order activities and growth in scale can occur. To use Aldrich *et al.*'s (1984) metaphor, entrepreneurs must seek expansion through the 'export' of goods and services to the general population beyond their ethnic boundaries. History abounds with instances of ethnic entrepreneurs who have succeeded in thus shifting from autarchy to export-led growth. As would be expected, the majority market can support far larger numbers of minority businesses, enabling many ethnic groups to develop self-employment as a leading occupational specialism. By definition such a specialism could never be supported by the ethnic population itself since, to paraphrase Hiro, no community can live by taking in its own washing. Classically described as 'middlemen minorities' (Bonacich, 1973), these commercially specialised communities are typified by US-based groups such as the Jews, Chinese, Japanese and Koreans who, according to Waldinger *et al.* (1990b, p. 120), 'exemplify those ethnic minorities whose overrepresentation in self-employment results from their success in finding customers outside their limited ethnic markets'.

Although most research on middlemen minorities (or 'entrepreneurial minorities' as Bonacich now chooses to call them for reasons laid out in Light and Bonacich, 1988) is North American-based, there is growing evidence of the emergence of this form in Britain and other European countries. In the case of South Asians in Britain, Ward (1985) argues that market reorientation was well under way by the 1980s, with a growing number of Asian businesses relocating, branching off or starting from scratch in areas relatively unpenetrated by Asian residential settlement. While the prime destination was middle-class suburbs in cities with an established inner urban presence, there was also penetration of peripheral council estates, exurban areas and localities not hitherto settled by the group in significant numbers.

However reorientation to the general market is not necessarily a second-stage progression as in the above case. In the case of Britain's Chinese population, it seems that almost from the first moment of postwar migration, business activity has been aimed at the non-Chinese mainstream. Moreover, with a self-employment rate over twice that of the general population and an almost complete absence of residential clusters or reliance on coethnic clientele, the Chinese fulfil all the criteria of entrepreneurial minority status in a more clear-cut manner than any of the other significantly large minority groups in Britain. At this point questions must be asked about precisely what comparative advantage racialised minority entrepreneurs enjoy in these open markets. Vulnerable and unprotected by coethnic customer support, *ceteris paribus* we might suppose them to be competitively disadvantaged rather than otherwise. What exactly are these 'market niches' so ideally suited to those against whom everything else in society is weighted? What is it that culturally distinct minorities possess which enables them to outperform in open competition those not thus handicapped? To answer these questions we turn to the forces of social and economic transformation outlined by Ward (1987a, 1991).

Changing demand patterns

One standard answer has to do with changes in lifestyle and consumer preferences, which act to create a greatly increased demand for convenience, flexibility, accessibility and general 'user-friendliness' in retailing and consumer service provision. To demonstrate through a specific case, we draw on accounts of the Chinese catering industry in Britain (Liao, 1993; Parker, 1994; Watson, 1977). Here a rapidly expanding market for restaurant and take-away food in general has been generated by social changes such as the rise in female employment and in the number of single person households. When this is coupled with changes in popular taste, the result is a vastly increased demand for 'exotic' food, a market space that can only be properly filled by caterers of foreign origin. This accounts not only for the dazzling proliferation of Chinese outlets, but also for the parallel rise of Mediterranean and 'Indian' equivalents (in the 'Indian' case these are very frequently Bangladeshi or Pakistani).

Not coincidentally, then, the catering sector is one of the two most densely populated middleman niches. The other is the even more heavily subscribed low-order retailing trade, which in Britain characteristically takes the form of South Asian-owned outlets for food and confectionery–news–tobacco (CTN), firms whose competitive *raison d'être* owes almost everything to customer convenience through long and unsocial opening hours. These two sectors together account for an inordinately large proportion of ethnic-minority firms in Britain. For the Chinese, things are still more extreme; as many as 90 per cent of the economically active population are accounted for by catering alone, either as self-employed or as employees of other Chinese (Bailey *et al.*, 1995). Evidently, then, these two areas of service activity have come to be ethnic minority specialisms, so much so as to have become embedded in British popular folklore – Mr Patel the newsagent, Mr Wu the take-away (though in a previous incarnation he was a laundry-man!). In both instances there has been a vigorous process of ethnic commercial succession, the newcomers directly displacing the incumbent indigenous shopkeepers or fish and chip proprietors.

Yet when we come to evaluate what this means for the entrepreneurs themselves we are confronted by a dilemma, a problem of distinguishing positives and negatives. In catering, for example, ethnic operators do seem to enjoy a positive advantage in that they are promoting a product that, because it is in its very essence derived from their own heritage cultures, is unique to them and appropriable by no one else. They are enjoying an ethnically protected monopoly but without the demographic and financial constraints of an ethnic clientele. In convenience retailing, too, it has been suggested that immigrant entrepreneurs flourish because of their very freshness, their attitudes and working practices uncluttered by hidebound notions of shutting shop at 6 p.m. on Wednesday afternoons and all day Sunday. This relationship between outsider status and the ability to see entrepreneurial possibilities in the most unpromising situations is convincingly demonstrated by Werbner (1990a).

Having recognised all this, however, there can be little dispute that far and away the principal competitive advantage possessed by ethnic firms in these sectors is labour intensiveness – sheer brute labour power. According to Jones *et al.* (1993), the average Asian CTN opens 14 hours longer per week than its white equivalent, a superiority that is absolutely crucial in a field where the prime consideration is customer convenience. Significantly, however, this competitive advantage is not mainly attributable to superior access to family labour, as is repeatedly argued, since family labour inputs turn out to be relatively minor for both Asians and whites. It is primarily due to the Asian owner working 17 hours more than his or her white counterpart. At 85 hours per week, this is more than double the normal West European working week and in itself is direct vindication of our claim that this kind of market niche imposes excessive costs on its incumbents.

As argued by Jones *et al.* (ibid.), Asian labour intensiveness in this sector ought not to be explained primarily by reference to cultural traits or communal resources but by the intrinsically demanding nature of low-order retailing, with its intense competitiveness and its premium on long hours of access for the customer. Seen in this light, the rapid colonisation of this niche by minority shopkeepers reflects not so much a vigorous response to an expansive new 'window of opportunity' as a withdrawal by white native entrepreneurs from a marginal activity offering paltry returns on sweated labour. All this perfectly illustrates Light's (1984, p. 199) comments about ethnic

entrepreneurs being obliged to 'obtain satisfaction from squalid propri-
etorships that would not attract native white wage earners'. Judged by
the yardsticks of capitalist accountancy, a fair proportion of small ethnic businesses in this market would be deemed uneconomic, only continuing to survive because their proprietors are prepared to accept
submarginal returns on human and monetary capital (Jones, 1989).
Even then they are subject to appallingly high individual failure rates
(McEvoy and Aldrich, 1986).

As if this were not sufficient disadvantage, there are two further
inescapable penalties. One is that because of the racialised nature of the
shopkeeper–customer relationship, ethnic entrepreneurs are compelled –
or feel they are – to work extra hard in order to overcome white resistance and place them on an equal footing with white competitors
(Jones *et al.*, 1993). In addition the white neighbourhood market
exposes them to all manner of racist harassment, abuse and occasion-
ally violence.[4] As outlined by Parker (1994), this applies equally
strongly to Chinese take-away food businesses, most of which are isolated in white neighbourhoods and reliant on young female family
workers, whose position is described by Parker (ibid., p. 627) as 'one of
the most vulnerable jobs in the world'. Such a chilling verdict is sufficient in itself to cause a rethink of the whole concept of opportunity
structures ripe for exploitation by minority entrepreneurs. When it
comes to exploitation, the boot is usually on the other foot.

A second condition, potentially even more damaging in the long
run, is commercial vulnerability in the face of competition from large
corporate capital, a product of the inbuilt structural disadvantage of
the small enterprise in an economy that, for all the rhetoric about a
new era of small entrepreneurialism, continues to be dominated by the
giants (Auster and Aldrich, 1984). In respect of retailing, Jones (1989)
argues that until roughly the 1970s this field was largely the preroga-
tive of the small operator simply because it generally yielded insufficient returns to justify the entry of large-scale capital. With the advent
of super/hypermarketing, all this changed drastically, opening up the
field for increasing penetration by the giants (so much for post-Fordist
decentralisation!).

In the latest phase of monopolisation, an invasion has begun of all
the hitherto ignored nooks and crannies so cherished by the ethnic
firm. Major supermarket chains in Britain have taken advantage
of changes in the law to stay open until late in the evening and
on Sundays; just before Christmas 1996 the Tesco chain kept certain
stores open 24 hours a day! The small retailers, to whom law enforcers

usually turned a blind eye, have lost the protected time niches they previously exploited. Simultaneously their spatial niches have been attacked by the arrival in Britain of highly competitive chains of discount grocery stores such as Aldi and Netto. These groups have chosen to locate their mid-scale shops in poorer areas of cities, normally at some distance from superstores. The poor and the relatively immobile now have a 'low price' alternative to the ethnic corner shop. A third prong in this attack on protected market space has been the spread of 24-hour convenience stores attached to petrol filling stations. Hardly unpredictably, then, the latest rash of 'ethnic' news headlines in Britain is peppered with such proclamations as 'Asian corner shop faces extinction' (*Guardian*, 17 September 1996) and 'Young Asians set to shun trade' (*Financial Times*, 10 September 1996).

What all this amounts to is that the 1980s expansion of the British Asian enterprise economy, as described by Ward (1985), was more a matter of simple spatial reorientation than structural transformation. The critical build-up of pressure on the ethnic niche market had to be relieved, either by targeting fresh customers in fresh areas for the same type of business, or by offering fresh products and services, preferably those with higher returns on financial and human capital. Or to redefine the distinction, either by shifting horizontally in space or vertically up the 'value-added chain'. Constrained by a persistent lack of personal and financial resources, new Asian entrepreneurs continue to concentrate on the established lines of business because of their low entry requirements and have merely exchanged the Asian for the non-Asian neighbourhood as their customer base. Indeed it is probable that they have become even more sectorally concentrated than before, because at least the Asian niche offered some room for specialists in culturally specific lines such as saree shops, sweet centres, Asian language bookshops and so on.

The absence of niche opportunities for African-Caribbeans in local ethnic space can also be interpreted as an impetus for some entrepreneurs to break out of the constraints of the ethnic market space in search of mainstream markets. The relative dearth of culturally specific necessities sought by the African-Caribbean community is such that entrepreneurs must eventually adapt their market orientation to serve the general society. The processes of market adaptation and adoption of a local non-ethnic role may follow an initial period in which the African-Caribbean firm targets the coethnic market. Arguably the need to break out is more urgent for African-Caribbeans than Asians owing to the shortage of specific in-group goods and services. No such break out has however occurred. As with South Asians, food retail and CTN are the most common business activities, but the number of enterprises is below the South Asian figure by at least an order of magnitude.

Manufacturing restructuring

More positively, other changes have opened up opportunities for a handful of ethnic firms to shift upwards, for qualitative development rather than horizontal duplication. The most obvious sphere in which to achieve this is manufacturing, which under post-Fordism has been subject to much decentralisation of ownership and a shift from mass to flexible production (Scott, 1988). This has created clear opportunities for small enterprise as a whole and also ideal niches for ethnic business (Ward, 1987a), notably in textiles and clothing (Phizacklea, 1990). For writers such as Werbner (1990) on Manchester Pakistanis and Clark and Rughani (1983) on Leicester Indians, the supreme competitive strength of Asians in this sector is the ethnic network: bonds of trust between producers, suppliers, middlemen, exporters and all else involved. Certainly the rag trade sector contains some of the most successful Asian enterprises in Britain, as measured by rapid growth, high profits and in some cases technical sophistication (Dhaliwal and Amin, 1995).

Even here, however – and at the risk of appearing mean-spirited – this optimism needs to be tempered. As Brah (1996) comments, the existence of a comparative minority of high fliers only goes to illuminate the acutely polarised nature of the Asian enterprise economy, whose more typical representative is still the diminutive shop surviving only by dint of a truly awesome working regime. In a widespread trawl of eleven diverse English localities, Jones *et al.* (1992) interviewed only 20 manufacturers out of a total of 174 Asian respondents. In line with Brah's comments, these did appear as a genuine though thin layer of cream, distinctly better performers than the general run – larger and with better earnings from far fewer working hours on the part of the owners themselves. Here we note that this finding deals a painful blow to the familiar mantra about ethnic entrepreneurial success being won by sheer industrious toil. In reality it is won by working 'smart' rather than simply working hard, in circumstances where owners have the opportunity to delegate and manage rather than sit behind a till until midnight. Yet again, however, there is a caveat. Even while entrepreneurial work appears less onerous and better rewarded in this sector, the evidence suggests that this advantage may be gained at the expense of a sweated workforce, many of whom are outworkers.[5] Once again this is a highly costly sector for those who work in it but with more scope for displacing the burdens from owner to worker.

A framework for further analysis

In common with most existing accounts of ethnic market patterns, the discussion so far has been somewhat unsystematic, with imperfect distinctions drawn between the various types of market space and the way the ethnic economy may progress from one dominant orientation to another. Even Ward's (1985) attempt to generalise about the way that immigrant groups progress from a replacement labour role into self-employment, with increasingly diversified market orientations, fails to go much beyond the well-known distinction between ethnic niche and middleman minority. What is lacking is a sense of geographical market hierarchy. What Ward implies is that all markets are local, whereas in reality it hardly needs stating that they can be city-wide, regional, national or even global. For example the South Asian retail cluster in Gerard Street East in Toronto exists in the almost complete absence of a relevant neighbourhood ethnic population but draws its Asian clientele from all over southern Ontario and from across the United States border.

In a bid to incorporate this added spatial dimension, Jones and McEvoy (1992) propose a fourfold typology based on the argument that ethnic firms are not only distinguished by ethnic versus non-ethnic market orientation, but also by whether their customer base is predominantly local or non-local. The latter derives from the fairly obvious assumption that larger scale and higher value-added activities such as manufacturing, wholesaling and high order retailing can only exist on the base of a market extending far beyond the local neighbourhood. Almost by definition such activities are geared to geographically extensive markets.

The resultant cross-classification by customer ethnicity and customer proximity gives four hypothetical market spaces:

- *Local ethnic* (Ward's ethnic niche): this is conceived as a double-bounded space in which entrepreneurial activity – type, size and performance – is constrained by localism as well as ethnicity. In addition to its quantitative restrictions on ethnic firms, such a space can support little in the way of sectoral diversity. We prefer the label 'ethnic enclosure' as accurately capturing the notion of ethnic enterprise as trapped, its potential repressed, only to be released by breaking out into more expansive environments.

- *Local non-ethnic* (Ward's middleman niche): most escapees from the enclosure have occurred in the direction of this space, which is relatively easy to enter, somewhat more expansive quantitatively but, as we have seen, still largely constrained to low-order sectors by the neighbourhood effect. Furthermore ethnic business is now subject to the additional hazards of customer and street racism and to actual shrinkage of customer potential. Real progress is likely to be confined to those who have made it to the two upper market spaces, where customer potential is not stifled by localism.

- *Ethnic non-local*: little recognised in the literature, this high-level ethnic market contains those firms which continue to sell mainly to their own coethnics but over a much wider, indeed theoretically infinite geographical orbit. Among South Asians the typical denizens of this market are wholesalers in the rag trade or selling to Asian retail outlets over a regional or national range; clothing manufacturers dealing through Asian wholesalers; high-order retailers such as those clustered in Southall in London or Gerrard Street East in Toronto, who pull in Asian customers from a very wide radius for up-market clothing, jewellery and other specialist goods; and self-employed professionals such as accountants serving other Asian businesses. In all these cases the ethnic network factor is retained but without neighbourhood constraints.

- *Non-ethnic, non-local*: unbounded on all sides, this final space represents a genuinely mainstream market, the ultimate stage in the progression, with ethnic firms selling to the open general market. As well as activities such as manufacturing and exporting, this space also contains 'Indian' restaurants that attract widely dispersed white customers, high-order retail outlets in strategic locations, petrol stations and hotels.

When we apply this typology to our own British and Canadian Asian retail and service firm samples we discover two things (Table 2.1). Firstly, the banal but vital hypothesis that earnings, scale and sectoral diversity are dependent on the availability of market space is clearly upheld in both countries. Whatever the political, economic and cultural differences between Canada and Britain, the pattern of difference between the four spaces holds good in each case: non-local markets are at an advantage on each indicator with respect to local markets. Secondly, in Britain the comparatively small number of firms in

Table 2.1   Selected characteristics of South Asian firms in four market spaces

		Percentage of firms in market space	Percentage with profits 'better than satisfactory'	Percentage with profits 'worse than satisfactory'	Average number of 'workers per firm*	Percentage of firms in food retailing**
Local	Canada	8.7	0.0	33.3	2.0	58.3
ethnic	Britain	18.7	0.0	42.8	1.4	46.4
Local	Canada	29.5	10.7	32.0	3.2	25.3
non-ethnic	Britain	51.3	8.7	26.1	2.4	68.6
Non-local	Canada	33.0	12.1	21.2	3.6	33.3
ethnic	Britain	12.0	0.0	9.1	10.7	8.3
Non-local,	Canada	28.7	13.7	9.8	4.6	7.8
non-ethnic	Britain	18.0	19.0	19.0	5.5	9.5

*Number of full-time equivalent workers per firm, including owner and counting each part-timer as 0.5.
**In Britain food retailers include CTN (confectioners, tobacconists and newsagents).
Source: Jones and McEvoy (1992).

non-local markets is testimony to the barriers – financial, managerial and psychological – ranged against those who attempt to move out of the stereotypically Asian market spaces (Ram and Hillin, 1994; Ram and Jones, forthcoming). That more progress in this respect appears to have been made in Canada is perhaps testimony to the more prosperous and open opportunity structure of that country (McEvoy and Jones, 1993). Given its obvious heuristic properties, this simple typology might perhaps offer a framework for future research in this field.

By way of summarising this chapter's arguments, we would suggest that the various processes affecting the market demand for ethnic entrepreneurs interact with factors affecting their supply. Entrepreneurial entry is an uneven process of selective allocation, a series of flows, blockages and diversions. These begin at the labour market stage, sifting out candidates for self-employment, and continue past that point as problems with securing resources (often originating in racism) divert most of these entrants into the lower levels of the market. What finally does all this tell us about the structural position of ethnic minority business in advanced capitalism? The central thrust of this chapter has been that any notion of an expansive flexible opportunity structure bristling with niches for minority enterprise is, at best, highly optimistic.

Notes

1 See also Light and Bonacich (1988) on the whole question of the role of 'acculturation lag' in minority business.
2 See Waldinger *et al.* (1990b) for numerous parallel examples elsewhere.
3 See Jones *et al.* (1989) for examples.
4 See Jones *et al.* (1989) on the drunken racism suffered by Asian restaurateurs in Bradford.
5 See Mitter (1986) and other relevant chapters of this volume.

3
Location Matters: Ethnic Entrepreneurs and the Spatial Context

Ans Rekers and Ronald van Kempen[1]

Introduction

A multitude of explanations have been offered for the start of ethnic enterprises.[2] The majority of these explanations emphasise cultural characteristics that are peculiar to ethnic groups, for example solidarity, a willingness to work hard for long hours, and flexibility (Light, 1979; Waldinger *et al.*, 1985). The same literature also suggests that immigrants may start an enterprise either voluntarily or under duress. They may be forced into business by circumstances such as unemployment or the lack of other ways to earn a decent living (Rekers, 1993). The presence of members of one's own group or network may make it easier to start certain kinds of enterprise. This group or network might serve as a potential consumer market or provide critical support in the form of financial or human resources.

One factor remains underdiscussed in the literature on ethnic entrepreneurs: the spatial context. The differences between spatial contexts and the influence of those contexts on ethnic entrepreneurs have not been given due attention. This blind spot is all the more remarkable in the light of the observation made some time ago that 'major variations between localities imply that opportunities are far from uniformly distributed and that this is the main determinant of the pattern of ethnic business, rather than whether members of particular groups have a flair for (or experience of) business (Mars and Ward, 1984, p. 10).

The point of departure in this chapter is that the spatial context is taken into account in explaining how (ethnic) enterprises are started. Following Dijst and van Kempen (1991), we call this the spatial approach. This chapter is not an elaboration of empirical data; rather it is an attempt to demonstrate relations by collating material that has already been published. In the event of there being a lack of necessary evidence in the literature, the relationships between the spatial context and ethnic enterprise and entrepreneurs should be seen as hypotheses requiring further research.

This chapter begins by demonstrating that the spatial approach is often lacking in research on ethnic entrepreneurs (section 2). In contrast the spatial approach is inherent in urban geography and urban sociology, however the literature of these disciplines is often very general and does not address specific developments in local circumstances. Section 3 demonstrates that this literature is not very helpful on this issue. Sections 4–7 describe the elements of the spatial approach, followed by a brief evaluation and some conclusions in section 8.

Missing links in previous research

Research on ethnic entrepreneurs has taken several directions. A major approach is the study of differences within and between ethnic groups, which can be considerable (see for example Jones, 1993). Sometimes these differences have been ascribed to characteristics of the ethnic group; in other cases they have been related to the structure of the host society. Surprisingly this kind of research has paid no attention to structural disparities between cities or regions. Some authors have conducted research in diverse locations (see for example Aldrich *et al.*, 1981; Waldinger, 1989), but skim over any variance in the number and type of ethnic entrepreneurship between these cities and do not attempt to offer explanations.

Because of this lack of spatial analysis, some important questions remain unanswered. Kasarda (1989), for example, explains the differences between black and Asian entrepreneurship in terms of fragmented family status, the lack of networks and the lack of economic solidarity among blacks. Yet he does not explain why only 19 per cent of the Koreans in Chicago are entrepreneurs while 35 per cent of the Koreans in New York have their own business (see also Dijst and van Kempen, 1991). Is family status less important in New York? Are the networks different? Or is the influence of the urban environment predominant, making group characteristics less important? Similarly Mars and Ward (1984) show a clear difference in the percentage of Pakistani entrepreneurs in two cities (6 per cent in Birmingham and Wolverhampton compared with 35 per cent in Manchester and Leicester), but they make no attempt to explain the discrepancy.

The literature also presents examples of networks, 'embeddedness' and social capital. Embeddedness in a social structure elucidates the (economic) acts of an individual (Granovetter, 1985; see also Chapters 8 and 9 of this volume). Portes and Zhou (1992) and Portes and Sensenbrenner (1993) have documented how embeddedness both promotes and impedes ethnic entrepreneurship. They stress that ethnic resources such as solidarity and enforceable trust derive their value from interaction with the host society. Implicitly, therefore, these are not cultural traits of an ethnic group. Unfortunately the authors do not mention which elements of the host society are important. Are certain preconditions required for embeddedness to arise? Is it, for example, conceivable that the use of social capital erodes faster in areas with an abundance of labour market opportunities than in areas where jobs are scarce? Lacking employment, ethnic groups could be more dependent on social capital.

Answering the above questions is interesting and important because it can help to identify the opportunities and constraints faced by potential ethnic entrepreneurs. Analysis aimed at describing differences between groups does not shed light on the differences in opportunities and constraints that arise from the spatial context. Moreover, by focusing on the cultural characteristics and differences between groups it is easy to ignore factors that apply to entrepreneurs and enterprises *in general*, ethnic or not. This implies that ethnic entrepreneurs are not necessarily different from other entrepreneurs. Actually the spatial context does show up in some research. Ward (1987a), for example, concludes that the structure of the local economy explains the differences in the settlement patterns of Asian entrepreneurs, as well as their chance of survival in diverse cities. However he does not identify which factors of the local economy are responsible and how they affect ethnic entrepreneurs in different spatial contexts.

Waldinger *et al.* (1990a, 1990c) state that the strategy of an ethnic entrepreneur is determined by a combination of group characteristics and his or her adaptation to the environment. This is called the interactive approach. According to the authors, the environment, or opportunity structure, consists of market conditions and access to ownership. Market conditions refer to the type of market. Ethnic entrepreneurs can target their own ethnic groups (internal orientation) or other groups (external orientation). The latter orientation can involve, for example, aiming at abandoned or underserved markets, at markets where scale advantages are unimportant, or at markets in which it is possible to create an extra demand by introducing new (ethnic) products. Finally, potential markets can be found in unstable or insecure sectors, such as the garment industry. Access to ownership is about entry barriers, or the accessibility of entrepreneurship. Necessary permits and the availability of premises for the enterprise are important factors.

The model developed by Waldinger *et al.* is quite useful for macro-level comparisons between countries, however for comparisons between or within cities it needs further elaboration.

The globalising economy and developments within specific cities

The internationalisation and globalisation of the economy, particularly the impact on urban change and developments within cities, have been central topics in many books and articles over the past two decades. Sassen, for example, made the concept of the global city world famous (1984, 1991a). Internationalisation and globalisation are discussed in articles on the forces that shape urban Europe (Hall, 1993). These processes are also important in the relation between the informational society and urban development (Castells, 1993). Other authors are less interested in urban developments but try to determine which factors and developments affect the success of certain types of industry (see Porter, 1990). Porter's work is mainly aimed at comparisons between countries.

The main drawback of this kind of literature is that the results are not automatically applicable to research on specific topics in a large number of spatial contexts (see also Kloosterman, 1996a). There are at least three reasons for this shortcoming. Firstly, many developments in cities such as New York and Tokyo cannot be compared with those occurring in smaller cities and do not necessarily trickle down to other spatial contexts. Rising employment in the financial sector of Frankfurt will not immediately – or even necessarily – affect ethnic entrepreneurs in Essen. Secondly, processes such as globalisation and internationalisation definitely do not explain everything. Other developments, which may be partly related or unrelated to these very general trends (for example specific demographic and socio-cultural developments), have their own impact. Thirdly, and perhaps most importantly, the general literature on urban and global processes is often vague about how the broad developments carry over into specific processes such as ethnic entrepreneurship. Authors seem quite able to demonstrate the fact that influences do exist, but they do not always make clear *which* factors and developments are responsible.

The spatial approach

The principles of the spatial approach have been formulated in an earlier paper:

> The developments that we consider pertinent to minority business are the deconcentration of employment and the changing urban population profile. The spatial trends in employment are caused by the emergence of flexible organizational forms of production. The changes in the urban population reflect the increasing differentiation in lifestyles and urban residential environments, which are generated by the rise in affluence throughout Western economies.
>
> (Dijst and van Kempen, 1991, p. 129)

Economic developments and changes within the urban population and environment are central here. In the same vein, a few important factors appear to have a potential effect on the start of (ethnic) enterprises:

- *Economic developments*: unemployment and the changing structure of functions; size of firms; subcontracting; the presence of other industries, agglomeration effects, and copying behaviour.
- *Population changes*: differentiation of lifestyles.
- *The urban environment*: availability of premises; local policies.

Some of these factors are related to processes of internationalisation and globalisation, others barely or not at all. Importantly, most of these factors influence (potential) entrepreneurs in general and are not specific to ethnic entrepreneurs. The basic idea is that these developments differ across spatial contexts, resulting in spatially governed opportunities for ethnic entrepreneurs. In other words, location matters. The focus here is on urban contexts[3] because ethnic entrepreneurs are concentrated in urban areas (see for example Ram and Deakins, 1996; van den Tillaart and Reubsaet, 1988). Of course this is a direct consequence of the urban settlement pattern of immigrants and their descendants.[4] We do not dwell on cultural differences between groups, because, as mentioned above, others have done this sufficiently.

Economic developments and their relation to ethnic entrepreneurs

Labour market restructuring – and in particular the impact on immigrants and their employment status – has been documented extensively (see Chapter 5 of this volume). However it should be pointed out that labour market developments foster the emergence of ethnic enterprises. A changing structure of functions can lead to redundancies, but at the same time unemployment or an insecure position in the labour market can prompt a person to set up a business. As the international organisation of the economy shifts, production may be relocated to other parts of the world, while specific tasks may be contracted out. Developments such as these can lead to greater opportunities for ethnic entrepreneurs. The presence of certain types of industry in an area may have implications for the emergence of ethnic firms. There is an interaction between group and individual characteristics on the one hand and economic developments on the other. How can these developments be related to immigrant businesses? How do they differ across urban contexts?

Unemployment and the changing structure of functions

The position of immigrants in the labour market is considered unfavourable in many countries, and most immigrants occupy the lowest segments of the labour market or are unemployed (see for instance Fainstein *et al.*, 1992; Özüekren and van Kempen, 1996).[5] In many Western European countries, former guest workers and individuals from former colonies are mainly found in these disadvantageous labour-market positions. They are dependent on the availability of jobs that require only a low level of education, and these jobs are continuously threatened by automation, computerisation and relocation to areas where goods can be produced less expensively. Competition from nationals with the same (low) level of education may further diminish their chance of obtaining a good and/or stable job.[6]

Global and national economic developments affect developments in the urban fabric of Western Europe. When countries in the Pacific Rim are able to produce ships relatively cheaply, this may have a detrimental effect on the shipbuilding industry in Amsterdam. The same holds for other industries, such as textiles, cars and computers. In many West European cities the consequences of global restructuring have been immense. As a result unemployment rates have been rising, especially among poorly-educated and poorly qualified individuals.

The prospects for people in the lower segments of the (regular) labour market are not very favourable. This is a result of a combination of group and individual characteristics (low level of education, language problems) and contextual developments (declining demand for workers with a low level of education, discrimination; see for example Özüekren and van Kempen, 1996). Moreover many jobs are now much less secure or less well paid than in the past. This happens when firms fill vacancies with temporary workers. In cities undergoing these economic developments, an increasing propensity to start an enterprise may be expected (Bovenkerk, 1982; Florax and Schutjens, 1996; Waldinger *et al.*, 1985).

Many cities in Western Europe are showing signs of an economic upswing (see for example Chesire, 1995). This could lead to an increase in the number of jobs[7] and a declining propensity to start an enterprise. It could, however, have the opposite effect: rising incomes could boost the demand for specific products and services, and potential entrepreneurs might pick up on this trend and move into gaps in the market. In this way developments in the labour market constitute a pull factor for potential entrepreneurs rather than a push factor.

The number of jobs within a region is important, but so too is the quality of those jobs. A changing (regional) structure of functions can have serious consequences, especially for people in positions that require few qualifications.

Theoretically, three developments are possible in the structure of functions. Polarisation occurs when the number of higher and lower functions rises while the middle segment decreases in size (Sassen, 1984, 1986). Upgrading denotes an overall increase in requirements for all functions; downgrading denotes an overall decline (see Huygen, 1989). Developments may differ between countries and across (urban) regions. The opportunities in local labour markets are determined by these types of development.

Dijst and van Kempen (1991) state that downgrading or polarisation can favour less educated migrants as downgrading generates opportunities for people with a low level of education (or at least if total employment remains at the same level), while polarisation may increase the demand for goods and services among those in higher positions. This may promote growth in lower-level functions (known as 'consumption linkage'), particularly in restaurants and bars and the cleaning sector (see also Sassen, 1991a). It should be noted that many of these positions are dead-end jobs. They provide little security, a low income and no career opportunities. Of course the spatial approach assumes that cities differ with respect to developments in the structure of their functions.

Size of firms

The presence or absence of enterprises may be important in explaining the opportunities for starting a business, although urban regions may differ in this respect. It has been demonstrated that the presence of many small firms (employing fewer than ten people) in a region is related to the number of new enterprises that are established there. In regions with many people in waged labour, however, the number of new enterprises is significantly smaller (Illeris, 1986). Socio-cultural factors such as an entrepreneurial mentality seem to play a role. This mentality is less prevalent in regions with a tradition of wage earning. Significant regional differences in the number of new businesses may be the result.

The size of firms may also determine career possibilities within the firm for employees with a lower level of education. Large companies (more than a hundred employees) can generally hire more less-educated people because of the fragmentation of work tasks. Because of this division of labour, in principle it is easier to rise in the hierarchy of jobs. In effect, large firms have a kind of internal labour market within the company (Gaspersz and van Voorden, 1987). Therefore a city or region with a relatively large number of small companies may be expected to generate more (ethnic) enterprises than a city or region in which large companies predominate.

Subcontracting

Subcontracting enables industries to minimise costs and insecurity and maximise the speed at which they can respond to market demand. Of course subcontracting also offers opportunities for small companies. Ethnic entrepreneurs can take advantage of subcontracting trends, for instance, by working within a flexible schedule and with family or other low-paid labour (Ward, 1987a). The effects of subcontracting are generally specific to a given branch and location. For example Amsterdam is seen as the fashion centre of the Netherlands. Companies that have contracted out specific tasks (for example sewing) have generally placed the jobs within the city of Amsterdam. The Turkish community in particular has profited from this.

Subcontracting is characteristic of industries aimed at the consumer market. It is also common in companies where internal economies of scale are not considered important and in sectors where technological development is rapid. It is also very typical of firms that serve an unstable, fluctuating market. Some examples include the garment industry and the automotive industry (Machielse and de Ruijter, 1988). But subcontracting is not limited to industrial tasks; it also occurs in the service sector. Public relations, accountancy, transportation, catering, cleaning and security can easily be contracted out. Furthermore subcontracting does not necessarily mean that the party contracting out the job is a large firm and the one taking on the task is a small enterprise. Rapid changes in market demand can also be accommodated by subcontracting between small firms (Brusco, 1982).

The opportunities for subcontracting are dependent on the character and mix of companies within a spatial context. This affects not only the launch of an enterprise but also its development, as Ward (1987a, p. 91) points out:

> In the Birmingham area cheap ethnic labour and cheap premises abound. But since Birmingham is not a shopping centre with large retail stores...there are few opportunities for full manufacturing firms to develop. By contrast, in Leicester, a traditional centre for hosiery and knitwear where retail buyers are located, more small Indian firms have been able to graduate from sweatshops to become full manufacturers with close links with major retail chains.

Agglomeration effects

Spatial clusters of ethnic entrepreneurs can create multiplier effects. Ethnic enterprises within a neighbourhood or larger area can attract customers from other areas, but also other kinds of enterprise in their immediate surroundings. In this way ethnic enclaves can develop into regional ethnic clusters such as those in Soho in London (Waldinger *et al.*, 1990c), the Westkruiskade in Rotterdam (a Surinamese cluster) and the Zeedijk area in Amsterdam (a Chinese cluster) (Bakker and Tap, 1987; Eskinasi and Kleine, 1995).

Clusters of ethnic entrepreneurs often emerge when an ethnic population is concentrated in an urban area. Sometimes this clustering of firms reflects the availability of cheap premises (see later in this chapter) or the presence of a daily street market. It is also possible for a cluster of ethnic entrepreneurs to stay put while the original population moves on, as happened in the Chinatowns of New York and Los Angeles. It seems only logical that cities will differ in this respect, with some cities having ethnic clusters and others having none.

Copying behaviour

Because the choice of a particular line of business is often less important than the desire to start an enterprise *per se*, many individuals start a business in which they already have some experience (Keeble and Wever, 1986; Mayer, 1987; Wever, 1984). Provided this experience has been acquired locally, the existing employment structure in an area can affect the character of the new firms. Consequently new firms add little to the diversification of the production structure of the area (Keeble and Wever, 1986; Wever, 1984). Of course the possibility of engaging in copying behaviour is dependent on the nature of the enterprises present. The Dutch literature shows that copying behaviour is frequent among ethnic entrepreneurs (van den Tillaart and Reubsaet, 1988). Furthermore differences between cities can be emphasised by this behaviour, and stiff competition between firms, leading to bankruptcies within the sector, can be a negative outcome of copying behaviour. Examples of this can be found in the literature (Dijst *et al.*, 1984; Rekers *et al.*, forthcoming).

In conclusion, economic developments and effects may differ between cities, leading to differences in the number and types of ethnic entrepreneurs.

Urban consumers

According to Reynolds *et al.* (1994, p. 446): 'No process is more fundamental than reactions to increased demand for goods and services. It is reasonable to expect that, as demand increases, more new firms will be founded to satisfy this greater demand.' To a large extent the population of an area determines the potential demand for goods and services.[8] The composition of this population (age, ethnic descent, income) is as important as its size.[9] Many cities are undergoing further differentiation in lifestyles as a consequence of individualisation and emancipation, immigration and the rising number of women in the labour market. New household arrangements have arisen alongside the traditional family system of a husband with a paid job, a housewife and one or more children. Incomes have increased, especially in dual-earner households. At the same time the number of (structurally) unemployed persons has grown in many cities, especially during periods of recession. This differentiation in households has resulted in overall differentiation as well as an increase in the demand for specific goods and services (Vijgen and van Engelsdorp Gastelaars, 1986). These developments create opportunities for new ethnic entrepreneurs (Boissevain, 1984; Ward, 1987a).

The urban mosaic of lifestyles is characterised by diverse financial budgets and diverse time budgets. These can be complementary, for example one category of people may use the goods and services another population category offers ('consumption linkage'). Individuals with family-based lifestyles spend more of their time and money in and on the house, while people with a more urban lifestyle do so in the city centre or elsewhere. These 'urbanites' are more accustomed to using the goods and services that others offer and tend to be more open to new and alternative products such as exotic vegetables, fruit and meals.

Heterogeneous populations are particularly manifest in large cities. Here the demand for goods is stretched on both sides: there is a growing demand for luxury items and exclusive goods, but the demand for cheap and sometimes inferior products has also increased. Opportunities have been created to set up speciality businesses to cater for very specific demands (such as antique shops or halal butchers). At the same time there is greater scope for shops aimed at meeting the specific demands of low-income households (second-hand shops, repair shops and so on). These are just a few examples of services that larger firms are neither willing nor able to provide. Small entrepreneurs, including ethnic entrepreneurs, have been able and willing to fill the niche – mainly in retailing and catering.[10] Consequently the shop structure within an area may change, with some shops disappearing because of lack of demand and others, such as delicatessens and ethnic-specific shops such as halal butchers, taking their places.

De Jong (1987) sees a growing and dynamic segmentation of market demand in which age, lifestyle, household composition and income are the determining factors. The outcome of this interplay between factors differs between cities. For example in the Netherlands comparisons have been made of the two largest cities, Amsterdam and Rotterdam (de Klerk and Vijgen, 1992; Rekers, 1993). In Amsterdam there are more people with an urban lifestyle; Rotterdam is known for more traditional lifestyles. In Rotterdam individuals are more focused on their home life; in Amsterdam people are generally oriented towards the city and its amenities. This is likely to be reflected in the amount of money people spend in restaurants and cafes, which in turn influences the number of establishments in this sector. Indeed the number of Turkish restaurants is five times higher in Amsterdam than in Rotterdam, even though the latter has more Turkish inhabitants.

The urban environment

The availability of premises

For many new entrepreneurs it is logical to keep the initial costs as low as possible. Consequently some entrepreneurs start up at home, with part of the house being filled with sewing machines, food or other products. Not everybody has the space or opportunity to do this, however. Furthermore suitable premises are not equally distributed within cities, so the character of the urban environment can affect the choices of the ethnic entrepreneur in a very definite way.

In earlier times, especially in the prewar period, the urban settlement pattern of enterprises was easier to explain than at present. New companies were often set up in older (often nineteenth-century) inner city neighbourhoods, which served as an 'incubation' base where weak businesses could make an easy start. After an initial period some were able to expand and move to other areas away from the centre (Hoover and Vernon, 1962). Many of these areas had a kind of reservation function for enterprises that could not develop into bigger businesses (Verhorst, 1989).[11]

This settlement pattern has become more diffuse. Only for a few lines of business are the older urban neighbourhoods the logical place to start. Developments in the size of the firms, government rules (with respect to, for example, noise and pollution) and communication techniques have removed the reasons for many enterprises to locate in these areas.

For Turkish businesses in the Netherlands, especially for retail shops, prewar neighbourhoods are still seen as a major settlement area (Rekers, 1993; see also Kloosterman and Burgers, 1996). For other businesses – restaurants, small offices, alternative shops, specific retail businesses – these areas provide potential customers, cheap labour, supplier firms, face-to-face contact and cheap premises.

'White flight' has sometimes created opportunities for ethnic businesses, especially in older urban neighbourhoods (Jones *et al.*, 1994). Aldrich *et al.* (1984) state that this is not a displacement situation, just a consequence of the unwillingness of the indigenous population to invest in older neighbourhoods. Hence members of minority ethnic groups take over the businesses of native entrepreneurs – a form of ethnic succession. The location of a new ethnic enterprise depends on the type of business concerned, the potential customers and the availability and cost of business premises. Entrepreneurs who target customers from their own group are likely to settle in an area where many of these potential customers live. Turkish coffee houses are therefore normally located in areas inhabited by Turks. Entrepreneurs who aim to attract other groups will not necessarily locate in these neighbourhoods. Restaurants, for example, are commonly found in areas with a good night life (Rekers, 1993).

The spatial structure of the city is important with respect to business premises. In many Western European countries an enormous difference

exists between prewar and postwar neighbourhoods. In older neighbourhoods, shops and other enterprises grew up more or less sponta-
neously around daily markets and in several streets throughout the
area. These premises are now being occupied by new users, including
ethnic entrepreneurs. Newer neighbourhoods, however, are often more
deliberately planned, in many cases very strictly. Sometimes rules exist
about who is and who is not allowed to establish an enterprise
(Schutjens, 1993). At least formally, it is far more difficult to start an
enterprise in these areas.[12]

But even in the older urban areas, both the supply and the use of
business premises are now more strictly regulated. Urban renewal activities have changed the structure of many old neighbourhoods. Many
buildings have been demolished, causing a reduction in the supply of
cheap premises and reducing the opportunity for new entrepreneurs to
start a business (Dijst *et al.*, 1984).

Not only aspects of the built environment but also the presence of
daily street markets can attract ethnic entrepreneurs (ibid.). The street
market is often a very important place to acquire speciality or inexpensive products for members of minority ethnic groups and nationals
alike (Veldkamp, 1985). A location on or in the vicinity of a street market is therefore attractive to many ethnic entrepreneurs. Unfortunately,
because of the popularity of such areas the cost of premises sometimes
rises to unaffordable heights. A location on the market itself is a possibility, but sometimes the waiting list is long.

The urban environment provides conditions that can be essential for
the location of ethnic enterprises. It is also a factor that can be influenced by local policy.

Local policy

The conditions under which potential entrepreneurs can start a business
often vary between cities. They may apply to education level, ethnic
descent, the number of years spent in the host country, the availability of
capital and so on. Conditions may be defined by local policy decisions.

Local policy can be active or passive. An example of passive local
policy is the non-enforcement of control, for instance in Amsterdam
the local government tolerated the presence of illegal Turkish sweatshops until the mid 1990s. This policy attracted even more (Turkish
and other) sweatshops. Other cities may be less tolerant, resulting in
large differences in the number of ethnic entrepreneurs between cities.
It is clear that even a passive local policy can influence the emergence
of ethnic businesses.

Local policy may also be aimed at actively encouraging ethnic entrepreneurs. For example the authorities might start supplying information to potential starters in their own language or providing favourable credit facilities. Opening up the roof space in houses where starters can rent inexpensive premises, make collective use of facilities, have a common reception desk and so on is another way of stimulating potential (ethnic) enterprise. One step further is to create deregulation or enterprise zones to provide an attractive climate for new entrepreneurs, with fewer rules and regulations or lower taxes, enabling their enterprises to grow into mature businesses. Such schemes can have a second function: the revival or renewal of run-down areas. This can be seen as a resurrection of the old incubation milieus.

The potential influence of local policy can hardly be overstated. However the enabling function of local policy is not put into practice very often.

Conclusion

The dynamics of cities are a result of external as well as internal developments. The globalisation and the internationalisation of the economy, the growing importance of information and services, sociocultural developments and migration affect most larger cities in the Western world. They create opportunities but also threats, especially for some population groups (see also Castells, 1993). Internal factors such as the structure of the local economy, the quality of neighbourhoods and the environment, the population structure of the city and of smaller areas within the city, and more abstract features such as ideology, history and tradition interact with broad international developments to give each city its own character and position in the national and international urban system (Jobse and Musterd, 1994).

In this chapter we have tried to demonstrate that the urban context can affect the emergence of ethnic entrepreneurs. Our message has been that the factors operating within the spatial (urban) context should not be ignored when researching ethnic entrepreneurs. Important relations cannot be explained if we lose sight of this context, for example we could not explain why there are more Turkish enterprises in Amsterdam and fewer in Rotterdam, even though Rotterdam has the larger Turkish population. With the spatial approach we can clarify this difference: Amsterdam has different population characteristics and a different economy (Rekers, 1993; Rekers *et al.*, forthcoming).[13] It would also be interesting to know why there are more Korean entrepreneurs in

New York than in Chicago (Kasarda, 1989), and why there are more Pakistani enterprises in Manchester than in Birmingham (Mars and Ward, 1984).

We do not suggest that our spatial approach should replace all other approaches. The cultural approach certainly does offer important insights into the emergence of ethnic enterprises, as does the structural or inter-active approach. Researchers sometimes forget that cultural factors are often only meaningful within certain spatial contexts. Only when cer-tain preconditions are fulfilled – such as the availability of affordable premises, the presence of customers for the products in question, the lack of stiff competition – is it possible to translate an inclination for entrepreneurship into the act of starting a business, ethnic or other-wise. Researchers applying a more structural approach also pay sur-prisingly little attention to local variations. The spatial approach should therefore be seen as complementary to existing approaches.

Finally, attention to the local context leads to better explanations, and perhaps better policies. Attention to the local context means that policies to stimulate businesses can be made on the basis of local opportunities. These will probably be more successful than policies at the national level or policies aimed at the cultural characteristics of ethnic groups.

Notes

1 The research upon which this chapter is based was made possible by the financial assistance of the Dutch Organization for Scientific Research (NWO). We are grateful to Veronique A. J. M. Schutjens for her critical review of an earlier version of this chapter.
2 In this chapter we use the term 'ethnic entrepreneurs' to denote (1) entre-preneurs who were born in one country and migrated to another and (2) descendants who have started a business.
3 Urban refers to the city and its suburbs. The influence of the city does not stop at the city limits.
4 This chapter is mainly about immigrants and their descendants with a low level of education. In Western Europe most of the people in this category are former guest workers, for example Turks and Moroccans.
5 Of course there is an enormous variation between and within subpopula-tions of immigrants. It is not the purpose of this chapter to elaborate on this point. Education, reason for migration, discrimination, competition and the availability of jobs are among the most important elements that affect the position of individual immigrants on the labour market.
6 See Rekers (1991) for further information on the competition between immi-grants and others in Amsterdam and Rotterdam.
7 This is not always the case. 'Jobless growth' is also possible.
8 Tourists and other visitors can also add to the demand.

9 We focus mainly on the entrepreneurs who do not aim exclusively at in-group customers. The internal market is not the subject of this chapter. It must be kept in mind, however, that the internal market can differ hugely between areas.

10 Of course informal services can also be supplied, such as house cleaning and childcare. It is very doubtful, however, that members of immigrant groups have profited much in this sector.

11 Some see the urban area as a series of incubator areas (Reynolds *et al.*, 1994).

12 In some new areas it is possible to carry out all kinds of activities, including illegal ones. This usually happens in areas where control is not strictly enforced. Kloosterman and Burgers (1996) mention Amsterdam's Bijlmermeer as an example.

13 Of course much more could be said about this, but space does not allow us to elaborate on it here.

4
Small Firm Financial Contracting and Immigrant Entrepreneurship

Robert Watson, Kevin Keasey and Mae Baker

Introduction

This chapter examines the financial management and contracting problems associated with starting and successfully operating a business. We focus on the areas where financial management theory appears to be helpful in analysing the particular distribution, character and problems experienced by immigrant owner-managed businesses in the developed market economies of Europe and the United States. Financial management is a discipline that uses economic reasoning to develop decision models to estimate, evaluate and manage the financial consequences of corporate investment, operating and financing activities. Creating and maintaining successful exchange relationships with other contracting agents (both inside and outside the business) are central to the achievement of corporate objectives. The structure of explicit and implicit contracts, which specify the duties and allocate the risks and returns accruing to each party involved in a transaction, governs economic activity and is a major determinant of economic possibilities and financial outcomes.

When investigating contractual relationships with external parties, the financial management literature has traditionally focused on the governance mechanisms appropriate for dealing with economic agents who are assumed to be motivated solely by self-interest and engaged in arms-length market exchanges. This has resulted in modelling the various financial incentives, bonding and formal governance mechanisms that attenuate opportunism via monitoring, aligning the interests of the contracting parties and/or imposing unacceptable costs (such as 'bonding' or so-called 'hostage taking') upon opportunistic behaviour. Nevertheless, a major difficulty confronting corporate decision makers is that the future state of the macroeconomy, the reactions of competitors, changes in tastes and so on are all difficult to predict, and therefore it is impossible to incorporate them into a contract *ex ante* even though they may have a significant impact upon the risks and *ex post* financial returns accruing to one or more of the contracting parties. Indeed when high levels of uncertainty (namely unquantifiable risks) are coupled with problems of bounded rationality, information asymmetries and conflicts of interest, the resulting contractual incompleteness may present insuperable barriers to arms-length market exchange.

In these circumstances, what is required is a corporate governance system that is able to ensure that agents perform not merely in accordance with the formal letter of the contract, but also encourages them to use their contractual discretion in a non-opportunistic manner whenever an *ex ante* unexpected event occurs. Corporate decision makers' willingness to undertake a course of action will therefore depend on their perceptions of their exposure to business risk and their confidence in the ability and trustworthiness of the agents they contract with. In the absence of formal governance mechanisms that create trust via imposing unacceptable costs upon the opportunistic party, the financial management literature has not addressed the issue of how trust may be engendered by other, less formal means. This is because the models have been developed on the assumption that the contracting parties engage only in arms-length exchanges, and therefore non-economic ties can be expected to have a minimal influence on economic behaviour. It is, however, clear that there are circumstances where social ties matter and that the type of exchange relationships between actors is not always of an arms-length or purely economic nature. Multidimensional 'embedded' relationships frequently characterise economic exchanges between firms and these relationships are governed by trust rather than by contract or any obvious economic rationality. Trust, as Uzzi (1996, p. 678) has stated, 'is a unique governance mechanism in that it promotes voluntary, non-obligating exchanges of assets and services between actors', which is of economic importance 'because it increases an organisation's access to resources and strengthens its ability to adapt to unforeseen problems'.

The various forms of 'social embeddedness' that create and sustain trust, but which are ignored by the financial management literature, may be effective substitutes for formal, contractually based governance mechanisms in circumstances where the latter are impossible or excessively costly to develop and maintain. Indeed, due to the formal financial contracting difficulties faced by many small firms, relationships based on embedded social ties and/or a stable network of partners may often be the only feasible way of operating a business. Following Waldinger *et al.* (1990b), and consistent with several of the contributions to this volume, it is clear that the socially embedded nature of some immigrant-owned businesses can give privileged access to the resources of an ethnic community. If such access provides a competitive advantage over native-owned businesses then this may result in relatively high rates of entrepreneurship amongst some immigrant and ethnic minority groups.

Social embeddedness has, of course, many dimensions and we argue that, whilst access to the resources of the ethnic community may have a positive effect upon entrepreneurship rates, the sectors these immigrant enterprises are concentrated in and the extent to which they are wholly or partially reliant upon informal inputs may limit their economic potential. For example, because of the problems external parties such as bank lending officers have in assessing risk exposure, many small firms, irrespective of the ethnic characteristics of the entrepreneur, can be expected to be refused financial backing simply because the entrepreneur is unable to reassure the potential lender that the investment does not expose it to unacceptably high risks.[1] Nevertheless any significant (real or perceived) differences between natives and immigrants in respect of their access to formal and informal capital market funding, along with differences in labour market opportunities, wealth, exchange relationships with suppliers and customers, can be expected to have an important influence on the character and viability of the enterprises created.

The chapter is organised as follows. We begin by examining the entrepreneurial decision, focusing on the economic motives for starting a business and the investment and financial requirements necessary to bring this about. The risk and return characteristics of small business operations and the difficulties both natives and immigrants face in obtaining formal capital market funding for their ventures are then discussed. The discussion also includes an assessment of the opportunities and limitations that informal market alternatives provide for some classes of immigrant entrepreneur. Although informal businesses tend to be very small and largely restricted to the service sector, the contract clothing manufacturing sector has many informally constituted, immigrant owned and managed enterprises. Indeed over the past 100 years or so this sector has provided business opportunities to successive waves of immigrants to Europe and the United States. We examine the production methods, labour and financial requirements and the supply and demand characteristics of this sector to see why – despite the low barriers to entry, low search and set-up costs and many substitutable enterprises – it is a sector in which atomistic market exchange relationships between firms are often untypical. We argue that, because of the characteristics of the market for the final product, interfirm pooling of resources, cooperation and adaptation are routinely required and/or necessary for survival and that this creates a competitive advantages to firms that are able to access a network of embedded relationships where opportunism is largely absent. The development of such networks is clearly facilitated when the owner-managers involved share other embedded social ties, such as a shared ethnic identity, value system or beliefs, which is another reason why this sector has proved to be particularly attractive to immigrant groups.

Much of this activity is undertaken by informally constituted enterprises and we discuss the difficulties owner-managers have to overcome to enable their businesses to make a successful transition to the formal economy, where contracting and regulatory costs and inputs such as labour services and financial capital can be expected to increase significantly. The future economic prospects for immigrant businesses are examined and the final section discusses some of the public policy implications that arise.

The entrepreneurial decision

In terms of understanding the motivations behind entrepreneurship, the economics literature has stressed that entrepreneurs are individuals who are prepared to commit resources to a venture because they believe they possess superior information regarding profit opportunities, or have specialised skills and/or access to input and output markets that provide them with an economic advantage over existing suppliers.[2] Economic theories of entrepreneurship generally make the assumption that the decision to start a business (or indeed to continue in business) is based upon the anticipation of earning a greater profit than that expected from the next best alternative (the opportunity cost, or if restricted to labour inputs, the 'reservation wage') available to the entrepreneur;[3] that is, the probability (p) that individual i will opt for entrepreneurship (E_i) is simply a positive function of the difference between the anticipated profits from the enterprise (π) and the individual's wage (w_i):

$$p(E_i) = f(\pi - w_i)$$

where $\pi = (R - C)(1 - T) =$ after tax profit from the venture, $R =$ revenues, $C =$ the costs associated with earning revenue R, $T =$ the rate of tax on business profits and $f > 0$.

This is a very simple model and, moreover, one which appears to be consistent with two contrasting views regarding the primary motivation for starting a business. The propensity to start (or continue) a business can be of a demand pull nature (that is, expected profit is high) or of an (actual or anticipated) unemployment 'push' nature (that is, the next best employment alternative is poor). Nonetheless, in spite of its simplicity the model is capable of generating a number of empirically testable hypotheses regarding the relationships between an entrepreneur's economic circumstances, the macroeconomic environment and the propensity to go into business. For example one implication of the model is that the primary motivations of new firm founders are likely to differ at different stages of the economic cycle, being predominantly demand pull (that is, driven by prospects of high profits) during periods of economic expansion and unemployment push (that is, poor employment prospects) during periods of economic recession.

For consistently disadvantaged groups in the labour force, the unemployment push motivation is likely to be strong irrespective of general levels of economic activity. The high rates of unemployment and constrained labour market opportunities experienced by immigrant and ethnic minority groups in many European countries and the United States may account for the higher than average rates of small business ownership and self-employment amongst these same groups. Somewhat more forcefully, Ram and Deakins (1996) suggest that, rather than being due to some assumed special 'cultural predisposition' towards entrepreneurship, the high rates of small business ownership amongst some ethnic minorities can be explained by the racial discrimination they experience in obtaining suitable alternative employment in their host country.

The model also suggests that low business-tax rates will tend to encourage the formation (continuation) of formally constituted enterprises and that high tax rates can be expected to lead to the formation of informal (unregulated and untaxed) enterprises. It can also be inferred from the model that individuals with marketable skills that command a high price in the labour market will choose to enter high profit sectors, whilst individuals with low skills and poor paid-employment prospects will tend to set up in sectors with few barriers to entry and/or relatively low profitability. This suggestion is consistent with the observation that large concentrations of ethnic minority businesses in low-profit sectors are found in many European economies where recent deindustrialisation has destroyed the traditional low-skill, low-wage job opportunities that attracted many of these immigrants to Europe in the postwar period.

Although the entrepreneurship model indicates the main economic motives of individuals *considering* starting a business, it is an inadequate conceptualisation of what is required actually to *start* a business. Briefly, it ignores the risk-time dimension typically associated with investment decisions and the contracting difficulties that have to be overcome in order for the potential entrepreneur to take advantage of his or her assumed superior information, privileged access to resources and/or skills.[4] By focusing exclusively on profits and labour market alternatives, the model fails to take into account the riskiness and timing of the relevant cash flows, particularly the usual requirement for the entrepreneur to incur significant upfront cash outflows prior to the commencement of trading (investment in premises, equipment, stocks and so on) and the receipt of any revenues.

In general the asymmetries in the timing of cash inflows and outflows means that although earning an adequate profit remains a necessary condition for starting a business, it is far from being sufficient. The ability to bear risk and, if the entrepreneur's own resources are insufficient to fund initial investment needs and operating requirements, the ability to acquire and bear the costs associated with obtaining external finance are also preconditions without which the potential entrepreneur will be unable to turn a potentially profitable opportunity into a business reality.

Within the financial management literature, the evaluation of investment opportunities using the 'net present value' (NPV) rule incorporates risks, initial investment needs and the timing differences associated with the incremental cash inflows and outflows from operations. The NPV method involves calculating the timing of cash flows and then discounting them by the 'risk adjusted' opportunity cost of capital in order to convert all costs and benefits received at different times into 'equivalent present values', as follows:

$$NPV = -C_0 + \Sigma(CF_t)/(1+r)^t$$

where C_0 = any initial investments required at $t=0$, CF_t = the expected incremental (namely, net of w_{it}) cash flow in period t ($t=1$ to n where n = end of project),[5] and r = the minimum risk-adjusted rate of return (opportunity cost) on the invested funds.

For an independent investment decision, the NPV rule is that the individual (or firm) should accept all investment opportunities when NPV>0 since the present value of the incremental net cash inflows exceeds the present value of the cash outflows. Clearly, projects with high initial outlays (C_0), with positive cash inflows ($CF_t > 0$) only occurring some time in the future, and where the opportunity cost of capital (r) is high, will have a much lower NPV than a pure arbitrage operation with the same (undiscounted) cash flows.

In terms of predicting the propensity to start a firm, the NPV model also indicates that, even with a project with a positive NPV, in order to commence trading the entrepreneur will first need to obtain the financial resources necessary to cover the initial investment outlay (C_0), plus additional funds to cover any possible cash shortfalls. Thus the size of this initial funding requirement, its cost and availability, the time period involved before it can be repaid and the riskiness of the future cash inflows are additional factors that the NPV model suggests can be expected to influence the entrepreneurial decision.

It is important to stress that profit, which is an attempt to measure the increase in wealth over a period, can rarely be equated with an increase in cash resources. Some of the increase in wealth may be invested in non-cash assets, such as plant, machinery and working capital (stocks plus debtors less trade creditors).[6] Although such investments in non-cash assets are expected eventually to lead to cash inflows, their immediate effect is a cash outflow, which not only requires financing but is also a major source of risk that one or more of the contracting parties will have to shoulder. Hence unlike the idealised competitive market model, which assumes that the only relevant criteria for entering into an exchange relationship are price and quality, the financial management literature recognises that issues of business risk, information exchange, the nature of the investment, the continuity of the relationship and the efficacy of governance mechanisms to attenuate opportunism are all important considerations.

The financial management literature has developed a number of theoretical models of the pricing of individual financial claims with particular risk, reward and governance characteristics. Central to these models is the notion of a market-determined, positive risk-return trade-off, that is, investments that appear to offer high returns will also tend to expose the investor to the most risk, whilst low-risk investments cannot be expected to be associated with high returns. Thus if the market pricing mechanism is functioning efficiently, the relative pricing structure of all financial assets and claims will be such that riskless arbitrage profit opportunities (the proverbial 'free-lunch') will not arise. Moreover an efficient market will ensure that all positive NPV projects that have been discounted at the correct risk-adjusted cost of capital will receive capital market funding.

The results of many hundreds of empirical tests of various pricing models on large publicly listed firms in the United States and Britain are somewhat mixed.[7] The assumed efficiency of the capital markets is, however, only relevant to large, well-established and publicly listed firms where a sophisticated investor and analyst clientele exist with strong incentives and resources so that risk exposure can be realistically assessed. As discussed below, the plausibility and relevance of these efficient market assumptions are, however, far from obvious in the case of small firms. Market imperfections in relation to assessing risk exposure will often mean that neither debt nor equity funding at any price will necessarily be forthcoming from the formal capital markets.[8]

Small business financial contracting issues

The small firm sector has certainly become an increasingly important part of the US and European economies in recent years.[9] It is generally recognised, however, that due to the high rates of failure characteristic of the small business sector, investors in such enterprises will inevitably be exposed to a high level of business risk (see Ganguly, 1985; Storey, 1994). The main financial contracting difficulty this creates is in reliably distinguishing between potential failures and successful businesses. The absence of reliable financial information, the inescapable uncertainties associated with business activities and the fact that the viability of the enterprise is wholly dependent upon the continued good health, energy, business acumen and financial probity of the owner-manager renders the task virtually impossible (Keasey and Watson, 1993).

There are a number of ways that owner-managers can reduce these uncertainties. The most obvious way is for them to increase the level of their personal equity investment in the business. The main economic function of equity is to provide long-term risk capital. Unlike equity holders, debt holders and trade creditors are not usually entitled to share in the profits of the enterprise. Normally these non-equity investors contract to receive a fairly low but certain (contractually fixed) return. They do not expect to have to bear risks for which they are not financially compensated, and the owner-manager's equity is therefore an essential financial buffer that enables the firm to absorb any unanticipated cash shortfalls whilst retaining the confidence of its creditors. If the owner-manager's ability to supply sufficient equity is constrained, then any inability or unwillingness to seek additional finance will restrict the size of the firm and/or result in persistent cash crises and, ultimately, corporate collapse. Even assuming that debt suppliers and trade creditors are willing to supply funds to firms with inadequate equity, they will have to incur non-trivial monitoring and information costs in order to protect the security of their investment.[10] The cost of financial resources supplied in such circumstances can be expected to incorporate a significant risk premium in order to compensate investors for the uncertainties and additional monitoring costs involved.

In addition the evaluation of investment opportunities, the negotiation of contracts and other set-up costs are unlikely to vary directly with the size of the investment, that is, there are likely to be fixed as well as variable costs involved in the evaluation and processing of applicants and subsequently managing the account. Hence in order to cover their total costs the return that investors demand will have to be inversely related to the size of the investment. Thus the total return required by investors will be made up of the following three components:

Required return $(r) =$ opportunity cost $+$ risk premium
$+$ fixed costs/size of investment

A number of theoretical asymmetric information models have, however, led to the conclusion that demanding high returns may create adverse selection and moral hazard problems, and therefore credit rationing of one form or another will exist if investors are unable to distinguish between good and bad risks (see for example de Meza and Webb, 1987, 1990; Stiglitz and Weiss, 1981).[11] Although, as Bester (1987) has argued, demanding collateral (which is equivalent to an injection of further equity) helps to safeguard the lenders' investment, the ability to provide collateral is a function of wealth. Moreover if borrowers are averse to risk, Stiglitz and Weiss (1987) have shown that relying exclusively upon collateral will not be sufficient to avoid credit rationing or the issues of adverse selection and moral hazard.

The above financial contracting problems have led to widespread complaints of a small-firm finance-gap.[12] To understand why such a gap exists and why it does not make any sort of commercial sense for banks to fill this gap themselves, a closer examination of the business objectives and organisation of banks is needed. In the first place, for portfolio risk minimisation reasons banks have to hold a diversified portfolio of investments and therefore, irrespective of the merits of the loan requests it receives, it would be both irrational and irresponsible for them to invest more than a small proportion of their available funds in the small business sector. In addition, in many developed economies the main clearing banks are in fact primarily retail deposit takers and do not see themselves as being in the business of providing risk capital to businesses. Moreover risk assessment is a difficult and costly activity that requires a range of specialised skills, experience and detailed knowledge of a variety of business sectors. As the main activity of bank branches is servicing customer accounts, it is rare for branch managers and other staff at the branch level to possess high levels of such skills. In Britain, for example, this lack of expertise in risk assessment is clearly reflected in the banks' small business lending policies. Loans and overdrafts generally attract interest rates of only some 2–3 per cent above the base rate (which represents a risk-free alternative return for the funds). Given this low-risk premium and the fact that banks have to make a commercially viable profit whilst not taking unreasonable risks with depositors' funds, it is perfectly reasonable for them to make loans available only to businesses that can provide adequate collateral or are otherwise able to make a convincing case to the bank that the risk borne by the latter is minimal.[13]

Corporate decision makers such as bank lending officers, trade credit specialists and purchasing managers with whom small business owner-managers have to deal are of course no less socially embedded than any other group in society. The credibility of business plans and other information on future financial outcomes will necessarily be ambiguous, and therefore if funding and credit applications are to be successful the decision maker has to be inclined to interpret favourably (that is, trust) the available information. Unfortunately for loan applicants, trust is not normally something that can be expected to develop automatically upon first contact or be equally forthcoming to all applicants. For example unfavourable racial and ethnic stereotypes are fairly common in both Europe and the United States and it would be surprising if a proportion of the corporate decision makers with whom immigrant entrepreneurs come into contact did not also share these attitudes. When they assess the risks involved in contracting with a small firm, their expectations, cultural biases and limited experience of what is required to run a small enterprise, particularly one run by an entrepreneur from an unfamiliar ethnic minority, can be expected to influence their decisions. Certainly, evidence from a number of surveys has tended to suggest that immigrants and ethnic minorities are significantly less likely to receive bank funding than native-owned businesses and some researchers have claimed that this reflects 'racial bias' (see for example Jones *et al.*, 1994; Phizacklea and Ram, 1996; Wilson and Stanworth, 1987).

It is, however, not clear from these studies that the differences in acceptance rates are of any statistical significance or that the native and immigrant applicants are 'comparable' in terms of risk, collateral, track record or the quality of the supporting documentation supplied.[14] Indeed it is clear that these writers have little conception of the relationship between business risk and return. Jones *et al.* (1994) for example claim that racial bias exists simply because they found that none of the UK Asian manufacturing firms in their sample were able to obtain 100 per cent bank finance to launch their ventures. The difficulties of such a view should be fairly obvious from the previous discussion: the high up-front cash outlays required for setting up a manufacturing enterprise creates high risks and makes a high level of equity funding from the entrepreneur (who will, after all, be the main beneficiary if the venture is a success) absolutely essential. Moreover, in our view any bank that offered 100 per cent finance for such a purpose would clearly be behaving in a most irresponsible manner with its depositors' funds. Hence on the currently available evidence, although there will undoubtedly be instances when a loan application is refused because of an inappropriate cultural or racial stereotyping of the applicant, the problems of insufficient collateral, high business risks and information barriers appear to be more plausible reasons for the majority of refusals.

The risks involved with investing in small enterprises, not surprisingly, results in many loan applications by small businesses to financial institutions being turned down. This, however, need not result in the firm being unable to start/continue in business since there may be informal capital market alternatives available. Indeed, in the early stages at least, the entrepreneur's own savings and free or cheap loans from family and friends often forms the main source of financial capital. The opportunity cost of this informal capital is usually low since most domestic savings can be expected to be currently earning a low return in deposit accounts. Moreover the relationship between borrower and lender, particularly when they are members of the same family or a close-knit ethnic or religious community, can be expected to be driven, a least in part, by a non-economic or 'embedded' logic characterised more by trust and non-obligating resource exchanges then considerations of risk and return. As noted earlier, entrepreneurs with few alternative employment and investment opportunities may also be willing to accept much lower returns for their labour and capital inputs than would be acceptable to large firm investors. Similarly other labour inputs – from family, friends, part-time workers, disadvantaged groups and those continuing to claim state unemployment benefits whilst working – may also be available at low cost. Regulatory costs – including compliance with health and safety and fair employment regulations, taxation and financial reporting requirements – are lower for small firms, and if the firm operates wholly within the informal sector they may even be avoided altogether.

Social relations make information interpretable and immigrant groups characterised by shared values and (bounded) solidarity (Portes and Sensenbrenner, 1993) can be expected to facilitate coethnic access to informal sources of capital from the extended family network and the wider ethnic community. In the United States for example, the widespread use of informal, ethnically based credit associations by Koreans (Light and Bonacich, 1988), Cubans and Indians (Leonard and Tibrewal, 1993; Portes and Zhou, 1992) is well documented.[15] Clearly these informal forms of contracting indicate that contracting difficulties can be overcome, and indeed may even provide significant cost advantages, particularly for firms operating mainly within the informal sector and requiring just a modest amount of financial capital. Only the very smallest of firms are, however, likely to benefit to any great extent since many of these advantages diminish significantly as the firm grows and enters into more and more areas of the formal economy. Hence continuation as an informal operation is unlikely to be a viable long-term strategy if the firm is to grow significantly. Eventually, for the relatively few enterprises with viable growth prospects, there will be a need to find ways of managing the transition from informal to formal status and finding new ways of solving the contracting problems discussed above.

Immigrant businesses in the clothing manufacturing sector

What should be apparent is that systematic differences in alternative labour market opportunities between social groups and differential access to input (resources) and output (consumer) markets can be expected to produce differences in observed entrepreneurship rates. As discussed above, the financial management literature focuses on the risks and returns and the financial contracting problems that need to be overcome in order for economic exchange to occur. This literature highlights the economic and other variables that influence an individual's motivation to start a business, the feasibility of the entrepreneurial option, the type of business and contractual relationships created and the probability that the business will survive, grow or fail. These variables act as a series of filters or barriers that limit the possibilities of those unable to pass through them. For example, due to wealth constraints, limited access to financial capital and low skill/educational achievements, the majority of small enterprises operate in retail and service sectors that require relatively little in the way of start-up capital and have few, if any, skill or other entry barriers. Also, ethnicity may form an effective barrier to competition and many immigrant businesses specialise in supplying goods and services specific to their own ethnic community, where they clearly have a comparative advantage over native-owned businesses.

For both native and immigrant, manufacturing businesses tend to be less common than service sector activities, not merely because manufacturing businesses typically have higher initial financial requirements, but also because of the need to invest relatively large amounts in non-cash, often highly illiquid fixed assets and working capital, all of which increase the exposure to risk. The manufacture of clothing is, however, a sector of economic activity that supports many immigrant-owned businesses. To understand why, we need first to examine the production and demand characteristics of this sector and secondly to examine the ways in which immigrant entrepreneurs are willing and able to supply this demand more adequately than are native entrepreneurs.

Clothing manufacture consists of several distinct processes: for example design, cloth manufacture, cutting, assembly (sewing) and packaging. Although there have been significant labour-saving technological developments in recent years in respect of both cloth manufacture and cutting, for example computer-guided laser cutting systems, such technology is expensive and requires consistently high output levels to justify its cost and minimise the investment risk. Moreover the cutting process can be separated from the highly labour-intensive final assembly (sewing together) of the garment, and these activities may often be undertaken by different firms (which means they are vertically disintegrated). The technology required for final assembly is well known and has hardly changed in several decades: one person using one sewing machine. Productivity improvements are therefore largely restricted to the learning effects associated with long production runs and splitting up the process into simpler tasks undertaken by different individuals. Even so the productivity benefits from both task specialisation and learning effects are likely to occur at low output levels, because the total number of tasks and their individual complexity is low. Hence economies of scale will be limited, and although there may be cost advantages associated with bulk purchasing of materials and transport, there will be few production cost advantages accruing to larger firms.

This simple technology creates few barriers to entry since the initial investment will be fairly low, particularly if the tasks are undertaken by outworkers using their own sewing machines in their own homes. Indeed if the small firm operates in or obtains some of its labour inputs from the informal sector, it can be expected to have lower wage costs, a smaller investment in working capital, a more flexible workforce and no taxes or other regulatory costs. Hence smaller firms can be expected to be able to compete with large firms in terms of the production costs associated with the final assembly of the garment. Thus large clothing manufacturing firms and retail chains generally find it cost advantageous to subcontract this process to smaller firms whose costs are lower than those which would be incurred by undertaking these tasks internally. The advantages for the subcontractor are that initially the entrepreneur may be able to manage with limited capital via the use of homeworking or premises in the poorest part of the local industrial infrastructure and second-hand machines from bankrupt firms or large firms that have decided to subcontract rather than continue in-house manufacture. For the final-assembly subcontractor, working-capital requirements may also be considerably reduced, since normally it is the customer that supplies all the materials. In short, many of the up-front fixed costs, and therefore risks, normally associated with setting up a manufacturing business may be avoided.

Whilst contracting out some processes to outside, small-firm subcontractors has the effect of significantly reducing investment, internal organisation and production costs, it does create the need for an external governance system to regulate interfirm relationships. Relatively low search costs and the existence of many potential and substitutable suppliers would appear to favour arms-length market relationships where economic exchanges are governed by formal contracts based purely upon price and quality considerations. However this is not universally the case since interfirm relationships in the contract clothing sector are frequently characterised by concentrated, embedded ties (Portes and Sensenbrenner, 1993; Uzzi, 1996).

As mentioned earlier, contractual incompleteness is inescapable in situations where high levels of uncertainty exist and this incompleteness significantly reduces the efficiency of governance mechanisms based upon formal contracts. The diversity of horizontal and vertical interfirm relationships that is characteristic of the clothing sector in most developed economies reflects the segmented nature of the consumer markets these firms supply. These market segments have very different average mark-ups, products and output volumes and require differing degrees of coordination and information exchange between the contracting parties to supply these market segments efficiently. High-quality items and fashion items, particularly those with highly promoted designer labels, can command a high mark-up on cost, which frequently makes speed of delivery and closeness to the designer, retailer and final customer more important than cost considerations. The demand for high-mark-up fashion items is also subject to frequent colour, style and fabric changes. This implies low production runs and a premium on speed of delivery, particularly when consumer demand is seasonal and unpredictable because of such things as weather and changing tastes.

Moreover the competitiveness of the sector, coupled with a highly volatile demand for the final product, can be expected to be associated with high subcontractor failure rates. Thus because of the high degree of coordination and information exchange required, plus the need to ensure that the subcontractor remains in business to complete the order, impersonal arms-length relationships governed solely by written contracts will frequently be too slow, inflexible and costly to administer effectively. In order, therefore, to reap the cost benefits associated with subcontracting, the manufacturer of fashion goods and other goods characterised by highly volatile demand will need to be concerned with more than simply the price and quality of the goods produced by the subcontractor. Contractually unspecified flexibility and favours will often be required of the contracting parties, which suggests that embedded relationships with a restricted number of firms may be more efficient if it encourages mutual trust, resource sharing, joint problem solving, information transfer, innovation and rapid feedback.

Clearly not all subcontractors will be equally able or willing to provide the required flexibility at low cost. Given the highly labour intensive nature of the production process, the greatest degree of flexibility and the lowest cost will occur at the point where all labour costs are variable. This requires the firm to have the ability to vary the number of employees and their hours of work directly in line with changes in demand. Clothing subcontracting may be particularly attractive to some immigrant groups if they have privileged access to such a flexible labour force. Also, such a business will not require access to large amounts of starting capital,[16] thus making it feasible for immigrants with relatively little wealth to begin operations, particularly in urban areas with large concentrations of coethnics. Clearly however, entry costs are not negligible and may require the combined wealth of several individuals or that of an extended family network. Moreover in recent years rising unemployment in the developed economies has impacted heavily upon many immigrant communities, thereby making the entrepreneurial option, even in areas of activity with low expected returns, relatively more attractive to such individuals. Acceptance of low returns is often compensated by a willingness to work much longer hours and to be more flexibly responsive to the fluctuating demands of their customers than the indigenous population (Portes and Zhou, 1996).

Generally poor labour market opportunities for coethnics may also provide entrepreneurs with cheap and readily available labour via the extended family network and the wider immigrant community (Sanders and Nee, 1996).[17] In particular, in some immigrant communities where there is a relative lack of 'culturally suitable' employment opportunities that meet the needs of the female population, or where there are many 'undocumented' immigrants, there is often a ready supply of low-cost, highly flexible labour working from within the home. Similarly the relative lack of suitable employment opportunities in the immigrant's country of origin may also mean that additional low-cost labour can be imported.

The above discussion indicates why immigrants may experience significant cost and organisational advantages relative to indigenous entrepreneurs. If privileged access to highly flexible and cheap labour and other inputs from the entrepreneur's own immigrant community are the main source of competitive advantage, then it is likely that many of these businesses will be operating in the informal sector. This, however, may have a number of consequences for the further development of the enterprise. Firstly, if the business is to grow significantly the resource requirements can be expected to outstrip the ability of the firm to finance this from its operating cash flows and/or its informal capital providers. Thus although the ability to operate in the informal sector is clearly beneficial initially, it may limit the further growth of the enterprise because the entrepreneur will possess little in the way of documentary evidence to convince external providers of his or her track record or the worth/potential of the business.[18]

This problem may be compounded by cultural misunderstandings, perhaps even an element of racism and/or simply a general lack of awareness of the nature of immigrant businesses by the external providers of capital. Furthermore, because of the perceived high risks involved, financial institutions will require a return that is commensurate with their risk exposure. Formal capital market investors may also impose other monitoring and control costs, such as the production of audited financial statements on a regular basis and perhaps even the employment of professional financial/accounting personnel with externally recognised qualifications to ensure compliance with regulations such as VAT, corporate tax, employment related taxes, health and safety and so on. What this suggests is that a move to the formal sector is required to facilitate business growth but that this is likely to result in a significant rise in the operating costs of the business. Consequently any move to the formal sector may need to be associated with a move to a higher mark-up business. Of course, even assuming that the financial resources necessary to accomplish this are made available, such a course of action is not without its dangers since it is likely to be associated with new forms of competition, often from indigenous entrepreneurs.

Conclusion

The financial management literature focuses on estimating the cash flow consequences – that is, the risks and returns – associated with corporate decision making. In terms of understanding the differing propensities to go into business and the types of business created, this involves assessing potential profits relative to the labour market alternatives to entrepreneurship, modelling the sources of risk, competitive advantage and the contractual problems that have to be overcome to obtain the financial and human capital resources needed to start and manage particular types of business. However market imperfections such as information asymmetries, which are costly to remedy, and difficulties in assessing risks and personal wealth constraints are characteristics that can be expected to lead to contracting difficulties for many small businesses. This is particularly important in the case of firms that require formal capital market finance to launch and/or expand their enterprises. Irrespective of the ethnic origins of the owner-manager, many small firms can be expected to find it difficult to obtain financial capital from the formal capital markets, simply because the legally enforceable contracting (governance) mechanisms available are often insufficient to protect the financial interests of these institutions due to the high and difficult to quantify risks involved. The perception that banks and other financial institutions discriminate against ethnic minority businesses and/or are simply less familiar with the *modus operandi* of such enterprises, further reduces the formal capital market's contribution to this sector of the economy. As we have indicated, banks are not in the business of bearing high levels of business risk and, in the absence of major retraining of existing staff and/or the recruitment of specialised risk assessment personnel, nor should they be if they are to take seriously their responsibilities to their depositors and shareholders.

Nevertheless, despite such problems many immigrant entrepreneurs, particularly those from communities with relatively poor formal labour market opportunities, appear to be willing and able to enter highly volatile and competitive sectors such as clothing manufacturing, even though these sectors are characterised by high failure rates and low returns. This suggests that these firms have been able significantly to reduce their cost base and exposure to business risks by having access to the relatively cheap and highly flexible coethnic labour that is commonly available in many urban locations, and/or have established themselves within a viable network of embedded business relationships that engender trust despite the high degree of contractual incompleteness involved. The development of embedded relationships between firms is clearly facilitated when the individuals involved perceive that they share a common ethnic identity, economic situation and/or value system. By engendering mutual trust, resource sharing and innovation, such embedded ties create a viable and less costly alternative to formal governance systems based on contracts.

As many of these immigrant businesses survive simply due to their informal nature, any state initiatives to force such firms into complying with the regulatory demands of the formal economy are likely to precipitate the collapse of many businesses. If such initiatives impacted upon a large segment of the host country's informal sector, this would be likely to result in a general raising of the costs of the finished product and/or the transfer of many of these activities overseas. Whether or not this would be beneficial to the host country's economic welfare is, however, less than certain. Any loss of jobs overseas would, given the relative lack of other employment opportunities available to the immigrant population, constitute an immediate economic loss (Simon, 1991). Of course such arguments have been used extensively by sweatshop employers since the beginning of the industrial revolution to justify their opposition to any improvements in employee pay and conditions of work. Certainly, closing down informal enterprises would be expected to result in an improvement in the pay and working conditions of the workers remaining in the industry. It has been argued that it may be more economically beneficial for public policy initiatives to focus on the relatively few informal (indigenous or immigrant) businesses that have significant economic potential (see for example Storey, 1994). Unfortunately, because of the high risks involved and the information and contracting problems detailed earlier, which render it very difficult reliably to assess risk, policies that attempt to identify such potential 'winners' would, in all likelihood, be an expensive and inefficient way of attempting to achieve a more internationally viable and prosperous small firm sector.[19] More modest objectives such as easing the difficult but not impossible process of a move towards more formal business operations, via offering subsidised loans, training, marketing and financial advice schemes may, however, prove cost effective.[20] Ultimately of course, the long-term economic prospects of both indigenous and immigrant businesses alike would seem to be dependent upon moving away from low-margin lines of business and into higher margin, less competitive, areas of activity.

Notes

1   In the case of bank lending, because the bank is not entitled to any profits from the enterprise other than the interest specified in the loan agreement it does not expect to share in any losses either. Hence from the bank's viewpoint an 'unacceptably high risk' may be any risk whatsoever, no matter how remote it may appear to the owner-manager.

2   See Casson (1982) and Clarke and McGuinness (1987) for reviews.

3   See Audretsch (1993), Blanchflower and Oswald (1990) and Evans and Jovanovic (1989) for reviews of the issues.

4   Indeed by focusing solely upon the margin of revenues over costs, it is only really strictly relevant to a pure arbitrage operation, which, because income and costs are received and disbursed simultaneously, involves no significant risk and requires no net investment (equity) by the entrepreneur.

5   It is worth emphasising that because annual profits and the enterprise's cash flows differ, the incremental cash flows in each period (CF_t) are not identical to $(\pi - w_i)t$ in the earlier model. The relationship between profits and cash flows are discussed in the following section.

6   The relationship between profit and cash flow for a period is as follows: $\text{Cashflow}_t = \pi_t +$ non-cash expenses$_t -$ net investment in working capital$_t -$ net capital investments$_t -$ dividends$_t +$ net new loans$_t +$ net new equity$_t$.

7   For a review of the recent evidence see Haugen (1995).

8   See Ang (1991) and Keasey and Watson (1993) for reviews.

9 See Stanworth and Gray (1991) and Chapter 1 of this volume for discussions of the international and macroeconomic factors that have fuelled this growth in small firm activities.

10 A high equity investment by the owner-manager also discourages opportunistic behaviour. See Keasey and Watson (1996) for a review of the issues and evidence.

11 Adverse selection occurs when investors are unable to judge the probability of success and demand a blanket rate of return, which results in low-risk, low-return firms exiting the market and thereby lowering the average quality of the investment portfolio. The problem of moral hazard occurs if high rates of interest induce firms to undertake riskier projects. Thus in both cases it is predicted that investors will choose to ration funds via methods other than a market clearing rate of return.

12 For evidence of this in Britain, see Binks *et al.* (1992), Keasey and Watson (1993) and the contributions in Buckland and Davis (1995).

13 See Keasey and Watson (1996) for a review of the issues and empirical evidence.

14 Recent immigrants can be expected to experience particular difficulties in obtaining finance from traditional lending institutions simply because foreign-acquired skills, education and other forms of human capital are often not highly valued and the fact that the immigrants will inevitably lack a business track record in their host country.

15 Financial institutions owned by coethnics are often a source of investment capital for some immigrant groups. See for example the evidence that Chinese immigrants in Los Angeles (Nee *et al.*, 1993) and New York (Zhou, 1992) are able to obtain much of their financial requirements from Chinese-owned lending institutions.

16 Due to cultural differences, language difficulties and/or discrimination by native controlled financial institutions, the problems outlined earlier regarding the lack of availability and/or costs of formal capital market finance are, moreover, unlikely to be made any easier for the immigrant entrepreneur.

17 See also Chapters 8 and 9 of this volume for analyses of the benefits of immigrant/ethnic networks.

18 See Peterson and Ragan (1994) for US empirical evidence of the value of long-term relationships with debt suppliers.

19 The British evidence in this regard is not encouraging, since public officials who lack incentive are not the most obvious candidates for evaluating potential winners, and tax subsidies seem to be largely treated as a 'windfall gain' without any significant impact upon business decisions. For a review, see Keasey and Watson (1993).

20 Despite their many differences, the one common feature that emerges from the many studies of successful small-firm-dominated districts throughout Europe is that local authorities and the firms themselves have evolved an efficient institutional mechanism that supplies essential public goods (for example physical infrastructure, information, education, skills training and so on). See Bagnasco and Sabel (1995) and Johannesson *et al.* (1993) for reviews.

5
Immigrant Entrepreneurship and the Institutional Context: A Theoretical Exploration

Robert Kloosterman[1]

The next stage in research on immigrant entrepreneurs

The entrepreneurial resurgence that started in the United States in the early 1970s was not recognised immediately. Buried in the annual avalanche of statistics, both this resurgence and the conspicuous role played by immigrant entrepreneurs were barely evident. In retrospect the United States turned out to be only the front-runner of a much wider renaissance that eventually occurred in many other advanced economies as well (OECD, 1992). Notwithstanding this clear international dimension, comparative research on immigrant entrepreneurs in different countries has thus far been very thin on the ground. There is, however, a rapidly accumulating literature on immigrant entrepreneurship within single countries. Case studies of specific groups (for example Boissevain and Grotenbreg, 1986), specific industries such as the garment industry (for example Waldinger, 1989b), of one group of immigrants in two or more cities (for example Min, 1996; Waldinger and Tseng, 1992) and of different groups of immigrants in one or more cities (for example Light and Rosenstein, 1995b; Razin and Langlois, 1996) do exist, but research mainly seems to stop at the border. Admittedly there has been some research presenting case studies from different countries (cf. Barrett *et al.*, 1996; Body-Gendrot and Ma Mung, 1992; Waldinger *et al.*, 1990a, 1990c). These studies, however, refrain from engaging in genuine international comparative research into immigrant entrepreneurship.

As this relatively recent history of research on contemporary immigrant entrepreneurship would lead us to believe – first case studies, then comparisons within one city or of one group in a number of cities, and more recently comparisons of different groups in several cities – the next stage will surely entail true international comparisons.

Some endeavours in this respect have already been made. The study by Ward (1987a) on ethnic entrepreneurship in Britain and Europe and, more recently, that by Razin (1993) on immigrant entrepreneurship in Israel, Canada and the United States (California) are rare examples of attempts to view the subject from a systematic comparative perspective.

This striking paucity in an age when comparative research has become *de rigueur* for social sciences is due partly to the difficulty of collecting the right data to compare immigrant entrepreneurship in several countries. Definitions of self-employment vary considerably more from one country to another than those of employment (see OECD, 1992). This data on self-employment, moreover, is prone to present a rather biased picture of economic realities, as many firms are just paper constructions for mainly fiscal reasons and not factual enterprises (Kloosterman *et al.*, 1998).

There is also a more fundamental obstacle that explains this notable scarcity of international comparisons. Comparing immigrant entrepreneurship among different groups in one city or comparing self-employment rates for one group of immigrants in two or more cities is difficult enough since the number of relevant variables, and thus possible interactions, rises substantially (Light and Rosenstein, 1995b; Razin and Langlois, 1996). However the problem becomes even worse when comparisons are made between groups of immigrant entrepreneurs in different countries. In the latter case differences in, among other things, the legal and institutional framework, the banking system and migration history also have to be taken into account. Migration laws, social benefits, economic policies towards small firms, the availability of venture capital and, for instance, legal impediments for immigrant entrepreneurs may influence rates of self-employment among immigrants at the national level. The two, rather exceptional, international comparative studies just mentioned acknowledge this immense complexity and both opt for specific strategies to cope with it. Razin (1993, p. 102), following Ward (1987a), argues that international comparison should stress

> (1) differences among receiving countries in the attributes of immigrants that, to a large extent, stem from the immigration policies of these countries; and (2) differences in economic characteristics, particularly the political-organizational attitude toward small businesses, and legal requirements and obstacles for starting a business.

What follows is an attempt from quite a different angle to provide some theoretical groundwork for this next, comparative stage in research on immigrant entrepreneurs. Instead of heeding Ward's and Razin's advice, we shall focus on the impact of the *national institutional frameworks*, on *opportunity structures* (and the corresponding chances for immigrant entrepreneurs to set up their own business), and on the *supply of immigrant entrepreneurs*. Migration policies, state policies towards small businesses in general and those on immigrants in particular, although clearly very important, are not the subject of this chapter, nor are inter- and intragroup differences among immigrants. Here the focus will be on the relationship between the welfare system and immigrant entrepreneurship from an essentially, socio-economic perspective; the emphasis is not so much on 'ethnicity' as on 'markets'. By focusing specifically on this relationship we are, to a certain extent, applying Esping-Andersen's approach, which has initiated considerable international comparative studies on both employment and unemployment trends in the advanced economies, and on the self-employment of immigrants (Esping-Andersen, 1990, 1993, 1996a, 1996b, 1996c).

Entrepreneurship and immigrants

In his path-breaking research, Esping-Andersen has repeatedly emphasised the importance of the national institutional framework for the structure of employment in this era of so-called globalisation. According to him, different types of institutional framework generate different types of *post-industrial employment trajectories*. More specifically, different welfare regimes create different economic opportunity structures (types and sizes of economic sectors) because of their distinct ways of interfering with the labour market. Here we shall explore, from a theoretical view point, the impact of these different institutional frameworks on trends in immigrant entrepreneurship in advanced economies, largely analogous to Esping-Andersen's approach. To analyse the relationship between the institutional framework and immigrant entrepreneurship, the latter will be treated as *a fictitious good* on a market with a supply and a demand side (cf. Light and Rosenstein, 1995b). Labour is, of course, almost always treated this way, notwithstanding the very specific historical process it took to create the modern labour market (Polanyi, 1957). Although this conceptual equation allows us to break down the impact of the institutional environment on (potential) immigrant entrepreneurs (the supply side) and on a specific part of the opportunity structure, namely the demand for entrepreneurs, in a rather convenient way, the attempt to equate the market for entrepreneurship with that of labour is not entirely without problems.

Firstly, in marked contrast to the labour market there is no *concrete* institutionalised 'market for entrepreneurs' with clearly advertised vacancies and a more or less easily identifiable supply. Opportunities for the self-employed ('vacancies') may go unnoticed or neglected for all kinds of reasons; furthermore, apart from those who are already active as entrepreneurs, it is usually totally unclear who else can be counted as part of the entrepreneurial supply. Secondly, most entrepreneurs are independently active economic actors checking out potentially relevant economic information, whereas workers are more passively involved and more or less accept the prevailing market conditions. This latter distinction holds especially true for the so-called Schumpeterian entrepreneurs, who constitute a small but usually significant minority among the group of entrepreneurs as a whole. In a sense, they create their own opportunities, circumventing existing constraints by introducing new products, new methods of production or new combinations, and are thus able to escape the dictates of the neoclassical market (Kirzner, 1997).

Notwithstanding these complexities, conceptualising entrepreneurship as a fictitious good allows us to analyse the supply and demand sides of potential immigrant entrepreneurs, as well as their interaction from a comparative perspective. We start with the supply side.

The supply side

The supply of immigrant entrepreneurs consists, in principle, of all immigrants who are willing to set up their own business. This very general definition does not bring us very far, so we have to look for a more specific common denominator for immigrant entrepreneurs without going into the socio-cultural characteristics of specific groups of immigrants. We shall focus on immigrants from less-developed countries, and hence we omit immigrants from other advanced economies. This allows us to construct a more specific *ideal-typical immigrant* who can be found, in principle, in all advanced economies. In doing this we shall ignore the processes of self-selection referred to by Razin (1993) and Borjas (1987, 1988), whereby immigrants with relatively high human capital opt for countries with a relatively unequal distribution of income, which offers them the prospect of high earnings, whereas immigrants who are less well endowed tend to go to more egalitarian countries with high minimum wages and substantial social benefits.

In our case, we assume that the typical immigrant distinguishes him- or herself from the indigenous population in general by having inadequate or inappropriate educational qualifications or skills, possessing little financial capital and lacking access to relevant indigenous social networks (social capital), and accordingly has difficulty obtaining essential information about certain vacancies (see Waldinger, 1996a; Waldinger *et al.*, 1990a). In addition this immigrant may lack sufficient proficiency in the language of the adopted country, and he or she may also suffer from discrimination. Consequently such immigrants are usually found at the end of the labour queue, being hired last and fired first, and if they do find employment it is mostly in poorly paid, dirty, dead-end jobs. However, such 'blocked mobility' can, according to Waldinger, act as 'a powerful spur to business activity' (Waldinger *et al.*, 1990a, p. 32; see also Barrett *et al.*, 1996; Boissevain, 1992; Chapter 2 of this volume; Kloosterman *et al.*, 1997a, 1997b; Razin, 1993). Hence if different institutional frameworks or welfare regimes generate distinct differences in the nature and level of obstacles to the labour market, all other things being equal, differences in the level of supply of immigrant entrepreneurs may result. These distinct supply-side characteristics of the ideal-typical immigrant not only shape the labour market position to a very large extent but are also important in determining the kinds of firm they can set up. Furthermore their range of options as entrepreneurs is restricted by their being limited in human and other capital in terms of the receiving country, and the likelihood that they will encounter discrimination.

Before going into specific types of business activity it should be noted that in general new businesses can almost only be started in markets that have certain characteristics. To be open to newcomers from whatever background, these markets must be free of high barriers to new entrants. Hence there should be no extensive economies of scale, high entry costs (for example expensive marketing or advertising campaigns will not be necessary) or closures of existing firms or other organisations as a result of government policies (Waldinger *et al.*, 1990a, p. 25). Such markets are to be found at the lower end of the overall market (low value-added production that requires no advanced knowledge) and at the high, innovative end of the market (high value-added production based on advanced knowledge). Ideal-typical immigrants, lacking appropriate educational qualifications and financial capital, are thus further constrained in the choice of market in which to set up a firm. They are channelled towards economic activities that require relatively small capital outlays, no specific educational qualifications and where technical barriers are low.

It should be pointed out that definitely not all immigrants from less-developed economies conform to the ideal-typical immigrant depicted here. For example the Indian and Chinese software engineers who have set up software businesses in large numbers in Silicon Valley (*The Economist*, 29 March 1997) are very well-educated, highly skilled, knowledgable and able to engage in highly specialised, high value-added production. They started their firms at the upper end of the market, and in this sense do not differ from highly educated indigenous entrepreneurs or immigrants from other advanced economies.

The ideal-typical immigrant entrepreneur, in contrast, can only start a business at the lower end of the distribution of firms: very small-scale, low value added and labour-intensive with a small capital to labour ratio. Given these characteristics, the success of immigrant entrepreneurs depends strongly on the size of the markets that support these specific kinds of firm. Which markets display these characteristics?

The demand side

Opportunities for small-scale, low-tech businesses that mainly depend on unskilled or semiskilled labour have become more limited in advanced economies as globalisation has enlarged the arena of international competition (Coffey, 1996; Dicken, 1992; Reich, 1991). Competitors in less-developed countries using cheap labour have pushed out many competitors in the advanced countries, which have responded by, among other things, upgrading their economic activities, namely increasing the added value by making use of sophisticated labour, mostly in combination with high-tech machinery. This globalisation of trade has changed the location of production: there has to be a specific reason for small-scale, labour-intensive, low-tech economic enterprises to be located in an advanced economy, otherwise they will be forced out of business by low-wage competitors from abroad.

This location factor can be either a direct physical need to locate in close proximity to customers, or a more indirect, transaction-cost-related need to be near customers. Personal service activities, almost by definition, fall under the first heading. Retailing, restaurants, childcare, hairdressing, clothing repair, strip-o-grams, house cleaning and valet parking, for instance, cannot be imported from elsewhere but at some stage need face-to-face contact and have to be produced on the spot. The same can be said for many producer services, such as security, cleaning or parcel delivery services. In general there are two main types of small-scale, low-wage services. According to Reich (1991, p. 215 ff.), these 'in-person servers' will be the only low-wage workers left in advanced economies.

The first category of services includes traditional economic activities that have bucked the trend towards ever-increasing scales of production, for instance because they are located in markets that are too small to support large firms or chainstores. In a sense these market niches are remnants of the preceding industrial era. Having almost no chance of expansion, they totter instead on the brink of survival. Many of those who are able to engage in more rewarding economic activities leave them behind. Thus even though such businesses may be on the decline, opportunities for newcomers arise as the departure of longer established entrepreneurs creates vacancies (Cross and Waldinger, 1992; Waldinger, 1996a). As the supply of indigenous small business owners decreases, immigrants replace them in a kind of economic counterpart of the invasion-succession model (Kloosterman, 1996b; Waldinger *et al.*, 1990a). This so-called 'vacancy chain' can be seen in a large part of the small-scale retailing sector (for example groceries and bakeries) and a certain part of the restaurant business (snack bars, cafés). As the increase in vacancies is clearly linked to the invasion and succession of residents, the clientele in these vacancy-chain businesses are in many cases coethnics.

The second type of small-scale service activities is, in marked contrast to the first, strongly related to the rise of post-industrial society; they can hence be considered as *new* activities. Post-industrial economies are, among other things, characterised by extensive outsourcing and the subcontracting of a variety of activities. This holds true for firms that increasingly concentrate on core activities and core skills and have to buy various services from outside suppliers. It is also increasingly the case for households. As the once traditional household with a male breadwinner working in the formal economy and a wife at home taking care of the children and the household chores has been replaced as the typical household by two-earner families, the demand for so-called social reproduction services (childcare, housecleaning) has risen. These processes of outsourcing by firms and households create opportunities for small-scale businesses in general and, more specifically, low-tech, labour-intensive firms (such as pizza delivery, dog-walking services, mail delivery and so on) that use low-skilled labour. Accordingly, at least some of these post-industrial services should offer opportunities for immigrant entrepreneurs (Sassen, 1991a).

Services generally involve a concrete transaction with the customer and this necessitates a location near to the customer. However some small-scale, low-tech manufacturing activities also have to locate near their main markets. This is particularly the case for markets characterised by highly volatile, uncertain demand and/or non-standardised, customised products (Scott, 1990). Large production series are not very feasible in such markets, and hence large-scale, capital-intensive firms have great difficulty coping efficiently with these markets. Moreover this kind of production entails close contact between producers and customers to enable the former to know what the latter want. Hence transaction costs in these markets are strongly related to physical distance and producers tend to locate near their markets. In many cases, highly specialised products requiring highly skilled, highly paid labour are involved (compare, for example, the animation film business in Los Angeles – Scott, 1990). However it also applies to small-scale firms using un- or semiskilled, low-wage labour, such as those run by immigrant entrepreneurs. Garment contractors are of course a prime example of the latter category and immigrant businesses traditionally abound in this sector. Even in advanced urban economies contractors are increasing in number. The Los Angeles garment industry, which is mainly run by immigrant entrepreneurs, keeps on growing and continues to demand low-paid workers despite its proximity to Mexico. The competitive edge of these contractors has to be attributed to their extremely flexible organisation, enabling rapid response, and also to its 'easy access to a squadron of trend-setting Californian designers' (*The Economist*, 9 August 1997).

The restructuring of advanced economies in the last quarter of this century has profoundly altered the demand for immigrant entrepreneurship. International competition, in combination with the shift to services, has changed the opportunity structure for small-scale, labour-intensive, low-wage, low-tech firms in both services and manufacturing. Although these broad changes have affected all advanced economies, significant differences among countries can be observed. Within a common postindustrial framework, diverging trends in national opportunity structures have emerged. These divergences are partly contingent on the kind of welfare state that exists. Minimum wage and social benefits, for instance, have deeply influenced the postindustrial employment trajectories. Below, we shall try to link the welfare state with immigrant entrepreneurship in a more systematic way by analysing the impact of the institutional framework on both the supply and the demand side of self-employment.

Institutional frameworks and immigrant entrepreneurship

In our market-oriented perspective we limit ourselves to the socio-economic aspects of the institutional framework and do not take legal restrictions, immigration policies, attitudes towards small businesses and so on into consideration. We focus primarily on the extent to which the institutional framework induces and facilitates immigrant entrepreneurship. In our case, then, the rate of immigrant entrepreneurship in a country hinges on (1) the extent to which mobility in other directions is blocked (namely access to regular jobs that will in time offer wages that are perceived by the immigrants to be in accordance with their human capital) and immigrants are pushed to become self-employed; and (2) the pull into self-employment, in other words, on the opportunities for small-scale, labour-intensive, low-tech firms that do not rely on advanced knowledge.

To assess the impact of the institutional framework on immigrant entrepreneurship we distinguish between two types of welfare state. We are aware that the categorisation offered here is a very stripped-down version of other, much richer typologies. Our purpose here, however, is not to provide a comprehensive welfare state analysis, but to point out the relationship between these two stylised welfare state models and immigrant entrepreneurship. Our typology is partly derived from Esping-Andersen's analyses (1990, 1993, 1996a, 1996b, 1996c) and (to a much lesser extent) Albert's (1991) juxtaposition of the so-called neo-American and Rhineland models. In his famous *The Three Worlds of Welfare Capitalism*, Esping-Andersen (1990) distinguishes three types of welfare regime, namely the American or neoliberal welfare state, the continental European or conservative welfare state, and the Scandinavian or social-democratic welfare state. By omitting the last one – which according to Esping-Andersen (1993) is moving anyway towards the continental European type – we have collapsed his threefold typology into a twofold one that embraces, as do all ideal-type constructions, a number of diverse characteristics that are to be found in different countries. In this way the – sometimes significant – differences between the individual Rhineland states can be bridged. We start with a brief outline of the American model and its impact on immigrant entrepreneurship. Then a similar kind of analysis will be offered for the Rhineland model.

The neo-American model

This welfare state model is first and foremost characterised by the near absence of government intervention in socioeconomic affairs (Albert, 1991). The minimum wage in this residual welfare state is relatively low and social benefits are strictly targeted at specific groups, such as female-headed households. In essence the American approach is one of low wages; thus keeping labour demand at a high level allows the unemployed and other job seekers to find a job within a reasonable

period of time. The rate of labour participation in this model is therefore very high for both men and women. The incorporation of female
labour into the formal economy is partly enabled by the rapid expansion of personal services, which in turn are made possible by low
wages. Social reproduction, then, is to a large extent provided by the
market; the contracting out of household and other chores takes place
on a large scale. This helps to sustain an impressive rate of job growth,
but on the other hand it also boosts inequality.

These two aspects of the American model are also linked in another
way. The growth of – predominantly less productive – personal services is
made possible by the low-wage strategy of the American model, but it is
also facilitated by a high level of income inequality because spending on
these services by high-income, two-earner households is extremely
elastic. Entry-level positions are not difficult to obtain in this job-growth-
oriented welfare state model, and this helps to 'integrate youth and
immigrants' (Esping-Andersen, 1996c, p. 258). Gauging the impact of the
neo-American model on immigrant entrepreneurship will be conducted
in two parts: first the implications for the supply side will be assessed,
and then the consequences for the demand side will be examined.

On the supply side, the blocking of opportunities could stimulate
self-employment. Immigrants who are unable to find a job are much
more likely to become self-employed. In the neo-American model,
high rates of job growth should preclude closures at the bottom of the
labour market. Openings at the lower end of the labour market for low-
skilled immigrants abound as a result of the low-wage strategy. High
rates of labour force participation for immigrants constitutes one of the
hallmarks of the neo-American model. There may still be local pockets
of stagnation, but at least at the macro level a structural blocking of
entry-level openings for immigrants is not very likely. In general, then,
these immigrants are not compelled to start their own businesses as
they can easily find work as employees. This, however, does not in
itself imply a low rate of immigrant business start-ups. Although jobs
may be plentiful, good jobs may be hard to find as immigrants may be
confined to the secondary segment of the labour market if their educational qualifications and other skills are not fully acknowledged by
employers. Those immigrants may do much better as entrepreneurs in
terms of money-returns on self-employment compared with the wages
paid in these entry-level jobs. This premium on entrepreneurship has
been widely documented (see Light and Roach, 1996).

Consequently opting for self-employment is not so much driven by
the lack of openings at the lower end of the job market as by blocked

mobility at higher levels. This implies that the more talented immigrants will opt for self-employment, lured by the possibility of (sometimes significantly) higher earnings as an entrepreneur. In the neo-American model, immigrants have more than one option for participating in the formal economy. This ability to choose will encourage would-be entrepreneurs with relatively good skills as their less qualified counterparts can easily find jobs as employees. The push towards self-employment will be experienced most strongly by those immigrants who bump their heads on the employment glass ceiling sooner rather than later.

The *pull* to become an entrepreneur is to a large extent shaped by the institutional framework, as this not only affects the supply side but also has far-reaching consequences for the demand side or opportunity structure. In the neo-American model a strong pull is exerted on immigrant entrepreneurs. Geared towards generating low-wage jobs, the model also creates room for small-scale, low-tech firms in both personal and producer services, and in location-bound manufacturing such as sweatshops. In particular, because personal services are diverse and usually only require a small capital outlay, this booming and expanding sector presents many openings for immigrant entrepreneurs. Vacancy-chain openings will also attract immigrants as openings continue to be created by the exit of upwardly mobile, longer-established entrepreneurs. There is, however, one snag. Whereas vacancy-chain businesses in many cases offer immigrant entrepreneurs coethnic markets, personal services are mostly geared towards non-ethnic clientele, and thus require a greater language proficiency.

Producer services are, on the whole, less cost sensitive than personal services as firms are able to pass their costs on to their customers (namely other firms). They are therefore less dependent on the low-wage orientation of the neo-American model. They nevertheless profit from the low wages, although this is less pronounced than in personal services. Driven by the process of outsourcing, they provide immigrant entrepreneurs with the opportunity to set up their own businesses. In contrast to vacancy-chain businesses, immigrant entrepreneurs cannot start by building on captive ethnic markets; from the very start they have to find customers and these are usually not coethnics. Therefore immigrants may find it difficult to set up businesses in these markets.

The low minimum wage seems to be more relevant in small-scale, location-bound manufacturing. Being able to pay relatively low (legal) wages obviously allows labour-intensive manufacturing to be competitive in an advanced economic setting. Therefore the opportunities for immigrant entrepreneurs should be comparatively extensive.

To summarise: given the institutional make-up of the neo-American model we should expect immigrant entrepreneurship to be driven more by the prospect of higher earnings than as a consequence of the blocking of entry-level jobs. Moreover there is wide scope for micro-businesses relying on low- or semiskilled labour in the rapidly growing service sector and sweatshop-type manufacturing activities. Personal services in particular should attract immigrant entrepreneurs as they provide ample opportunities for further growth and are not marked by the cut-throat competition that characterises vacancy-chain businesses that cater to declining, saturated markets. The neo-American model, then, appears to be rather conducive to immigrant entrepreneurship by selecting the better-endowed on the supply side and providing all kinds of opportunities to set up small-scale, labour-intensive firms using semiskilled labour.

The Rhineland model

From our admittedly very broad perspective, the Rhineland model is by and large the opposite of the American model. In continental Europe the hand of the state is very much present: redistributing income, furnishing all kinds of services at prices below market level (for example education, public transport, health care, housing) and providing extensive social benefits to persons without paid work (Albert, 1991, p. 121). Labour is, as Esping-Andersen puts it, strongly decommodified: protected against market forces by high and easily obtainable social benefits, minimum wages and strict labour regulations. This protection of labour, however, has its price.

On the whole, employment growth in continental European states has been very sluggish. The Rhineland model is consequently characterised by high levels of unemployment. This unemployment is, of course, not evenly spread, and women, youth and immigrants are the first to be excluded from the labour market (Esping-Andersen, 1990, 1993). Continental European states are split in two along a marked 'insider–outsider' cleavage. 'The employment conditions in continental Europe', according to Esping-Andersen (1996b, p. 79), 'display all the characteristics of 'insider–outsider' labour markets'. As immigrants have great difficulty finding entry-level jobs they are to a large extent excluded from the labour market, and accordingly are strongly overrepresented among the unemployed outsiders. Notwithstanding the relatively high social benefits, for many immigrants social mobility is blocked altogether. However those talented immigrants with contacts and luck who are able to find a job and thus enter the ranks of the insiders are rather well off. In contrast to the neo-American model, these immigrants do not have a strong incentive to set up their own business, whereas the less talented (the excluded) immigrants have a much greater incentive to become entrepreneurs. This selection of immigrant entrepreneurs on the supply side is thus the exact opposite of that which takes place in the United States, where there are abundant opportunities for low-skilled immigrants lacking in financial resources to start their own business. How, then, is the opportunity structure or demand side with respect to these kinds of business affected by the continental welfare regime?

The relatively low level of female labour participation in some European countries means that the traditional division of labour between the male breadwinner and the female homemaker is still in force. Social reproduction is therefore still largely taken care of by the households themselves. This typical continental European nexus between welfare state/family/work has restricted the growth of personal services by depressing demand and setting too high a price (namely a high minimum wage).

These specific welfare state characteristics have significant implications for both the level and direction of job growth in continental European states. According to Esping-Andersen the

> lack of service job growth (except in high-end services, such as business, finance and the like) can be attributed to the classical cost-disease problem... Since most personal and social services enjoy only modest, if any, productivity improvement they will fail to create jobs if wages and labour costs follow trends in high-productivity sectors. Egalitarian and high-wage (family wage) structures, as exist throughout Europe, will therefore render private sector services, like laundry, carwash, bellhops, or day care inordinately expensive.
>
> (Esping-Anderson, 1996b, p. 79)

In the Rhineland model the opportunities for immigrant entrepreneurs to set up business in personal services are therefore slim. The same reasoning could be applied to location-bound, small-scale manufacturing activities. High minimum wages block the growth of these activities, however if the demand for products in these volatile markets is strong enough, firms could cut corners and resort to informal production. This tempting escape route is partly dependent on the level of surveillance, and partly on the level of trust that groups of immigrants can generate (Kloosterman *et al.*, 1997b). Although the scope for legal production remains limited in continental Europe, vacancy-chain openings do occur and the succession process in neighbourhoods affects local businesses as long-established, native shopowners leave and are replaced by immigrants.

Driven by the lack of employment prospects and the limited demand for personal services, we can expect immigrant entrepreneurs in continental European states to flock towards these kinds of opportunity. In the Netherlands, for instance, Turkish and Moroccan entrepreneurs abound in the grocery, bakery and small restaurant businesses (Kloosterman and van der Leun, forthcoming); a similar situation exists in France (Ma Mung, 1992). Although many of the entrepreneurs' coethnics are unemployed, the relatively high social benefits that characterise the Rhineland model help to support their businesses. On the other hand most of these markets are nearing saturation, given the easy entry to them and the push to become self-employed due to exclusion from the labour market. Inevitably, cut-throat competition will evolve in these already shrinking markets and immigrant entrepreneurs often seem to be veering towards a permanent *Lumpen bourgeoisie* existence.

A rather different case is offered by producer services. The outsourcing of tasks by large firms may provide an efficient way out of restrictive regulations, as buying services from outside small producers allows the circumvention of corporatist regulations and promotes flexibility. Small firms that cater to these producer services can, then, be seen as part of an 'atypical employment' pattern and as an example of 'labour market actors dodging the rigidities and high costs of the regular economy' (Esping-Andersen, 1996b, p. 81). In this sense, these small firms can be put under the same heading as, for instance, temporary workers and those engaged in informal economic activities (cf. *The Economist*, 3 May 1997; Kloosterman *et al.*, 1997b, 1998). As mentioned above, many producer service activities are hard to enter for immigrant entrepreneurs wanting to start their own business. The extent to which immigrants can participate in these producer services depends largely on their social and cultural capital (language proficiency and relevant networks that link them with potential clients).

To summarise: continental European welfare states push mainly unemployed immigrants towards self-employment but seem to offer little scope for the setting up of small-scale businesses with strong growth prospects. The growth of personal services is severely curtailed by high wages and lack of demand due to social reproduction being provided by either the state or the households themselves. This funnels immigrant entrepreneurs towards sunset activities in vacancy-chain businesses, competing fiercely in shrinking markets with little hope of progressing beyond mere economic survival. Producer services may offer a way out, but accessibility may constitute a severe obstacle to this.

Conclusions

We have tried to provide a theoretical starting point for international comparative research on immigrant entrepreneurship as it now seems that such comparisons will be the next stage in the process. International comparisons of immigrant entrepreneurship inevitably have to take account of differences in national legal systems, policies on immigration, policies on firms in general and immigrants in particular, and differences in the socioeconomic institutional framework. Our analysis has focused on the latter aspect, thereby complementing recent comparative research on employment and unemployment. In doing so we have deliberately disregarded the other aspects and the cultural characteristics of immigrants. Instead we have concentrated on structural processes on both the supply and the demand side of entrepreneurship to create a socioeconomic framework for comparison at a high level of aggregation. Further research will be needed to reveal the extent to which, for instance, the opportunities offered are seized, under what circumstances and by whom. As research has shown, entrepreneurship is causally significant; opportunities may go unnoticed or may be otherwise neglected (Light and Rosenstein, 1995b, p. 6 ff.) Empirical comparative research inevitably has to include both immigrant group and city characteristics in order to account for the observed patterns. In order to conduct such research, however, a more all-embracing theoretical framework is needed that can serve to frame research questions more precisely and provide a start for explanations.

We have attempted to fill this gap by combining three theoretical building blocks. The first comprises notions on immigrant entrepreneurship. We have assumed that immigrant entrepreneurs in most cases lack both human (educational qualifications) and financial capital to start a business at the higher end of the market. They are therefore largely confined to small-scale, low-wage, low-tech firms.

The second building block consists of a brief analysis of socioeconomic trends with respect to low-wage activities in advanced economies in general. Globalisation and the emergence of post-industrial societies has led to extensive reshuffling of the low-wage, low-tech segment of advanced economies. Low-wage manufacturing has become increasingly confined to specific, location-bound activities. In services, however, an expansion of low-wage activities is more likely as households and firms increasingly switch to outsourcing.

The third building block comprises two broad and contrasting institutional frameworks. A neo-American model was juxtaposed with a Rhineland model, thereby abstracting from differences between, for instance, the Netherlands and France or Germany. In both models the impact of the institutional framework on the supply of immigrant entrepreneurs, as well as on the demand side or opportunity structure was examined.

Using our theoretical framework we have found marked differences between the models' expected impact on immigrant entrepreneurship. The neo-American model, with strong, low-wage job growth as one of its hallmarks, offers ample opportunities for immigrant entrepreneurial activities in general and personal services more specifically. Moreover, as immigrants can easily find work as employees, only those who are confident that they can earn more from self-employment are lured into entrepreneurship. Vacancy-chain businesses offer opportunities as well, but being in very constrained markets they offer less promise for aspiring entrepreneurs.

The Rhineland or continental European model presents a rather different picture. Hampered by high wages at the lower end of the market, these states are characterised by high unemployment and a sharp division between insiders and outsiders. Immigrants are clearly overrepresented in the outsider group. Subject to long-term unemployment, they are trapped in a situation of exclusion. This may push them towards entrepreneurship, despite the social benefits they receive when unemployed. In contrast with the neo-American model the expansion of low-wage activities is much less pronounced and work that pays more than the immigrants receive in social benefits is rather scarce. Most entrepreneurial opportunities are found in vacancy-chain businesses, which because of their concentration in declining markets invariably involves cut-throat competition. Producer services and informal production also offer opportunities, but the first requires a specific kind of social capital (access to networks that include native businesses) and the second either stays very marginal or requires a legal facade, and falls mainly under the category of vacancy-chain business. Unemployed workers encounter exclusion; the self-employed may face rigid segmentation.

Both the level and the incidence of immigrant entrepreneurship differs along these lines in welfare states of the neo-American type and those of the Rhineland type. Further research will determine how groups of immigrants and individual immigrants cope with these structural opportunities and constraints in a concrete way.

Note

1   I would like to thank Ivan Light for his comments on an earlier version of this chapter.

6
State Regulatory Regimes and Immigrants' Informal Economic Activity

Gary P. Freeman and Nedim Ögelman

Introduction

Immigration scholars tend to agree that democratic states possess only a modest capacity to control the movement of peoples across their borders and are structurally vulnerable to illegal migration, mass asylum claims and other forms of unwanted migration. Whether such sweeping assertions about the inability of states to control international migration are warranted or not (cf. Freeman, 1994a; Joppke, forthcoming), discussion of this issue rests on a good deal of empirical evidence. In contrast the role that state regulation can play in shaping the economic behaviour of immigrants inside national borders is not as well-studied or understood.

It would seem reasonable that domestic 'immigrant' policies would be even less successful than those directed at regulating entry. States that cannot regulate their borders – a police function that operates at the literal frontier of national sovereignty – ought not to be expected to manage effectively the more demanding tasks of ensuring that migrants, authorised or unauthorised, follow the established rules of economic life, participate only in lawful activities, are protected from exploitation by employers operating outside the law, and contribute in the most efficient way to the nation's economic health. Such policies, it would seem, would fail in the face of the same powerful economic forces, political pressures, administrative incompetence and lack of will that were obstacles to immigration control in the first place.[1]

The central concern of this chapter is how the policies of liberal democratic states interact with the economic strategies of migrants to shape their entrepreneurial and working behaviour. We are especially interested in the impact state regulations have on the decisions of migrants to set up their own enterprises and on the tendency for migrant entrepreneurs and workers to operate in the informal economy. Immigrant entrepreneurs warrant particular attention due to their position as profit-maximising economic risk takers who have links to places in which alternative laws, norms or customs govern market transactions, employee recruitment and working conditions. We focus on three sectors of state policy that have special salience to the economic activities of immigrants: immigration regulation and control, economic regulation and the provision of social benefits.

Regulatory regimes and immigrant incentives

State regulations create a legal framework (which we shall call the regulatory regime) within which immigrants and nationals make choices. With respect to migrants, the most interesting choices are whether and how to enter the host country in the first place; once there, whether to become wage earners or launch entrepreneurial endeavours; and whether to operate inside or outside the formal sector.

Our approach to regulatory regimes is guided by recent work in the 'new institutional economics'.[2] The major theoretical insight of this approach is recognition of the importance of the transaction costs of economic exchange, which neoclassical economic theory assumed were zero (Feige, 1990, p. 990). According to new institutionalists, the institutional structure of societies has an independent role in shaping economic outcomes. Institutions are conceived as sets of rules governing behaviour. They 'establish and guarantee rights, bestow privileges, and administer regulations and penalty structures that serve to foster adherence to the rules' (ibid.). Rules may be formal or informal. With respect to the former, we are especially concerned with those economic rules which define property rights: 'the bundle of rights over the use and the income to be derived from property and the ability to alienate an asset or a resource' (North, 1990, p. 47).

By informal rules we have in mind the social organisational structures and norms that characterise the political economy of the labour market in particular countries. These involve the representative institutions of labour and capital, their structured interactions with the state, and the norms by which relations among the three sectors are governed. The informal rules and institutions of society have a major impact on the implementation and effectiveness of formal rules laid down by the state (Putnam, 1993). An institutional perspective is relevant to the analysis of immigrant economic activity, their choice between labour and entrepreneurship, and their contribution to the emergence of informal economies in advanced societies (Reynolds, 1991; Tokman and Klein, 1996). The essential difference between formal and informal activity is whether the activity complies with the currently established rules of the game.[3] Because informal activity is defined in terms of institutional arrangements imposed by the state, 'any positive or negative outcomes associated with the emergence of the informal economy can, in principle, be either reinforced or weakened by policy actions which modify the institutional setting' (Feige, 1990, p. 993).

Entrepreneurs, who make a living by discovering and exploiting niches of inefficiency in the market system, are more prone than other members of society to test the limits of state regulations that interfere with short-term profit maximisation. Immigrants exhibit a marked propensity for entrepreneurial pursuits. The disjunction between their status aspirations and the status opportunities available to them in host societies leads them to seek to overcome these structural barriers through innovative and creative economic ventures. In a sense, they try to build their own opportunity structures through entrepreneurship. Immigrant entrepreneurs, moreover, are likely to be less familiar with the institutional framework in which they must operate and they are more likely to have ideas that differ from host country practices. State policies are central to the obstacles immigrants face in their strategies for integration, but they may also play a role in facilitating integration (Reynolds, 1991; Waldinger *et al.*, 1990b). Altogether, immigrants are likely candidates for entrepreneurship and informal activity.

As Feige (1990, p. 990) has noted, there are many sets of institutions in any society and they constrain different types of behaviour. One must locate the institutions that are linked to the behaviour one is seeking to understand. Regulatory regimes, for our purposes, involve the laws and policies governing immigration, market and welfare.[4]

Our working presumption is that as a consequence of their proximity, salience and directness, immigration policies are the most significant determinants of the scale and character of migrants' economic behaviour, followed by economic regulations and social benefits, in that order. Immigration policy sets the conditions under which foreigners enter a country and the terms of their sojourn. Because they control the opportunities for entry and the range of activities that may be legally pursued once admitted, migration rules are a central component of the immigrant's economic choices. A nation's immigration law determines the number and types of immigrants, and thereby contributes directly to the emergence of the populations that are the chief focus of our analysis.

Policies regulating markets, on the other hand, establish the rules within which land, labour and capital are bought and sold, and thus create the framework within which individuals obtain and hold jobs, act as employers and create and distribute wealth. The effects of welfare state programmes are less direct. Social benefits constitute, for recipients, that part of the individual's income and living standard that is derived indirectly, that is, from the state rather than directly from the employer or via business activities. This is sometimes referred to as the 'social wage'. These benefits affect the marginal utility of work for those who are eligible. For employers, on the other hand, social benefit programmes are a principal element of the 'social charge' and add to the cost of doing business.

Regulatory regimes constitute the rules of the game as it is played in particular societies. If institutions differ from one society to another, the behaviour of immigrants should differ as well. Our goal in the following sections is (1) to suggest how particular policy instruments and objectives affect the incentives of migrants and natives, (2) to classify states according to the types of policy they adopt in each sector and (3) to discuss how policies governing the three sectors are linked.

Our analysis is hampered by the absence of systematic and authoritative data for such key dependent variables as rates of entrepreneurship among immigrants in different countries, the size and composition of informal economies, and the scale of illegal immigration and unauthorised employment. Most of these phenomena are inherently difficult to measure because of their clandestine nature. With respect to the size of informal economies, we rely on rough estimates. We consider the Scandinavian and Northern European states, as well as Britain, to have relatively small informal economies. France and Belgium, we suspect, fall somewhere in the middle range. The United States and the Southern European countries appear to have relatively extensive problems (Tanzi, 1982; Weiss, 1987; Williams, 1994). The weakness of the empirical base of our discussion of informal economies and immigrant entrepreneurship, as well as the sketchy discussion of particular national cases, make our argument more an attempt to develop an agenda for research than to test hypotheses in a rigorous manner.

Immigration policy

We discuss three important ways in which national immigration programmes differ: (1) their purposes and methods in recruiting and accepting immigrants, (2) the means by which they enforce rules constraining immigrant participation in the economy and (3) the methods they employ to assist or direct immigrant settlement and incorporation.

A few states have a formal, long-standing and institutionalised practice of receiving new immigrants for permanent settlement; most states, however, do not operate an explicit immigration system. There are three sets of countries among the Western democracies with divergent historical experiences in this regard (Freeman, 1992, 1995; cf. Cornelius *et al.*, 1994a, pp. 11–27; Papademetriou and Hamilton, 1996, pp. 5–7).

The English-speaking settler societies are traditional countries of immigration. Australia, New Zealand, Canada and the United States have formal systems that provide for the annual admission of new immigrants for permanent settlement (Betts, 1988; Dirks, 1995; Freeman and Jupp, 1992; Hawkins, 1989; Jupp and Kebala, 1993; Richmond, 1994).

The European states with post-colonial and guest worker migrations (Germany, France, Belgium, Britain, Denmark, Sweden, Norway, Austria and the Netherlands) do not claim to be countries of immigration, although some of them (such as France) have admitted large numbers of migrants over the years. Their principal experience of migration in the post Second World War era has involved guest workers recruited to satisfy a high labour demand, many of whom have subsequently become *de facto* settlers. While family reunification characterised subsequent migration in the late 1970s and early 1980s, in recent years the most important avenue of legal entry into these countries has been through asylum claims (Meissner *et al.*, 1993; Rogers, 1985; Thränhardt, 1992). In the wake of the guest worker experience these states have had to confront the incorporation of peoples from diverse cultural backgrounds – a problem that was not on the policy agenda of many of these host countries until quite recently.

Finally, economic growth and changes in the global economy have transformed a number of West European countries that only a few years ago were significant sources of emigration (Spain, Italy, Portugal and Greece) into receiving states. They are in the process of setting up immigration regimes that can control illegal immigrants and organise and regularise the new immigrant flows (Fassmann and Münz, 1994; Miles and Thränhardt, 1995).

Although it seems reasonable to expect that countries with such diverse approaches to the admission of migrants would experience varying levels of success in managing their economic activities, it is difficult to uncover any obvious pattern of outcomes. The traditional countries of immigration certainly have more experience with migration and they possess more institutionalised recruitment and selection mechanisms. Furthermore it is often claimed that the best defence against illegal immigration is the establishment of an annual quota for permanent entries because otherwise would-be migrants have no legal alternatives for entry. This implies that states with settlement policies should have less difficulty with illegal immigration. Nonetheless the United States, which is the leading country of settlement in the world, arguably has the most pervasive problems with unauthorised work, illegal immigration and informal economic activity by immigrants. Canada and Australia, on the other hand, appear better able to cope with these matters despite operating immigration programmes that are as large or larger than that of the United States (Birrell, 1994; Garcia y Griego, 1994). On the whole, therefore, the settler societies show no clear pattern with regard to deterring unwanted entry, unauthorised work and informal business activity.

Two aspects of the admissions programmes of the settler societies relate directly to the decision of immigrants to operate businesses: business or investor visas and a process for the recognition of overseas credentials. Canada, Australia and the United States have provisions in their immigration laws that are designed to admit entrepreneurs, that is, individuals who are able and willing to invest specified sums in economic ventures with employment-generating potential or who intend to set up a business (Jenks, 1992). These programmes have been sharply criticised in some quarters (Economic Council of Canada, 1991, p. 34) and the Canadian and Australian operations have been temporarily suspended and revised due to charges of corruption (Borowski and Nash, 1994). Britain also operates an investor programme for those with sufficient means. The number of visas granted under these schemes is significant. For example about 10 000 persons entered Australia in 1989–90 under various business-investor categories; over 17 500 persons were granted visas to Canada in 1989 as either entrepreneurs, self-employed persons or investors; almost 10 000 investors were admitted to the United States in 1992; and 330 persons entered Britain in 1990 as either persons of independent means, business investors or self-employed (INS, 1993, p. 8; Jenks, 1992). Clearly these countries encourage entrepreneurship and investment among immigrants as an official policy, but convincing evidence that such policies are effective, desirable or necessary is unavailable.

A second aspect of the immigration programmes of the countries of permanent settlement is the recruitment of highly skilled migrants.

Programmes designed to achieve this are complicated and, on the available evidence, only modestly successful (Freeman, 1994b). Although one reason for pursuing the highly skilled, including those with professional training and credentials, is to ensure that they contribute economically once admitted, a number of obstacles lie in the way of professional and skilled immigrants pursuing their vocations in their new countries. A major study in Australia (Hawthorne, 1994) found that immigrant engineers experience considerable difficulty finding and holding jobs in their profession due to the 'transferability gap': the disjunction between the experiences and qualifications of immigrants in their native countries and the assessment of those experiences and qualifications by host country employers. The gap seems to derive from a reluctance to recognise overseas qualifications, linguistic and other cross-cultural factors, as well as discrimination (cf. Castles *et al.*, 1989; Chapman and Iredale, 1993; Woldring, 1994). Highly educated and professionally qualified individuals who are unable to practice their vocations of choice often end up unemployed, but many decide to go into business for themselves. Hence an ineffective programme for vetting overseas qualifications can inadvertently promote immigrant entrepreneurship.

One might presume that those European states that administered guest worker programmes until 1974 would be in a better position to control the unauthorised economic activity of immigrants than states that admit tens of thousands of settlers annually. Guest workers, after all, were recruited for their specific skills, given permits that limited the type and duration of work, and generally lived under much more stringent formal controls than immigrants with permission to settle permanently. Guest worker programmes tended to develop institutional capacity only slowly, however. Administration tended to be *ad hoc* and the enforcement of rules lax. The result, though it varied from country to country, was a massive disregard for the law by employers, immigrants and state officials alike, contributing to the growth of a veritable culture of illegality in some European labour markets. Informal recruitment, illegal entry followed by regularization, amnesties, visa overstaying and unauthorised employment became the rule rather than the exception and were widely tolerated, despite ritualistic complaints about exploitation.

The new countries of immigration in Southern Europe are scrambling to erect immigration laws and programmes where only a few years ago none existed. Even so, officials have been tempted to turn a blind eye to illegal immigration and the extra legal economic behaviour of immigrants on the justification of shortages (Freeman, 1995, pp. 893–6). These countries appear to have a systematic tendency towards unauthorised work and immigrant concentration in the informal sector because of the combination of fledgling immigration programmes, internal labour market conditions and external pressures for entry.

In all the immigration countries the cultural distance between the immigrant community and the host society seems likely to be related to the participation of immigrants in the informal economy, whether as an employee or an entrepreneur. Immigrants who bring with them ingrained habits, methods or expectations of what is acceptable business practice that clash with the norms of the host society may generate underground activities (Reynolds, 1991). In this respect, recruitment and admissions policies that promote the migration of culturally distant groups (Turks in Germany, for example) may contribute to a high rate of entrepreneurship, much of which may be undertaken in the informal economy.

The principal immigration policy that seeks directly to enforce constraints on the economic activities of immigrants, our second category, is the regulation of authorisation to work. The most commonly employed method of regulation is employer sanctions, which turn the focus of policy away from preventing illegal entry or overstaying towards the elimination of the attractive pull of employment. A recent review concludes that sanctions are 'the immigration-control policy of choice' of the industrialised societies, used primarily 'as a tool for checking the spread of the underground economy' (Papademetriou and Hamilton, 1996, p. 14).

While employer sanctions are widely thought to have been ineffective since their adoption in the United States in 1986 (Calavita, 1994a; Fix, 1991; Martin, 1994b; North, 1994; Perotti, 1994), recent political trends have been in the direction of reinforcing rather than repealing the law, as had earlier seemed possible. The evidence from Western Europe, Australia and Canada is mixed. Most European states adopted sanctions after they halted temporary labour migration in the mid 1970s, although the new states of destination have acted more recently. The best evidence suggests that sanctions were not effective early on, but that modifications made as time passed gave them new life (Marie, 1994; Miller, 1987, p. 46; but compare Calavita, 1994b, pp. 314–17; Cornelius, 1994, p. 347; Martin, 1994a, p. 220; Suarez-Orozco, 1994, pp. 252–3). The Canadian and Australian experience is more clearly, if imperfectly, sanguine (Birrell, 1992, 1994; Burstein *et al.*, 1994; Cox and Glenn, 1994).

The drawbacks of an employer sanctions strategy against unauthorised work are that enforcement, which is expensive and difficult, tends not to be extensive enough and penalties are not severe enough to deter employers from hiring illegal workers, especially if they are in possession of apparently valid documents. As for the immigrants themselves, they have little to lose in accepting such jobs if they already have an illegal status. This suggests that the states that will be most successful with employers' sanctions have strongly organised trade-union federations and employers' associations that engage in extensive self-regulation – a topic to which we shall return.

With respect to the third category of immigration policy – incorporation and settlement – all other things being equal, states that assist migrants in the process of settling – temporarily or permanently – (employment and housing assistance, language training and so on) should do a better job of avoiding the concentration of immigrants in the informal economy and should facilitate the entry of immigrants into the ranks of the self-employed. Due to the absence of systematic data on settlement policies, however, it is only possible to speculate about possible patterns. In the case of the United States it is clear that not every settler society considers it useful to create a comprehensive settlement programme. Indeed the United States has no formal settlement policy for immigrants, apart from refugees.[5] This *laissez-faire* attitude surely contributes to the large number of immigrants who enter the informal sector as employers or employees or who engage in unauthorised work in the United States. Legislation passed by the US Congress in 1996 pushed federal policy even further in this direction, placing new restrictions on the access of legal immigrants to publicly funded benefits.

Australia and Canada have divergent settlement policies, but both are elaborate and well-institutionalised, especially when compared with the United States (Jupp, 1992; Lanphier and Lukomskyj, 1994). The fact that the informal economy is apparently less well-developed in both countries is consistent with our hypothesis. Likewise the evidently greater success of the Scandinavian countries in coping with underground economic activities may be related to their extensive settlement programme (Hammar, 1985; Ornbrandt and Peura, 1993).

Regulation of economic behaviour

State policies affecting opportunities for work and entrepreneurship impinge directly on the lives of migrants. Our discussion will deal more or less exclusively with the regulation of employment, though we will look at it from the perspective of both immigrant workers and employers. We distinguish between labour market regulation on the one hand, and policies responding to national employment trajectories on the other. Labour market regulation is concerned with setting labour standards and protecting workers' rights. Because they involve monitoring and enforcing rules of behaviour, labour market regulations are fundamentally police functions. Among the most important regulations for our purposes are those that pertain to working conditions: hours, wages, work-place safety, child labour and the like. Beyond these are regulations that lay down the rights of workers to organise, bargain collectively, obtain due process, avoid forced labour and generally enjoy the protection of the law.

In important respects, all the Western democracies have adopted a common set of labour market regulations that adhere to the standards of international organisations such as the ILO (Commission for the Study of International Migration, 1990, p. 73). Nevertheless there remains considerable variation in how committed and effective states are in enforcing such regulations, especially with regard to economic immigrants (Weiner, 1995, p. 186). Much of this variation may be attributed to the difference in the effectiveness of administrative institutions; some must surely reflect varying commitment on the part of officials.

Employment trajectories, the second policy forum we address, involve the projected changes in the sectoral composition, skill requirements and size of a country's workforce. Here policies entail a set of broader programmes and decisions that are directed not so much at working conditions and rights as at reconfiguring rules to conform to changes in the basic structure of the economy. To take one example pertinent to our discussion, the wealthy states must all confront the challenges of their rapid transformation from primarily industrial to service or post-industrial economies (Wieczorek, 1995). This involves the growth of highly skilled, well-paid work at one end of the job market and the continuing need for, or even proliferation of, unskilled, unattractive and poorly remunerated work at the bottom. It also involves the looming problem of long-term mass unemployment at rates well above those that had become conventionally acceptable in the growth years after 1945. States may adopt some combination of three strategies in response to their perception of their employment trajectories. They may permit a low-wage sector to develop within the national labour force, producing what may turn out to be a permanent underclass. This seems to be a major part of the United States' response to its economic development (Piore, 1979a). On the other hand, governments may try to export jobs at the low end of the employment hierarchy to low-wage, Third World countries. This has been the principal path taken by Japan, for example. This may not be feasible for many low-wage positions as the personal services involved must be performed on-shore. States may therefore import foreign labour to take up these jobs and tolerate low-end service subcontracting, in or outside the formal sector, within their national borders. All the Western democracies have done this in one form or another. The major differences among them relate to whether they have admitted permanent settlers or temporary migrants.

The experience of the settler societies has not been uniform. The United States is unique in its willingness to admit vast numbers of unskilled settlers, legal and illegal, and acquiesce in the development of an extensive system of low-end subcontracting, much of it outside the legal system. Migrants are not necessarily confined permanently to the lower reaches of the income ladder, but they tend to enter the economy at that level and in their continuing flow constitute a partial solution to the low-end services demands of the US economy. Australia and Canada, on the other hand, try at least to discourage poorly skilled immigrants through the use of the points system of selection, although their family reunion and refugee categories include a significant number of less skilled persons.[6]

The importation of temporary workers to satisfy demand in particular productive sectors was a tactic adopted by most European states in the 1960s and 1970s. They hoped to 'import labor that does not have to be absorbed into the social or political system' (Weiner, 1995, p. 77). Assuming that guest workers, most of whom had only limited skills, would remain within their borders only temporarily, states initially adopted restrictive and exclusionary social, political and economic policies regarding foreign residents. With the dawning realisation after the mid 1970s that guest workers were likely to remain indefinitely, states relaxed their rules and began to permit or encourage more complete social and economic integration.

Nevertheless the immigrant populations of most of these states, including the descendants of the first generation of guest workers, today tend to be found disproportionately in low-wage, low-status jobs and in small-scale entrepreneurial endeavours (Castles and Kosack, 1985, pp. 57–112; Remy, 1991). Quite apart from the human capital characteristics of immigrants, bureaucratic inertia, discrimination and a policy framework that is unresponsive to the market requirements of immigrant enclaves contribute to their entry into the semiformal or informal economy as small business owners or workers. Despite the differences among the Western democracies in the formal labour market regulations and employment policies they adopt, the more interesting variation is probably the extent to which formal policies are actually implemented. This may in part reflect the capacity of different states to carry out policies and in part it may be the result of what might be called purposeful failure to follow through with official rules. To understand these issues we need to investigate the informal institutions that operate in the labour market. How are workers and employers organised? How do they interact? What norms and traditional practices govern labour, management and state relations? And finally, how adaptive are governing institutions to changes in the structure of the market? We believe that answers to these questions can be found in the strength and mode of the organisation of trade unions and employers' associations and the manner in which they engage in consultations and negotiations with state officials.

In a well-known typology, Lehmbruch (1984, pp. 65–6) identifies five categories of democratic states according to the extent and durability of the 'concertation of major economic interests'. States are arrayed along a continuum running from 'pluralist' systems with negligible concertation (the United States, Canada, Australia and New Zealand), through 'weak corporatism', where organised labour enjoys institutionalised participation in policy formation (Britain and Italy), 'medium corporatism' (Ireland, Belgium, Germany, Denmark, Finland and Switzerland) to 'strong corporatism' (Austria, Sweden, Norway and the Netherlands).[7]

There are reasons to expect the institutional arrangements and norms associated with corporatist concertation to be positively related to strict enforcement of labour regulations and the development of extensive and activist labour market policies. Corporatist decision-making structures should contribute to a social climate in which there is significant respect for workers' rights and a large degree of self-enforcement of labour standards on the part of trade unions and employers' associations. These aspects of the corporatist structure should work against the development and expansion of dual labour markets, large informal sectors with numerous businesses operating off the books and immigrant participation in them.

On the other hand the strict enforcement of labour market regulations, as well as extensive and activist labour market policies associated with corporatist concertation, could contribute to a rigid policy environment that is not responsive to market dynamics. Decision makers in corporatist systems are less free than those in pluralist states to respond to the shifting forces of supply and demand when changing labour market regulations. Existing policies in corporatist states will be the result of a more or less formalised interest-group compromise and establishing new policies will require significant bargaining and input from labour and capital. Policy may be slow to respond to market transformations and impatient entrepreneurs may not wait for regulations to catch up with their own views of what the market demands. These aspects of corporatist systems may produce effects that are contradictory to those associated with cooperative decision making and self-regulation. Whether they will produce underground activities on a significant scale may depend on the effectiveness with which the organisations police their own constituencies.

The situation in corporatist societies contrasts sharply with that in pluralist states where labour–management relations are often adversarial. With labour unions less well-established and employers' associations less hierarchically organised, labour market policies result from a less structured and formally negotiated process. Two consequences should result. Firstly, state officials should more readily be able to restructure policy in the light of perceived competitive pressures, even if the vested interests of labour unions are threatened. Secondly, states should take a more casual attitude towards the violation of formal rules if the ends of economic efficiency are being served. Pluralist social institutions and processes, therefore, should be associated with higher levels of illegal immigration, more unauthorised labour and more pervasive business activity on the borders of legality.

Looking at the order in which countries appear in Lehmbruch's typology, it appears roughly compatible with these arguments, if we take our estimations of the extent of informalisation discussed earlier as indicative. On the whole, the corporatist states appear to have been most successful in suppressing illegal immigration and underground economic activity, while the pluralist states have been least successful. There are some anomalies, however. Among the pluralist states, the United States and Canada seem to fit, but Australia and possibly New Zealand do not. The former certainly have significant informal sectors, but not the latter.

Likewise, within the category of weak corporatist states, both Britain and Italy are out of place, the former having a smaller informal sector than predicted, the latter a larger one. In the cases of Australia and Britain it may be that labour, while not brought into an institutionalised decision-making process, is nonetheless capable of exerting considerable pressure on conditions in the workplace, including the elimination of unauthorised work and the suppression of underground enterprises.

One might quibble about particular cases among medium and strong corporatist states, but they surely include those European states that are relatively most successful in combating informalisation. With the exception of Ireland, all these states recruited guest workers, a decision that produces pressures conducive to the development of an informal sector. Hence there are contradictory forces at work: the guest worker experience leads to informalisation, while the self-regulating mechanisms of corporatism deter it. The result is a mixed picture with the results depending on the relative weight of these contradictory forces in particular societies.

We should stress that it is not obvious that the elimination of illegal immigration, unauthorised work and immigrant business outside the formal economy is an unconditional benefit to the countries that achieve it. Our analysis suggests that effective regulation is sometimes attained at the cost of labour market rigidity. Corporatist concertation may mean more effective enforcement of labour market regulations, but those regulations may not be suitable for a rapidly changing market. The flexibility exhibited in the weak corporatist and pluralist states may be messy and at the expense of certain groups of citizens and immigrants, but it may also contribute to economic dynamism and job growth.

The welfare state

Social benefits are the aspect of state regulation least directly connected to immigrant economic behaviour. Nevertheless the complex array of taxes, cash and similar benefits that make up contemporary welfare states obviously weigh importantly on the economic calculations of immigrants in their roles as workers and employers. But how? Three logical, but contradictory, general propositions are commonly heard.

The first is that the generous social benefits distributed by the rich welfare states draw poor immigrants from the Third World. This seems reasonable, as does another proposition: that the attraction of welfare benefits encourages immigrants to find employment in the formal sector, where such benefits are guaranteed. Unfortunately a third proposition is equally plausible, namely that the cost of social benefit 'contributions' encourages employers (indigenous and immigrant) to push their activities underground in order to avoid them. Moreover immigrants themselves might well prefer underground employment or operating an informal business enterprise in order to escape paying social security and other welfare-related taxes. Obviously the relationship between the welfare state and the immigrant's economic life is not simple.

The hypothesis that welfare state provisions act as a magnet pulling immigrants into the rich countries may not be as persuasive as it appears if immigrants are primarily motivated by the desire to work. Such benefit programmes as old-age pensions, health insurance, housing subsidies and so on may be of only marginal interest to job seekers or small-scale entrepreneurs, especially if they see themselves as temporary residents and are primarily concerned about savings and sending remittances home. Nevertheless, once they are working or in business, immigrants may exhibit a more pronounced tendency to stay on, even in the face of unemployment, because of the cushioning effect that social benefits produce.

Immigrants, like other workers, may prefer good jobs in the formal sector that bring with them the full range of benefits. Again, this may be especially true of those who intend to stay. But the payroll deductions that such benefits entail suggest that for many it may be more attractive to forego them. On the whole it seems that welfare state benefits are probably more important in pushing immigrants into the informal economy than they are in drawing them into formal activity. This would seem even more clear in the case of employers, national or foreign. Generally, the growth of the welfare state, especially the escalating costs of pensions and health programmes, are a prime factor in the global movement towards economic restructuring (contracting out and so on) that is integral to the rise of informal economies in the first place. Employers, caught in an environment of intensifying competition, seek various means of eliminating the cost of social benefits for employees, programmes that can amount to half or more of total labour costs.

If social benefits seem, on the whole, likely to contribute to the growth of the informal economy and to immigrant concentration there, what can we say of the experience of different types of welfare state? Although all the rich democracies are welfare states, they vary considerably in the level and types of benefit they guarantee. Esping-Andersen's (1990) useful typology divides welfare states into three broad categories: liberal (the United States, Australia, Canada), conservative/corporatist (Austria, France, Germany, Italy) and social democratic (Scandinavia) (cf. Castles and Mitchell, 1993). It would seem plausible, all other things being equal, that those states with the most extravagant benefit structures would produce the strongest incentives for employers and workers to move out of the formal sector in the face of high fiscal burdens. We would find the most thriving informal sectors in Scandinavia, more modest ones in countries such as Germany and France, and the smallest of all in the stingier welfare regimes of the United States and Australia. This of course is not consistent with the facts as we can know them. Indeed roughly the reverse seems to have happened.

The best explanation for this is probably that the level of taxation for social benefits, even though it varies considerably across the Western states, is sufficiently high everywhere to be thought of as a constant in the calculations of businesses and workers. In all the states it produces strong incentives for those businesses that can, to move their economic activities out of the formal sector or to displace as much of their production costs as possible onto firms and workers outside it. The incentives for immigrant employers to do the same are also strong. But the opportunity to act on these incentives is not constant across the industrial economies. The opportunity structure for informalisation, so to speak, is a function not so much of the welfare state but of the political economy of the labour market, as discussed in the previous section. Those countries with strong social-economic institutions are better able to deter tax avoidance and non-compliance with labour and business regulations.

Conclusion

State regulatory regimes designed to monitor and change the economic behaviour of native and foreign economic actors vary considerably within Western democracies. Without more precise data it is difficult to draw conclusions, but it appears that outcomes, as indicated by the extent of unauthorised immigrant work and small-scale enterprise, especially in the informal sector, vary even more widely than formal rules and policies. Some of this variation is clearly a function of the size and characteristics of the immigrant populations in particular countries. Generally, the larger the immigrant pool and the more culturally distant it is from the host society, the greater the tendency of immigrant workers and entrepreneurs to move into the informal sector. Moreover the greater a country's capacity to absorb and integrate immigrant populations, the weaker the trend towards informalisation.

Beyond these matters, however, regulatory regimes are clearly important. The strongest conclusion to emerge from our analysis is that outcomes are less a function of the content of the regulatory regimes
adopted in particular countries than of the effectiveness with which
they are implemented. This in turn seems to be significantly affected
by the degree to which the rules and regulations on the one hand, and
the socioeconomic institutions and norms of civil society on the other,
fit. States cannot enforce regulations on either native or foreign
workers and employers who have strong incentives not to cooperate,
without incurring political and fiscal costs that are unacceptable in
democracies. States have more success when they are dealing with
institutions, such as trade unions and business associations, that can
engage in self-regulation and share with state officials the objective of
strict adherence to labour laws.

Notes

1 Just one reason why this would be so is that the rights would-be immigrants
already enjoy in national and international courts are much more extensive
once they are legally inside a country's borders. The protection of these
rights in liberal democracies constrains the ability of the state to regulate
migrant behaviour. On the rights of prospective immigrants, see Bauböck
(1994) and Soysal (1994); on the role of rights in domestic immigration
policy, see Hollifield (1992).
2 The chief intellectual progenitor of this field is North (1990), but it has taken
a number of directions in disciplines adjacent to economics. See also the
work of Olson (1982) and Weaver and Rockman (1993).
3 The informal economy can be defined as comprising those economic activities that circumvent the costs and are excluded from the benefits and rights
incorporated in the laws and administrative rules covering 'property relationships, commercial licensing, labor contracts, torts, financial credit and
social security systems' (Feige, 1990, p. 992).
4 Fiscal systems are also a critical element in any discussion of economic
incentives and the development of informal activities. Our discussion will
deal with taxation primarily as it relates to the costs of social benefit programmes that fall on employers. Lack of space precludes a fuller discussion
of taxation systems in their own right.
5 This is somewhat misleading because private agencies spend large sums and
offer a range of services, although these are targeted mostly at refugees
(Bach, 1992).
6 Australia amended its immigration policy in 1996 to reduce overall numbers
and shift the intake away from family reunion to skills (*Australian Financial
Review*, 4 July 1996).
7 Lehmbruch is unable to classify Japan and France, concluding that they
exhibit corporatism without labour.

7
The Economic Theory of Ethnic Conflict: A Critique and Reformation

Roger Waldinger[1]

Introduction

The 1960s and early 1970s represent a period of fertile theorising on race and ethnicity. Conflict sociology bore fruit earlier in this field than in others, mainly for circumstantial reasons. The consensual assumptions of earlier theories, such as Park's concept of the race relations cycle, were too incompatible with the events sociologists saw around them; looked at in the same light, the micro focus of the social psychological literature, while not inherently objectionable, appeared fundamentally incomplete. But whatever the precise causes there can be little question about either the theoretical trend or its import. Theories such as Lieberson's (1961) 'societal theory of race and ethnic relations', van den Berghe's (1978) 'taxonomy of paternalistic and competitive race relations system' and Rex's (1970) 'Weberian class analysis of race relations', to take just the most prominent of examples, were bold departures that sought to address macrosociological dimensions with a particular emphasis on power and conflict.

However penetrating these insights may be, they are now mainly found in textbooks. There is little in this earlier body of theorising that clearly influences research on race and ethnicity today. Only one body of work appears to have escaped this fate: the 'split labour market' and 'middleman minority' theories developed contemporaneously by Edna Bonacich. Several factors appear to explain why Bonacich's work has stood up so well. In contrast to the grander objectives of Rex and van den Berghe, Bonacich's work was somewhat more narrowly focused. In the case of the split labour market theory, that focus converged with the topic that has since come to preoccupy research in this field – economic differences between white Americans and other ethnic groups.

In the case of the middleman minority theory, Bonacich turned out to be prescient in identifying a phenomenon that would soon turn from an object of historical interest to one of contemporary concern. Immigrant business is now an activity of significant quantitative dimensions throughout the industrial West; its determinants and consequences are subjects of considerable empirical as well as theoretical work.

Though Bonacich's work has been influential, it has not been fully recognised for what it is: an attempt at an integrated theory of ethnic conflict, deriving antagonism from underlying economic oppositions. In practice the two theories receive little consideration as a theoretical whole. Since each seeks to illuminate different empirical problems, they are invoked in isolation from one another. For example Stone's (1985) book on sociological thinking about racial conflict first applies split labour market theory to black–white relations in South Africa, and thirty pages later employs middleman minority theory to treat the problem of entrepreneurial minorities – without ever mentioning a conceptual affiliation between the two ideas. Yet as I shall show, the theories not only share a common intellectual approach, but are essentially similar in logic of argument, causal connections, underlying assumptions, objectives and conceptual tools.

An integrated reading of Bonacich's work has two objectives: to examine the scope of her intellectual agenda and the boldness of her effort, and to analyse her intellectual framework. As I shall show in the critique that follows, both split labour market and middleman minority theories are afflicted by two fallacies.

The first of these is the *competitive fallacy*. In both theories Bonacich argues that conflict is the result of economic group competition at the initial contact point. This assumes that competition characterises the underlying economic reality that migrant labour and middleman minority groups encounter at the time of their incorporation into capitalist societies. I will argue for an alternative, emphasising structural processes that place both migrant labour and middleman minority groups into non-competing economic segments.

The second is the *culturalist fallacy*. As economic explanations of ethnic conflict, split labour market and middleman minority theories should view behaviour as flexible adaptations that alter with varying economic situations. However Bonacich explains behaviour as a consequence of prior cultural differences that are resistant to economic changes.

The basic strategy of this chapter is to recapitulate these theories, underlining common elements and emphasising ideas that have been insufficiently appreciated, and then to present a critique, discussing each of the problems identified above and offering alternative formulations.

The theories recapitulated

Split labour market theory

'Ethnic antagonism' is the explanandum, as Bonacich indicates by the title of her first article on the subject.[2] 'The central hypothesis is that ethnic antagonism first germinates in a labor market split along ethnic lines' (Bonacich, 1972, p. 549). Thus the labour market is split *prior* to conflict between groups. But under what conditions does this occur? The split labour market must contain at least two groups of workers whose 'price of labour differs for the same work, or would differ if they did the same work' (ibid.). These 'price differences' have two sources: (1) disparate 'motivations', which include income goals and commitment to industrial work and 'are related to the worker's intention of *not remaining permanently in the labour force*' (ibid., p. 550, emphasis added); and (2) differences in 'resources', a concept which includes standards of living, extent of information and trade union experience among competing groups on the labour market. Not only do expectations play a crucial role in determining the 'price of labour', Bonacich argues that they are generated outside, not within the workplace or the broader labour market institutions to which they are attached.[3] Thus Bonacich considers the white settler colonists who established themselves as independent farmers and artisans as 'high-priced' labour, even though, as she concedes, they were 'not strictly speaking "labor"' (Bonacich, 1981, p. 243). More important for the theory are the factors that affect the expectations of lower-price labour. Bonacich argues that 'the fate of (lower-priced) labor is determined by their lower *initial* price of labor, an attribute they bring with them into the capitalist economy' (ibid., p. 242). Indeed the examples that Bonacich uses to develop her theory – Africans recruited to work in mines in South Africa; Asians recruited for work in California; attempts to recruit Indians, Chinese, and Japanese for work in Australia; the recruitment in the United States of black southern sharecroppers to northern factories; and so on – all involve migrant groups recruited into capitalist economies from less developed or even non-monetised economies.

The dynamics of the split labour market are propelled by the motives of capitalists and the two classes of labour. 'Capital will *naturally* gravitate toward the cheaper group' (Bonacich, 1979, p. 25) and cheaper labour can be used by the employer 'to undermine the position of expensive labor, through strike breaking and undercutting'. This threat by competitors who are willing to take a lower wage generates antagonism among higher-paid workers, who seek to retain their advantaged wage position by excluding cheaper labour altogether, or restricting them to low-level, 'caste'-like positions (Bonacich, 1972, p. 554).

Three additional points are worth noting. Firstly, the concept of 'price of labour' is unusual, meaning neither labour cost nor wage. Rather it is the wage needed to attract a particular group of workers to a specific activity; the closest counterpart is the economist's notion of a 'reservation wage'.[4] In effect, Bonacich contends that sociologically distinct groups of workers will differ in their reservation wages, which are in turn determined by premarket factors. Secondly, the theory presumes no prior contact between groups, since it is precisely conflict resulting from a contact situation characterised by 'price differences', and not simply cultural differences, that the theory seeks to explain. Furthermore the concept of 'price differences' itself presumes no contact. For low-priced labour to entertain distinct expectations it must be both independent and external to the labour market. Were there contact, *interdependent* wage expectations would quickly take root.

Thirdly, the 'split labour market' is not only different from but also the opposite of the similarly sounding concept developed by segmented or dual labour market theory (see Bonacich, 1979, pp. 35–7). Since 'price differences' exist prior to contact, labour markets 'are split by the entrance of a new group' (Bonacich, 1972, p. 549). One consequence of the split is 'caste', the consignment of low-priced labour to subordinate, dead-end jobs. 'That women and racial minorities are confined to secondary firms and industries is explained by these efforts of primary workers to protect themselves' (Bonacich, 1979, p. 36). By contrast, in segmented labour market theory, segmentation comes first, caused by technological and societal factors, followed by the recruitment of subordinate ethnic groups to low-level segments from which upward mobility is difficult or impossible. This difference is most apparent in Bonacich's article 'Advanced capitalism and black/white race relations in the United States' (1976), where she argues that the principal cause of unemployment among blacks is their displacement from 'high-priced labour' jobs. By contrast segmented labour market theory explains black unemployment as a consequence of dependence on secondary sector jobs; blacks' confinement to the secondary sector creates a high level of frictional unemployment (Piore, 1979a).

To reiterate, 'split labour market' theory is an attempt to explain ethnic antagonism. The split in the labour market refers to price differences between two groups with no prior history of contact with one another; price differences are principally determined by non-labour-market factors; institutional barriers result from the conflict between capital and differently priced groups in the labour force.

Middleman minority theory

In this case, ethnic antagonism is *not* the explanandum. Rather the theory seeks to explain the development and persistence of a particular configuration or form: ethnic minorities concentrating in intermediate positions where they engage in trade, commerce or other activities with outgroup members. By persistence, Bonacich means the survival of the middleman form, from the precapitalist situations with which it has been historically identified, to modern capitalist societies. Persistence is a particular problem for contextual theories that 'predict that middleman minorities arise only in certain kinds of societies', namely those characterised by a status gap or a derogation of trade. But middleman minorities are 'found in environments that do not conform to the specified type' (Bonacich and Modell, 1980, p. 26); hence one must look to other factors for an explanation of middleman minority persistence.

Middleman minority theory has undergone two permutations. In the original elaboration the argument hinged on the importance of sojourning, which Bonacich (1973, pp. 585, 588) identifies as a necessary though not sufficient condition of the form. Middleman minorities, Bonacich argues, begin as sojourners, enduring short-term deprivations for the long-term goal of return and choosing specialisations that are easily portable to other societies or liquefiable for return home. Sojourning also breeds in-group solidarity and distance from the host society, thereby providing mechanisms for controlling intragroup tendencies for conflict or competition. These characteristics made middleman economic behaviour 'closely akin to preindustrial capitalism' (ibid., p. 588). The 'universalism' of the modern industrial capitalist, 'the isolation of each competitor is absent in middleman economic activities, where primordial ties of family, region, sect, and ethnicity unite people against the surrounding, often individualistic economy' (ibid., p. 589). The characteristics and behaviour of middleman minorities in turn induce hostility from host society groups, especially business and labour, who find themselves in competition with price-cutting middleman minorities. Bonacich emphasises the fundamentally interest-based aspect of this conflict, arguing that conflict occurs because 'elements in each group have incompatible goals' (ibid.). Contending that 'each party to the conflict has a "reasonable" point of view' (ibid.), Bonacich argues that 'the difficulty of breaking entrenched middleman minorities, the difficulty of controlling the growth and extension of economic power, pushes host countries to ever more extreme measures...until, when all else fails, "final solutions" are enacted' (ibid., p. 592).

A somewhat different approach appears in Bonacich's book on Japanese-Americans, coauthored with John Modell in 1980. Here Bonacich and Modell skirt explanatory issues, taking an agnostic position on how best to account for the middleman form and back-pedalling on the earlier central focus on sojourning. Although they concede that contextual theories have some validity, they point to the many examples of middleman minorities in advanced capitalist societies and emphasise again that persistence is a problem that contextual theories cannot explain. This second permutation otherwise resembles the original version. Bonacich and Modell emphasise the interrelationship of three distinctive traits: group solidarity, economic position in non-productive business lines, and the characteristically hostile reaction of host society groups. They argue that 'the essence of middleman minorities lies in the way they organize their economic activities' (Bonacich and Modell, 1980, p. 23); in this respect a key factor is that 'middleman minorities are not modern capitalists in orientation' (ibid., p. 32). The 'social form' of middleman minorities 'dictates' concentration in small establishments, 'limits the size and nature of the firms they establish', and makes it 'imperative that people (in middleman firms) know each other well and in many contexts' (ibid.).

The common elements

The following summaries help us identify key elements that are common to both theories.

Outside, culturally distinctive groups

The driving force in both split labour market and middleman minority situations is the importation of outside groups with distinctive cultural norms. In the split labour market situation, 'motives' are obviously cultural in content. So too are such aspects of 'resources' as 'level of living', in which case the standard of living in the home society determines a group's labour price in the host society, and 'information', in which a key factor is how much 'people know about conditions pertaining to the labour market to which they are moving'

(Bonacich, 1972, p. 550). In both versions of middleman minority theory, the middlemen are immigrants whose imported attributes, particularly sojourning, solidarity and a 'petit bourgeois' form of economic organisation, set into motion the whole train of events described above. Given the centrality of these original cultural norms, the question of their malleability bears strongly on the theories' internal consistency.

Wage and price competition

Wage and price competition are pervasive in both theories, driving conflict and antagonism. Clearly if the employers of high- and low-priced labour were not competing on the basis of wages, or if low-priced labour did not present a competitive challenge to the wages of high-priced labour, 'price differences' could exist and still not engender conflict or antagonism. Similarly competition flows from Bonacich's rejection of contextual theories of middleman minorities, since if middlemen filled a gap or niche, the likelihood of competition between native and middleman groups would be much lower. Yet again competition is crucial in fanning host society hostility and thereby reinforcing the original middleman traits.

Undifferentiated categories

In both theories Bonacich regards opposing groups as essentially undifferentiated – a logical correlate of the emphasis on competition. Price differences are the only relevant aspect distinguishing one group of labour from the other; disparities in skill, social organisation in the workplace, orientation towards work and so on do not affect their role in the system of production. Similarly 'business is business', and there is no differentiation between the needs of resource-exploiting and manufacturing businesses, as in Greenberg's (1980) comparison of South Africa, Alabama and Northern Ireland, or as in the better known taxonomy of segmented labour market theory. Similarly consumer, business and labour groups are all pitted against the middleman minority.

Critique

The competitive fallacy

Without economic competition among groups at the time of contact there would be no antagonism, and hence none of the dynamics that drive Bonacich's theories. But Bonacich assumes economic competition and never provides any plausible reasoning to back up that assumption.

By contrast I will argue that for both migrant labour and middleman minority groups the contact point is more likely to be characterised by *non-competition*.

Competition and the split labour market

For Bonacich, the wages of low-priced labour are almost entirely determined by external factors. But this view implies conflict between 'high-' and 'low-priced' labour only if one adheres to a view of labour market reality in which these groups compete against each other. Rather than assume competition, as does Bonacich, one can instead argue in favour of non-competing labour market segments, with roots in technological or political factors, as does Michael Piore (1979b). In this model labour mobility across segments is impeded and wage determination processes are similarly disconnected, therefore 'low-priced' labour can be recruited into one segment without threatening the interests of the 'high-priced' workers in the other segment. Indeed Piore goes further, arguing that migrant workers do not pose a competitive threat as long as they possess those same characteristics – a sojourning orientation, wage norms deriving from a different wage hierarchy, and so on – that Bonacich views as the source of 'low-priced' labour's competitive threat. As long as migrants retain this distinct set of work orientations their recruitment may actually be in the interest of 'high-priced' labour, who would otherwise be forced to bear the costs of instability that instead are absorbed by the migrants.

There are two ways of adjudicating between these two interpretations – one theoretical, the other empirical. The logic for Bonacich's competitive view of the labour market rests on her assumption that the relevant actors are essentially undifferentiated, as noted before. But that assumption seems entirely grounded in the types of empirical material that Bonacich used to generate her theory. As a close reading of her 1972 article shows, *all* of the clearly specified examples involve two types of extractive industry with undifferentiated labour requirements: capitalist agriculture (Australia, Guyana, southern US, West Indies, California) and mining (South Africa, Pennsylvania). Clearly the mobilisation of labour is a generic problem of these extractive industries that emerge at early or geographically peripheral stages of capitalist development; hence the incessant recourse to heavily coerced labour from non-capitalist areas. Not only that, they are also particularly sensitive to wage pressures, since as Greenberg (1980, p. 135) points out, 'profitability depends on their ability to hold down costs at the most vulnerable point – the mass of unskilled workers'.

Whether a theory of split labour markets in extractive industries can be further generalised is another matter. Outside the extractive industries there are other concerns besides labour costs. One need not subscribe to a technological explanation of internal labour markets (Althauser, 1989; Doeringer and Piore, 1971) to agree that employers are concerned with securing and maintaining their trained labour force and have striven hard to increase stability (Jacoby, 1985). These considerations have implications for the labour demands that specific types of employer or industry generate. The 'secondary' industries of advanced capitalist societies can and do make use of unskilled, temporary migrant workers precisely because they are like extractive industries in the sense that their labour is interchangeable and replaceable (Böhning and Maillat, 1974). But where there has been substantial investment in training, where the labour force is skilled or where long-established interdependencies among workers play a crucial role in the production process, unskilled migrant workers cannot readily serve as substitutes for skilled labour.

These issues bring us to the empirical question, in which resolving the dispute hinges on the question of timing. Did contact between competing groups lead to the creation of a structure that produced 'caste' and thereby diminished the competitive threat posed by low-priced labour? Or did the structure come first, and then the recruitment of culturally distinct, low-priced groups? Consider the circumstances under which African-American workers were recruited into US industry, a decisive case for the theory and one on which Bonacich's own analysis pivots. The sequence of events strongly suggests that structure preceded contact, not the other way around as Bonacich insists. Firstly, blacks did not make substantial headway into manufacturing industries until the outbreak of the First World War cut off the flow of migrants from South and Central Europe.

Secondly, the jobs to which immigrants from Southern and Central Europe (SCE) were recruited were circumscribed in well-defined ways that limited competition with native-born or North European immigrant workers. In part, such circumscription has roots in very early attempts by skilled workers to achieve employment security and advancement. As Elbaum (1984) shows, the development of internal promotion practices in the steel industry goes back to the 1860s, with protection from competitive market conditions yielding wide occupational wage differentials. The steel industry is a key case: it was an important employer, first of SCE immigrants and later of blacks; moreover circumscription resulted from management strategy. Management objective, as Brody

(1960) shows, was to maintain a stable cadre of skilled, albeit non-union workers alongside a floating supply of unskilled immigrant workers. While some immigrants could gradually enter skilled ranks over time, many 'moved out at the first depression or with a satisfactory accumulation of capital' (ibid., p. 108). Thus the transience of the SCE immigrants fits in with the industry's need to accommodate economic fluctuations. That same characteristic excluded them from competition for skilled jobs.

Finally, when large-scale black recruitment into industry began, it involved replacement not displacement. The advent of labour shortages led to recruitment from the south by agents, starting around 1916 during a period of relative labour stability and before the 1919 strike upsurge in which black–white competition played an important part (Marks, 1989). Moreover the role of labour agents and direct recruitment by northern business appears to have been greatly overplayed. Recent historical studies find little evidence that black settlement or colonisation in an industry resulted from direct employer efforts (Bodnar *et al.*, 1982). Rather information flows through informal networks and community institutions such as newspapers, galvanised a northward movement (Gottlieb, 1987; Grossman, 1989) that had begun as early as the 1870s. Thus it appears to have been opportunities that precipitated migration, not recruitment that created opportunities. There is also little evidence that industry suddenly rearranged its job structures when it shifted from an SCE immigrant to a black labour supply. Rather, as Nelson (1975, p. 146) notes, the 'experiences of southern black emigrants...demonstrate the persistence of the informal system' by which SCE immigrants had earlier been recruited.

Competition and middleman minorities

Contending that middleman minorities 'persist beyond the status gap', Bonacich (1973, p. 584) concludes that the explanation for middleman persistence *must* lie in the characteristics of the groups, and not in the characteristics of the societies in which they arise. But Bonacich never considers alternative contextual explanations that do not emphasise status considerations. This is particularly damaging to her theory, since the same structural factors that create opportunities for middleman minority-type groups also limit competition with native groups.

An alternative contextual explanation, which is outlined here, emphasises those processes that create entrepreneurial niches into which minorities can move without competing with or displacing native workers or businesses. In rapidly developing capitalist societies the key factor is the growth of new industries; under these conditions, business opportunities for immigrants or minorities arise through *niche creation*. In fully developed capitalist societies, by contrast, a more important factor involves the limits to economies of scale, leading to *niche maintenance*. In these persisting niches, replacement processes, akin to the ways in which immigrant workers succeed native-born labour, produce vacancies for immigrant or minority business owners; thus the emergence of opportunities can best be characterised by *niche succession*. In both cases systemic conditions lead to the emergence of *non-competing segments*, placing immigrant or minority business owners into lines of business where competition with natives is minimised.

The process of niche creation characterises the transformation of European Jews under the impact of industrialisation. In this case industrialisation pulled Jews away from their traditional middleman activities, while creating new activities in which they remained distinct from the broader Jewish population. Thus the early nineteenth century saw Jews in Western Europe move away from their traditional concentration in money lending and peddling into new business lines in commerce and industry (Sorkin, 1987). While trade and commerce continued to exercise a disproportional influence on the Jewish employment profile, in the late nineteenth and early twentieth century, the Jewish share of commerce and trade declined. Simultaneously, expanding opportunities for professional self-employment provided new avenues for niche expansion in cities such as Berlin, Vienna, Budapest and Prague (Cohen, 1983; Goldscheider and Zuckerman, 1984; Rozenblit, 1983). Indeed, the rapidity with which Eastern Jewish migrants to the Central European cities moved up, at a pace that compares favourably with the much celebrated experience of Jews in the United States, testifies to the extraordinary opportunities they found (Rozenblit, 1983; Wertheimer, 1987). In the West European and US cities to which Jewish immigrants from the Pale moved in the late nineteenth and early twentieth century, the clothing industry provided a particularly supportive environment. In these cases the influx of Jewish immigrants coincided with a burgeoning demand for factory-made clothes from the 1880s onwards; Jews provided the industry with its petty entrepreneurs, and for a while its labour (Green, 1985; Rischin, 1962; Schmiechen, 1984). In these large cities Jews subsequently entered new niches as they arose, reducing their role in wage and salaried employment, all the while maintaining a disproportionate presence in clothing and related industries. Thus entry into new and growing industries, such as construction, real estate, entertainment and high technology, led to niche diversification (Aris, 1970; Glazer and Moynihan, 1962).

By the late twentieth century, American Jews had entirely transformed their niche, while retaining a distinctive economic role. Though still highly concentrated in a relatively narrow set of industries and occupations, American Jews in such cities as New York and Los Angeles had largely shed their traditional economic base, retaining only a handful of small clusters in trade. In all respects but one, namely the persistently high rate of self-employment, the Jewish niches of the late twentieth century have an utterly post-industrial cast, with education, legal services, publishing, advertising, public relations and theatres topping the list (Waldinger, 1996a; Waldinger and Lichter, 1996).

In advanced capitalist economies where growth proceeds more slowly there are two crucial factors: processes that maintain a favourable environment for small business, or *niche maintenance;* and processes that create vacancies in those niches, characterised here as *niche succession.*

Niche maintenance. The structure of industry, namely the number of businesses, capital and technological requirements, is a powerful constraint on the creation of new businesses. New firms are unlikely to arise in industries that we characterised by extensive scale economies and high entry costs. However most Western economies contain niches where techniques of mass production or mass distribution do not prevail. Five such niches can be identified:

- *Underserved markets.* These are markets that are underserved by the large, mass-marketing organisation. In the United States and Western Europe, immigrants mainly reside in core areas of urban centres that are both illsuited to the conditions of large firms and favourable to small enterprises (Simon and Ma Mung, 1987; Waldinger, 1986; Ward, 1987b).
- *Markets with low economies of scale.* Since returns to scale in these markets are limited there are few or no capital-intensive, high-volume competitors. Hence small immigrant business owners, especially those in urban cores, can successfully pursue a strategy of self-exploitation (Ma Mung and Guillon, 1986; Orlick, 1987).
- *Segmented product markets.* When demand falls into stable and unstable portions, and the two components can be separated from one another, industries may be segmented into non-competing branches (Piore, 1980). One branch is dominated by large firms handling

staple products; a second, composed of small-scale firms, caters to the unpredictable and/or fluctuating portion of demand. The small-scale sector, with its low entry barriers and high capital-to-labour ratios, offers ethnic entrepreneurs an accessible route to the general market.

- *Ethnic consumer markets.* These are 'protected' markets that arise when ethnic communities have a special set of needs and preferences that are best served by those who share those needs and know them intimately. Under these conditions ethnic entrepreneurs have an advantage, since servicing these needs involves a direct connection with the homeland and specialised knowledge of tastes and buying preferences – qualities that are unlikely to be shared by larger, native-owned competitors (Aldrich *et al.*, 1985; Light, 1972).
- *Markets for exotic goods.* Native interest in exotic goods allows immigrants to convert both the contents and symbols of ethnicity into profit-making commodities. Immigrant entrepreneurs are likely to be the only business owners who either possess the special product or can supply or present it in conditions that are seemingly authentic (Palmer, 1984).

Niche succession.   This involves the relationship between the supply of native entrepreneurs and ownership opportunities. Should the supply of native owners for a small business industry dwindle, immigrants may take over as replacement owners. Niche succession occurs under a variety of conditions. At the neighbourhood level, replacement opportunities for immigrant owners selling to their coethnic neighbours arise as a result of ecological factors (Aldrich *et al.*, 1989).

In the general economy the crucial factor is that the petite bourgeoisie does not often reproduce itself, but survives through the recruitment of owners from lower social classes (Bechhofer and Elliott, 1981). To some extent, it is the very marginality of the small business position that discourages heirs from taking up their parents' modest enterprises (Berteaux and Berteaux-Wiame, 1981). In the central cities of the United States, where small business has been concentrated among European immigrants and their descendants, the rising social class position of Italian, Jewish and other European ancestry groups has weakened recruitment into small enterprise; similar processes have been observed among the long-established Jewish population in Britain (Pollins, 1982). When native groups weaken in their recruitment to small business their share of the small business sector inevitably declines, if for no other reason than the high failure rate to which all small businesses are prone. Birch's (1987) studies, for example, have shown that 8 per cent of all firms in US metropolitan areas close down each year, which means that almost half of all firms in any area must be replaced every five years for the area simply to break even.

The burgeoning of immigrant business in New York's clothing industry shows how the diverging appeal of small business for immigrants and natives creates a favourable environment for immigrant entrepreneurs by reducing the competition for business positions. Immigrant clothing factories fail at a higher rate than their native-owned counterparts, but the crucial difference is that immigrants establish new businesses at a very high rate. By contrast there are virtually no natives replacing other natives whose factories fail. However, higher-profit and higher barrier-to-entry lines in the industry retain white ethnic entrepreneurs. Immigrant factories have burgeoned, but they function as contractors, producing to the specifications set by manufacturers, which are invariably Italian- or Jewish-owned concerns. This relationship makes new and old small business groups complementary rather than competitive (Waldinger, 1986).

In the end, opportunities are a necessary though not sufficient condition of the persistent business activity of immigrant or minority groups. A full explanation of middleman persistence need only consider immigration, since some immigrants in virtually all modern capitalist societies respond to the disadvantages of their situation by seeking out business opportunities. Of course in order to explain which immigrant groups concentrate on business we would have to emphasise the interaction between opportunities and those group characteristics that provide a predisposition for entrepreneurial activity. For the purposes of the issues at hand, however, the crucial argument is that the secular trends creating opportunities for ethnic entrepreneurs systematically *reduce* competition with natives, thus short-circuiting the conflictual cycle prescribed by middleman minority theory.

The culturalist fallacy

Both middleman minorities and 'lower-priced' groups of labourers come from very different backgrounds when entering host societies. The fundamental factor producing conflict is the new groups' distinctive attitude towards work and income generation – in other words their cultural attributes. But if this attitude is economically conditioned it should also be malleable, altering rapidly as economic circumstances change. But in Bonacich's treatment economic orientation, as well as the antagonisms it supposedly produces, is highly resistant to change. Indeed both theories rest on attitudinal and cultural stability, since otherwise the interaction chains linking interest, economic pre-disposition and conflict would be decoupled.

In the case of middleman minority theory, Bonacich is particularly emphatic on the invariant nature of their economic orientations. As noted in the summary, she contends that middleman minorities will not take advantage of economic opportunities in the same way as members of host society groups. In particular middleman minorities will not hire out-group members nor will they seize chances to expand their firms. Clearly this general line of argument is entirely consistent with Bonacich's views of middleman–host society interactions, as pointed out in the summary above.

But is it true that middleman minorities will *not* be 'modern capital-ists' – regardless of the opportunities they confront? There is little evi-dence to support this proposition. American Jews have been active in numerous large-scale enterprises in which gentiles comprised the majority of employees; even in the garment industry Jews ceased to be the dominant workforce group as early as the 1920s (Kessner, 1981). In Germany 79 per cent of all department store trade took place in Jewish-owned stores, with the not surprising result that anti-Semitic propa-ganda made much of the fact that non-Jewish women were employed in these Jewish-owned stores (Gross, 1975). In Poland, Jewish-owned textile mills employed an exclusively gentile workforce (Mendelsohn, 1970). The behaviour of Jews in this respect is not exceptional. When immigrant streams dry up, ethnic entrepreneurs have repeatedly shown their willingness to tap into other labour pools when in-group members are no longer available. Thus the typical Greek restaurant in US cities sells to American customers, employs Greek waiters but hires non-Greek immigrants to work in the 'back of the house' (Bailey, 1987). Nor are Korean merchants in US cities, perhaps the classic case of the contemporary middleman minority, averse to hiring non-Koreans (Min, 1989).

In split labour market theory, invariant views of the distinctive cul-tural traits apply to both 'low-' and 'high-priced' groups. Bonacich's characterisation of the distinctive occupational and wage orientations of 'low-priced' labour is plausible; what is questionable is how long those distinctive traits last. To begin with, the social structures that keep the target earner's wage aspirations low do not last for long (Piore, 1979b). As a migration stream continues over time, the later arrivals are increasingly influenced by the experiences and expectations of those who preceded them; consequently the presence of settlers brings the later arrivals more closely into line with the norms of the host society. Even this assumption of fundamental discontinuity in work orientations between early temporary or circular migrants and their hosts is unlikely to hold true. Long-distance migration from Europe or countries south of the United States was often the culmination of earlier, shorter moves during which migrants from rural areas were likely to have obtained some exposure to industrial work and small city life (Bodnar *et al.*, 1982; Gottlieb, 1987). In many cases the birds of passage were the veterans of several earlier long-distance sojourns (Thistlethwaite, 1960). Moreover the relationship between stayers and migrants leads to a secular increase in earnings expectations: remittances produce gains in consumption, which in turn lead to greater consumption demands and therefore spiralling expectations of the remittances that migrants will send home (Massey *et al.*, 1987). Thus the wage expectations of migrants and host groups undergo strong pressures towards convergence right from the very start.

Of course these arguments flow from a rather different conceptualisation of labour migration from the one Bonacich adopts. For Bonacich, migration is the consequence of employer recruitment, occurring when 'employers turn to cheaper sources' (Bonacich, 1972, p. 553). But direct employer recruitment, though not insignificant, is far less important than the social networks in which labour migrations have been rooted (Bodnar, 1985; Portes and Rumbaut, 1990). Because networks provide for efficient flows of information (Massey *et al.*, 1987), labour migrants are neither as unfamiliar with prevailing wages and conditions nor as distant from the living and consuming norms of their host society as Bonacich asserts.

Thus the 'low-priced' group is likely to become *more* like the 'high-priced' group, with substantial changes in its wage and working-orientations occurring over a short span of time. Yet if the 'labour prices' of the two groups converge, what happens to the antagonism of the 'high-priced' group? Bonacich never says; indeed in her 1976 article she discusses the contemporary economic problems of African-Americans without ever mentioning the issue of white antagonism. Nonetheless her theory clearly implies that white antagonism should have undergone drastic decline, since the rational roots of the antagonism no longer apply. Whether or not African-Americans were originally resented because they were 'low-priced' labour, this no longer applies today. Compared with current immigrants, African-Americans belong to the class of 'high-priced' labour, having 'rejected the sweatshop as had white workers before them' (Bonacich, 1976, p. 48). Consequently one rarely hears the complaint that African-Americans are potential strike-breakers who are pushing down wages; the view more commonly expressed is that blacks, like whites before them, 'are unwilling to work under rough conditions for low wages' (ibid.). The advent of immigrants has had two consequences: the displacement 'of black industrial workers who had made important gains under the New Deal', and 'the persistence of peripheral or marginal firms operating on cheap labor [which] means that the split labour market is not dead' (ibid.). But the arrival of immigrants should also diminish white antagonism towards blacks, since from the perspective of realistic group conflict it is immigrants, not blacks, who provide the greater potential for wage undercutting. Thus, either split labour market theory implies that white workers' antagonism towards blacks has drastically diminished – a contention belied by the unions' extraordinary resistance to integration and affirmative action (Gould, 1977), or else we can conclude that white antagonism atavistically persists long after its original causes have disappeared, which would violate the interest-based assumptions of the theory.

A reformulation

If outsider groups enter as complements to dominant, native-born groups, how then do we account for the types of ethnic conflict that Bonacich has sought to explain? Though space constraints prohibit more than a brief exposition, the following alternative formulation is suggested.

The instability of capitalist economies persistently generates opportunities at the bottom of the ladder. Growth pulls the topmost group up the ladder and lower-ranking groups seize the chance to take their place; in their wake they leave behind vacancies at the bottom, which are filled by persons from outside the economy – namely migrants.

Outsider groups thus enter the economy in response to shortages at the bottom and then gravitate towards the next tier of scarce positions, remaining in that ambit as long as their (low) economic orientations match the (low) requirements and prerequisites of the jobs. What happens next tends to follow one of several scenarios. In the succession scenario, the *shape* of the labour queue can change if later economic expansion further tightens the supply of established groups, pulling the low-ranked group up the ladder. In the leapfrogging scenario, the characteristics of the low-rank group, in particular its education levels, substantially improve, making them more desirable to employers, which thereby *reorders* the labour queue. In the persistence scenario, the *preferences* of the low rank group remain unchanged, in which case their tolerance for low-level work stays more or less the same.

But one can also imagine a sequence of events resulting in conflict, in which the preferences of low-rank groups change faster and more extensively than either the order or the shape of the labour queue. In this case the ambitions of outsiders extend to higher-level positions, to which established groups remain firmly attached. Under these circumstances competition becomes overt and leads to ethnic conflict, as newcomers seek to enter the occupations and industries controlled by dominant groups, and incumbents try to maintain the structures that have protected their group's economic advantages. Consequently ethnic conflict is activated not by differences in the aspirations and expectations of outsider and in-groups, but rather by growing similarities between insiders and outsiders, as well as the ability of outsiders to mobilise the resources needed to gain access to full membership.

Notes

1 This chapter has its origins in conversations with Thomas Bailey. I am grateful to him and to Greta Gilberston for their sceptical reactions to my ideas. Thanks is also due to Eric Leifer for his close reading of an earlier draft.
2 The following summary is based on Bonacich (1972, 1975, 1976, 1979, 1981a, 1981b). Though the 1979 article does not use the identical terminology developed in the initial piece, it essentially hews to the original argument, while placing greater emphasis on the factors creating a globally mobile labour force. The ability to mobilise a 'cheap' labour force is clearly a precondition of the dynamics of the split labour market; once that condition is satisfied the dynamics do not change.
3 Consequently 'the price of a group of workers can be roughly calculated in advance and comparisons made even though two groups are not engaged in the same activity at the same time' (Bonacich, 1972, p. 549).
4 Killingsworth defines the 'reservation wage' as 'the highest wage at which the individual will not work. Thus, when the wage is below the reservation level, *changes* in the wage will not change behaviour' (Killingsworth, 1983, p. 8).

8
The Social Capital of Ethnic Entrepreneurs and their Business Success

Henk Flap, Adem Kumcu and Bert Bulder[1]

Introduction

In the last two decades the long-term trend in Western industrial societies of a steady decline in the number of small enterprises has drawn to a halt (Steinmetz and Wright, 1989). Karl Marx's assertion is refuted as the old middle class seems to be growing again. Newly founded small enterprises are contributing to economic growth, and are often a source of innovation and new jobs, more than larger enterprises, including multinational companies (Granovetter, 1984; Loveman and Sengenberger, 1991). Given this reversal of a basic trend, it is no wonder that small enterprises have lately become a fashionable research topic.

There is considerable turnover in any population of business enterprises. Studies on the ecology of organisations show that, in general, within five years nearly half of new businesses disappear, go bankrupt, are taken over or stop for other reasons (Carroll, 1984, p. 75). The decline and growth of small enterprises contribute to a restructuring of whole industries, since most firms start off small before becoming big. Small new firms have a high rate of decline, it has been discovered, as they combine what is called the liability of newness with the liability of smallness (Brüderl *et al.*, 1992). Within Europe the survival chances of newly founded small firms are best in Germany and the Netherlands; yet even here as many as 40 per cent go out of business after five years (EIM, 1995). This high turnover rate makes the question of what determines the start-up as well as the success of small firms more pressing.

The definition of business success is not unequivocal, however. What is success and what is failure? The usual measures of business success, such as profitability and growing numbers of employees, may be oversimplistic as they probably contain biases. On the one hand they probably underestimate success, since although an entrepreneur's business might not be growing, he or she might be accomplishing other goals that are important to him or her, such as learning hard-to-acquire entrepreneurial and technical skills, securing a job for his or her children or being able to start another business. Moreover, having sold the old business he or she might be left with more assets than before (Light and Karageorgis, 1994). On the other hand success is overestimated in that some small entrepreneurs evade tax, laws and labour regulations, employ illegal workers and the like. Sometimes entrepreneurs close down their businesses just to avoid controls and the possible confiscation of their assets. And even if an entrepreneur is successful, one should take into account all the hours and energy put into the business.

Given that one has to be cautious about the definition of success, the question remains: who starts up a small enterprise and who is successful? Well-known psychological accounts refer to personal characteristics such as leadership qualities, locus of control or need for achievement. These are much criticised on empirical grounds. The common sociological and economic explanations that point to the amount of financial and human capital brought to the start-up process fare somewhat better in empirical research (for a review see Brüderl *et al.*, 1996). This human capital includes, next to general education, schooling in business, previous knowledge of the field and previous experience of self-employment. A matter of some concern is whether persons with more human and financial capital try sooner to become self-employed, meaning that those starting a business already form a particular sector of the general workforce. Of course business survival and success is dependent on many other factors, most of which are beyond an entrepreneur's control. In many industries, especially highly competitive ones, market forces are dominant (Aldrich and Reese, 1993).

Almost simultaneously with the growing research on small enterprises, the study of what has become known as ethnic enterprises became popular (cf. Waldinger *et al.*, 1990b). Perhaps they could better be called migrant or minority enterprises, since that is what the term actually refers to, given that native entrepreneurs can be regarded as a particular category of ethnic entrepreneurs. Although ethnic enterprises are nominally a special case of small enterprises, until now research into both areas has been somewhat disconnected (Aldrich, 1991). Lately ethnic enterprises are receiving more attention in research and public debate because they form a niche in which ethnic minorities perform better than elsewhere in the labour market. Given their human capital, self-employment provides them with a better income than being an employee (Light and Roach, 1996). Small ethnic entrepreneurs sometimes even outperform their native counterparts. Thus politicians and other policy makers place hope in the founding of small businesses as a means of improving the prospects of ethnic minorities.

A major question within the research area is why members of some groups enter business ownership in numbers disproportionate to the size of their group, whereas other ethnic groups shun entrepreneurship almost altogether (Aldrich and Waldinger, 1990, p. 112; for a review see Barrett *et al.*, 1996). For example in the Netherlands Turkish immigrants have a self-employment rate of up to 10 per cent, which is higher than that of the Dutch population, who have a self-employment rate of 6–7 per cent, and much higher than that of, for example, Moroccan immigrants (Blaschke *et al.*, 1990, p. 93).

Existing explanations for differences in the success of ethnic entrepreneurs look to very diverse causes, such as prior experience in the business as an employer or employee, the characteristics of the settlement or servicing a particular, often coethnic clientele (Waldinger *et al.*, 1990a). Light and Karageorgis (1994, pp. 654–63) make a useful distinction between market conditions on the demand and supply sides. On the demand side of the market they identify five conditions that are favourable to success: the special consumer demands of coethnics, the local industrial mix, the resurgence of small and medium-sized business, vacancy chains emerging from the retirement or exit of existing business owners, and political encouragement.

Special consumer demands of coethnics refer to ethnic products or services that coethnics know best how to produce and distribute. A local industrial mix that favours small and medium-sized firms, for example, with a large share of service industries, also favours ethnic enterprises. The general revival of small business enhances the chances of ethnic entrepreneurs. Major opportunities for ownership result from the process of ethnic succession: vacancy chains emerging from the retirement or exit of existing business owners offer opportunities for minorities to take over an existing line of business. Moreover it is an established fact that the takeover of an existing business enhances the chances of its success.

The final condition identified by Light and Karageorgis can be formulated as the absence of encouraging policies. Government measures often affect ethnic minorities in such a way that – as they are not fluent in the official language, have little or no formal education or are illegal immigrants – they are forced to work in informal or illegal circumstances (Portes, 1994). For example in the Netherlands both employers and employees are subject to a high degree of labour market control. Prospective entrepreneurs cannot officially open a business without a residence permit, which they only receive after several years of residence. Rules on licensing and apprenticeship requirements, health standards and the minimum wage law raise the costs of entry and operation for small firms. The impact of these labour market and business policies is most severe in countries such as the Netherlands, which continues to bear the imprint of its traditional artisan or guild-like past, placing heavy constraints on commercial competition (Light and Karageorgis, 1994, p. 650).

Another well-known explanation for the relative success of ethnic entrepreneurs, not mentioned by Light and Karageorgis, is that they operate in product markets where entry barriers are low, for example in markets where one can start production without much technology, where little capital is needed to finance this and other necessities and where competition is minimal.

Demand factors alone do not fully explain why some groups of ethnic entrepreneurs have grown much faster than small business in general. One needs to consider the interaction with conditions on the supply side, such as financial and human capital. Human capital also consists of knowledge of the chosen field and what it takes to conduct a business. It is also helpful to be proficient in the national language and to know the cultural codes of the ethnic majority (see Ericsson, 1996). Light and Karageorgis call these 'class resources'. Note that most of the causes named also apply to native entrepreneurs and only some, such as a special ethnic clientele, qualify as a possible explanation for the success of ethnic entrepreneurs.

Finally Light and Karageorgis (1994, pp. 661–3) mention ethnic and family resources. These are networks based on common ethnicity and family and the solidarity that flows from these. These resources are examples of what will be discussed in the remainder of this chapter, that is, the social capital of entrepreneurs and would-be entrepreneurs.

Social capital: the newly discovered factor

A prominent idea in recent research on ethnic minorities and ethnic entrepreneurship is the idea of social capital. Social networks as a resource explain why a new business is started, its chance of survival and why some ethnic groups are particularly successful in small businesses.

Developments within the social sciences prepared the way for this interest in what social capital does for ethnic enterprises. The new economic sociology emphasises that transactions in real markets, whether consumer markets, labour markets or product markets, are embedded in ongoing relations and social networks (Powell, 1990). The textbook image of firms acting autonomously in free markets is incorrect for yet another reason. Market-type relations are common within organisations, as illustrated by transfer pricing between units of organisations, (Eccles and White, 1988). The discovery that markets are interlaced with social networks has also stimulated interest in the role played by social networks in ethnic entrepreneurship. Furthermore sociologists in the field of stratification, labour markets and social mobility have demonstrated that, next to economic, cultural and political resources, social networks can be resources as well (Boxman *et al.*, 1991; de Graaf and Flap, 1988).

Economists have recently embarked, often from a transaction cost perspective, on organisational studies in which the social structure is incorporated. They realise that modern organisations do not suffer from high production costs but from transaction costs, including the cost of information and of making and enforcing agreements, and that social structure has a vital bearing on these costs (Williamson, 1985). In particular the notion of transaction-specific investments connects transaction cost economics with the idea of job and work-specific social capital.

These developments also affected ethnic studies, and it was soon discovered that ethnic entrepreneurs are also embedded in all kinds of social network. Moreover if social networks are helpful for the careers of employees and managers, they are probably also helpful to self-employed persons, primarily in reducing transaction costs (Werbner, 1990b, p. 70).

The idea of social capital entered the social sciences almost simultaneously from a utilitarian, rational-choice point of view (Boissevain, 1974; Coleman, 1990; Loury, 1977) and from a combined Marxist and neo-Weberian stance (Bourdieu, 1973, 1981). The notion of social capital ties in with the classic neo-Weberian core of sociology: people achieve better results if they have more economic, political and cultural resources, and institutions and other social conditions determine what kind of resources one has and how useful they are.

The theory of social capital offers more than a simple choice-constraint model (Fischer, 1982) in which networks are just another constraint under which individuals decide upon the course of action to be taken. Staying with the analogy of social capital to human and financial capital, the focus comes to rest on the production side. Social capital theory assumes that individuals are active and want to build a good life. Social networks are a capital good that helps to produce goals that would otherwise be hard to achieve. The central questions, then, are: how can one realise one's goals more effectively, how can social capital enhance the productivity of one's labour and human capital, and how can people invest in each other, not only for instant rewards but also with an eye to the future (see also Flap, 1988)? This is called generalised reciprocity: a favour is repaid at a later, unspecified date with an unspecified service, if possible and if necessary. Many actions are also investments, conducted with an eye to future returns on one's own labour, and on connections with other persons. There is a discount rate for social capital: the faster that the value of social capital has to be discounted, the smaller the expected value of support will be. The future is less important than the present because players tend to value pay-offs less as the time of their obtainment stretches into the future, and there is always some chance that the players will not meet again (for instance the 'debtor' moves away, changes jobs, dies or goes bankrupt). Generalised reciprocity is possible only if the shadow of the shared future is long.

Thus the core of the social capital research programme is quite simple. Firstly, people with better social resources – in the sense of their social network and the resources of others they can call upon – are more likely to attain their goals. Secondly, people will invest in social relations according to the expected value of the social resources made available by these relations. The notion of social capital entails a whole series of research questions, which jointly constitute a research programme (see Flap, 1988, 1996).

Social capital refers to the importance of the resources that are available to a person through his or her social relations with others. These social resources – comprising the wealth, status, power and social ties of those other persons – are aptly called by Boissevain (1974, pp. 158–63) 'second-order' resources. The resources of affiliated individuals are substitutes for one's own resources. The basic constituents of social capital are the number of persons in an individual's network, their preparedness or sense of obligation to help when called upon (usually approximated by the strength of the tie) and the resources they make available. Bourdieu and de Saint Martin (1978, p. 28) have proposed including the density of the social network as well.

Social capital has a structural aspect too. There are two views on this. Coleman (1990) emphasises (Bourdieu had already hinted at it) that a dense network constitutes a resource to its members by promoting a willingness to cooperate and provide help. In such a community type of network people have a great deal of mutual credit that they can call upon. In addition people can be forced to fulfil their obligations in the interests of maintaining their reputations. Burt (1992), on the other hand, stresses that individuals have a comparative advantage in competitive situations if they have 'holes' in their network, for example if those who are connected to them do not have ties with each other. Autonomous persons – meaning that the ego has many alternatives to establish social relations – have information and control advantages. They will hear about business opportunities sooner and thus can extract higher yields from their financial and human capital. They can play their relations off against each other. An entrepreneur who is in the middle will enjoy a favourable exchange rate in his dealings with clients and suppliers. Of course these others could try to turn the tables against him or her. So ego has an interest in not becoming estranged with his competitors.

Social capital theory has had an impact on ethnic studies. Ethnic entrepreneurs or would-be ethnic entrepreneurs with more social capital should fare better. Ethnic studies usually favour the community notion of social capital. Coleman's now famous description of the force of social capital is a case in point:

> Wholesale diamond markets exhibit a property that to an outsider is remarkable. In the process of negotiating a sale, a merchant will hand over to another merchant a bag of stones for the other to examine in private at his leisure, with no formal insurance that the latter will not substitute one or more inferior stones or a paste replica. The merchandise may be worth thousands, or hundreds of thousands, of dollars. Such free exchange of stones for inspection is important to the functioning of this market. In its absence, the market would operate in a much more cumbersome, much less efficient way. Inspection shows certain attributes of the social structure. A given merchant community is ordinarily very close, both in frequency of interaction and in ethnic and family ties. The wholesale diamond market in New York City, for example, is Jewish, with a high degree of intermarriage, living in the same community in Brooklyn, and going to the same synagogues. It is essentially a closed community. Observation of the wholesale market indicates that these close ties, through family, community, and religious affiliation, provide the insurance that it is necessary to facilitate the

transactions in the market. If any member of this community defected through substituting other stones or through stealing stones in his temporary possession, he would lose family, religious, and community ties. The strength of these ties makes possible transactions in which trustworthiness is taken for granted and trade can occur with ease. In the absence of the tie, elaborate and expensive bonding and insurance devices would be necessary – or else the interactions could not take place.

(Coleman, 1988, pp. 98–9)

There are also instances in which a social resources interpretation of social capital is used to explain the fate of ethnic minorities, or immigrants for that matter. Well known is that of Wilson (1987), who claims that the bleak life of black migrants in the urban ghetto is not produced by cultural differences and discrimination, but mostly by physical and social isolation from the more well-to-do section of the black community. The latter moved out of the inner cities into the suburbs because they could afford it and because large companies transferred their production sites out of the inner cities. To quote Wilson (ibid., p. 60):

Inner city social isolation makes it much more difficult for those who are looking for jobs to be tied into the job network. Even in those situations where job vacancies become available in an industry near or within the inner-city neighborhood, workers who live outside the inner-city may find out about these vacancies sooner than those who live near the industry because the latter are not tied into the job network.

Fernández Kelly (1994) added that poor immigrants are not always isolated, as is often thought. Frequently they are well-connected, but do not profit from their networks because they contain few resources. Underlining this, Borjas (1990) shows that, deprived of the resources that usually influence the attainment of education and income, and given neighbourhood poverty, there is a negative effect of living in a community of coethnics with few resources. Portes and Sensenbrenner (1993) emphasise that it is because of this relative lack of viable alternatives that these minorities develop a bounded solidarity, which means that minorities have more social capital in the sense of a greater willingness to help each other. According to Light and Karageorgis (1994, p. 660), such 'reactive ethnicity' enhances ethnic entrepreneurship by enhancing group solidarity.

The general thinking on social capital in ethnic entrepreneurship is that ethnic groups with extended families that are tightly integrated, not only within the confines of their own household but also within the wider family circle of uncles, aunts, brothers-in-law and nephews, have an advantage if they go into business. They employ family members at lower wages, they have more trust: their own family and they raise more capital by pooling or borrowing from family members. This factor could explain differences in rates of self-employment between ethnic groups (Zimmer and Aldrich, 1987), especially since most ethnic groups have larger families or a more elaborate family system than natives. Similar arguments can be made about the larger number of friendships and other ties within ethnic groups. Of course native entrepreneurs can also employ members of their family, borrow money from them and the like, but they usually have smaller immediate and extended families, who furthermore may not live in the same neighbourhood. They are also less likely to be forced together by common adversities. Ethnic entrepreneurs profit from coethnics' lack of alternatives by hiring them as cheap labour (ibid.). Although ethnic entrepreneurs cannot compete with coethnic entrepreneurs who have better educational and financial resources, ethnic entrepreneurs do better than coethnics with a similar education who are working as employees (Bates, 1994).

Portes (1995a; see also Portes and Sensenbrenner, 1993) has reviewed the types of social capital that are relevant to ethnic entrepreneurship. He describes four types: (1) introjected values that prompt people to behave in ways other than naked greed; (2) reciprocity transactions based on previous good deeds; (3) bounded solidarity emerging from a situation in which a class of people face common adversities; and (4) enforceable trust flowing from group membership. Type 2, social capital based on reciprocity, refers to the second-order resources that are available through ties to a particular person. Type 4 is the already discussed community type of social capital. Type 3 is a special condition that increases the strength of the relations implied in types 2 and 4. With regard to type 1, although there are some (for example Coleman, 1987) who agree with Portes, we object to internalised norms being categorised as a type of social capital as this overextends its meaning. The concept should refer to how persons use their actual social relations as a resource. After all, one should not forget that the social capital idea came about as a criticism of functionalistic theories that explain human actions as the result of shared cultural norms (Boissevain, 1974).

The multifaceted nature of social capital has resulted in an array of definitions and measures. It is our contention that for further progress we need to pin down the concept and standardise its measurement. To evade circular reasoning, any definition of social capital must distinguish between structure and effects. Moreover measurements should take into account the multidimensional nature of the social capital idea.

It is clear from Portes' typology and other publications that little attention has been paid to Burt's (1992) argument about the advantages of a structural autonomous position within a network of clients and suppliers. This argument still has to make headway within the research on ethnic minorities.

Too much or the wrong kind of social capital

Two assumptions are basic to the literature on the role of social capital in the life of an ethnic entrepreneur. Social capital is generally seen as positive, as a good thing to have, and furthermore is thought to be instrumental in the achievement of many goals. But not everything is as bright as it looks. We are not the first to pay attention to the negative sides of entrepreneurship and social capital. Light and Bonacich (1988, pp. 429–34) have discussed the social costs of immigrant entrepreneurship to individuals and society. They paint a rather dark picture. Migration is wrenching, disruptive, makes for hard work and causes many family problems. The majority of migrants will never climb up the social ladder as they originally hoped. Immigrant entrepreneurship leads to labour exploitation, creates intergroup competition along ethnic lines, stimulates a dual ethnicity that hinders the emergence of a moral community of all people and stimulates the unrestrained, ruthless pursuit of profit in dealings with people from other ethnic groups. Finally, it also lowers labour standards for society as a whole.

Portes and Sensenbrenner (1993, pp. 1138–44) give examples in which social capital has detrimental effects. Firstly, people become trapped in their network by their investments in their local community, and if they try to escape from their fate they are ridiculed as 'wannabes'. Secondly, those who are successful will be approached by job and loan-seeking kinsmen who lay claim to their profits. We will elaborate on this later, but first we want to emphasise a general point that is often taken for granted.

All resources, be they financial, human or social, are distributed unequally among the population. There will always be the 'place in the row' effect: the first is able to attain scarce goods more easily than the last in the row. An ethnic group that is successful at its trade, in combination with the social embeddedness of its business, can, for example by hiring only employees from its own group, wittingly or unwittingly prevent other ethnic groups from entering a field of business (Waldinger, 1995). Grieco (1987, pp. 97–117) has described how a particular ethnic group appropriated a whole line of business by favouring own-network members. The occurrence of vacancy chains and differences in social capital between ethnic groups makes eminently clear how business opportunities are conditioned by social networks. In his study of small businesses in the New York garment industry, Waldinger (1986) describes how this originally Jewish industry was taken over by the Chinese, mainly due to their more aggressive use of their social network.

The capture of a whole line of business contributes to the rise of an ethnic economy where a particular minority has a controlling ownership stake, or even an ethnic enclave economy with a local clustering of interdependent firms and coethnic employment (Light and Karageorgis, 1994, pp. 648–9). If a particular group has more coethnic social capital and prefers coethnic business partners, jobs and business ownership in whole branches will become closed to other ethnic groups (see Flap, 1991).

The wrong kind of social capital

There is a further aspect of networks in ethnic enterprises that has not received enough attention. Social capital is not a means for all purposes. Entrepreneurs make differential use of their social capital when starting and maintaining a business. They need help in three areas: the raising of financial capital, the gathering of information on markets and operating a business, and finding labour. To whom do they turn and for what kind of support?

Entrepreneurs themselves distinguish between two different parts of their network: close and extended family and close friends on the one hand, and more casual friends, colleagues and other acquaintances on the other. The network of ethnic entrepreneurs is often largely coethnic. Often people from their home region predominate. Identification with former coresidents is probably stronger in agrarian than in industrial societies. Thus interest seems to determine whether they are treated as 'kin' or 'friends'.

These two broad categories of ties were given a theoretical meaning by Granovetter's (1973) famous 'strength of weak ties' argument. Weak ties provide people with information they previously did not possess. Strong ties promote inbreeding in a network and can never bridge disconnected parts of the network, unlike weak ties, which can facilitate information from distant sources. A growing body of empirical evidence shows the manifold ways in which personal networks contribute to a small entrepreneur's success or staying capacity. Such evidence is provided in case studies (for example Waldinger, 1986; Werbner, 1990b) as well as large-scale surveys (see for instance Brüderl *et al.*, 1996; Preisendörfer and Brüderl, 1995). Entrepreneurs use different social circles to solve different problems. Depending on what they want or need they turn to different sources. Our own research among small Turkish entrepreneurs in the Netherlands revealed a division of labour between strong and weak ties. For example money is borrowed from extended family members, while information on markets and how to run a business, as well as advice on the hiring of labour is obtained through weaker ties such as acquaintances and colleagues. Often these are the elderly or those with a reputation of being good businessmen (Kumcu *et al.*, forthcoming).

Official agencies could also provide help, but small ethnic entrepreneurs often avoid enterprise-assistance agencies as previous experience has taught them to distrust bureaucrats. Moreover small ethnic entrepreneurs are frequently discriminated against by banks, probably because the latter think it will cost too much energy, time and money to assess the financial value, credit rating and risks of ethnic business enterprises. Furthermore ethnic entrepreneurs often have no property that can used as collateral (compare Chapter 4 of this volume).

Although many aspiring ethnic entrepreneurs have some financial capital of their own, they frequently need to borrow considerable sums of money to buy an existing enterprise, which usually involves a large payment for the goodwill of the business. In the Netherlands, for instance, the purchase price of a restaurant can be more than 300 000 guilders, but first-time ethnic entrepreneurs usually only have 20–50 000 guilders of their own. Given the amount of money that they need, lending requires a high degree of trust so they have to turn to family and close friends. To amass the money they often borrow from a number of different people, from other friends and from extended kin. However all this money has to be repaid within a year or two. In our research we found that loans are hardly ever requested from the nearest family members or very best friends (Kumcu *et al.*, forthcoming).

The amounts borrowed in other industries, such as the garment industry, are lower, ranging from a few thousand guilders to 50 000 guilders. Apart from setting up a garment factory which does not require much capital as the building is usually rented, these loans are used to buy fabric or to pay the workers. Because of the time lag between buying the fabric and being paid for the final product, entrepreneurs frequently run out of cash. The sewing machines are leased in order to prevent confiscation by the authorities and to enable the use of up-to-date equipment. Loans for such purposes are short term and are expected to be paid back within a couple of weeks or, at the most, months. Interest is neither charged nor expected.

To stay in business entrepreneurs have to retain their workers. The turnover of employees tends to be higher in small enterprises as they do not offer opportunities for internal promotion. In this case hiring coethnics, friends and relatives has the advantage of greater trust, reducing the chance that workers will quit. On the other hand an entrepreneur cannot treat friends and relatives in too businesslike a manner, and they cannot be pressed as hard as other employees (see also Waldinger, 1986, pp. 34–7, 160–4).

Friends and family are also a mixed blessing as customers because they expect a special price, quality or credit. In general, if the business is to grow, contact with other ethnic groups is needed, especially with majority groups. Waldinger (1995) points out that the opportunities for black contractors in the United States are relatively poor because they usually lack contacts among a richer white clientele.

Our own research among Turkish entrepreneurs indicates that those who use weak rather than strong ties for business information fare better in the garment trade, restaurants and groceries. When borrowing money, however, there seems to be no choice but to borrow from a strong tie, that is, a relative or good friend.

The combination of differences in the number of strong and weak ties, the division of labour between these ties in the help they provide, and the differential benefits they bestow, leads to the preliminary conclusion that new entrepreneurs will not always have the right kind of social capital to become successful.

Too much social capital

There are still darker sides to the use of personal networks when doing business that are initially even harder to understand from the perceived positive view of social capital. Although large sums of money are sometimes required, in practice amassing this kind of money is often not a problem for aspiring ethnic entrepreneurs as many relatives and good friends are prepared to lend money. But why do they do so in the absence of collateral?

They do so not only because they expect future returns, but also, especially if they are entrepreneurs themselves, because they have a status to uphold or gain. Others refer to this status when asking for a loan and make them feel obliged to honour their request. In many ethnic communities there is great eagerness to become an independent, self-employed entrepreneur as this is seen as the road to wealth and respectability. Status is always local, but it is even more so in local immigrant communities where networks are mainly restricted to coethnics.

The outcome of this competition for status is that money is often readily available without the need for collateral. The downside is that if it becomes known that a particular person is interested in buying a property in order to make it available to a new enterprise, there is hardly any room to reconsider because of loss of face. So starting a business may not be a problem, but staying in business is, mainly because money that is borrowed to start up a business has to be repaid at short notice. The moment that some profits are made these sizeable short-term loans have to be repaid.

Tight ethnic communities produce a great deal of social capital in the sense of enforceable trust, as Portes (1995a) calls it. People fear getting a bad reputation or even being ostracised. Not living up to the implicit repayment agreement certainly means losing face. Thus business owners may lie about their financial situation, and in some cases they may in desperation even sell family properties in the home country.

Our research demonstrated that people who have acquired a business but have found that keeping it going is not that simple, let alone getting rich, give bad advice and hide the true state of their affairs out of fear of damaging their reputation and ruining their chance of selling their business and goodwill. Since it is often the case that some of the money with which they started their business was borrowed and they have to pay it back, it is unwise to tell the truth. Besides the danger of losing the invested capital, they do not want to lose face. By upholding the impression of being a successful entrepreneur they encourage new would-be entrepreneurs. In line with former observations, we found that Turkish entrepreneurs who came to the Netherlands alone and stayed on their own, and thus had little social capital, were doing better than those with large extended families to support them.

Thus new ethnic entrepreneurs often start their business with little of their own capital, few skills, little experience and inadequate information (Barrett *et al.*, 1996, p. 887) but too much social capital. The rather tight ethnic community, the eagerness to become a successful businessman and to attain status, the wide availability of money and incomplete and often faulty information about what it takes to run a successful business creates a vicious circle that is hard to break. The strength of this vicious circle may vary according to type of trade. It is probably stronger in the restaurant business and green-grocery than in the garment industry. In the latter, the entry and exit barriers are far lower, mainly because far less money is needed to start up and not much is lost in the event of closure.

How to interpret the adverse effect of too much social capital

Social capital can be helpful but there are also indications to the contrary. In the previous section we discussed the strange phenomenon of having too much social capital. Accordingly a question for future research has to be: why and under which conditions does social capital have detrimental rather than beneficial effects on the business success of ethnic entrepreneurs?

As a start, two interpretations for such adverse effects will be given: a cognitive-cultural one and an instrumental one.

A cognitive-cultural interpretation

The classic account of why individuals can have too much social capital is found in the works of Weber. Is the situation of 'too much social capital' an instance of what Weber called 'Binnen und Aussenmoral'? (Weber, 1923, pp. 234–7, 269; cf. Geertz, 1963). For example does a specific culture contain a double ethical standard: traditional taboos against making profits from others in one's group and a completely unrestricted drive for profit *vis-à-vis* other people? Or as a contemporary sociologist states: strong solidarity within one's own group and no solidarity at all with the out-group, making business transactions with close friends and family, as well as with outsiders impossible (Lindenberg, 1988, 1992). Such an ethic would not be conducive to a rational economy since in dealings with the in-group economic calculation is forbidden and the out-group is not accepted as a partner in any lasting economic exchange, but is only there to be exploited for quick and maximum profit.

According to Weber (1923), the Protestant ethic put an end to moral codes that prescribe a different treatment for strangers and fellow believers. This more universalistic faith enables barter with persons from the in-group, as well as long-lasting exchange relations with strangers. There are indeed differences between cultures, religions and ideologies (we shall not go into these differences here) as to the extent to which they distinguish between 'us' and 'them'. Portes (1995a) provides the example of entrepreneurs in South America who switch from the Catholic to the Protestant faith to prevent claims on their wealth by relatives.

The examples given above indicate that small Turkish entrepreneurs also find it difficult to act in a business-like way in their dealings with coethnics, especially friends and family. There is no evidence that the small Turkish entrepreneurs in our research were especially ruthless in their business dealings with strangers, or no more so than other small entrepreneurs. Moreover, although Islam – the religion shared by most of the small Turkish entrepreneurs interviewed – formally forbids the extraction of interest on money lent to fellow believers, these entrepreneurs, just like entrepreneurs in general, do not insist on a strict interpretation of their faith (see Geertz, 1963). Most cultures are not opposed to making money and acknowledge that earning money makes one respectable.

Cultures differ in how clearly they draw the boundary between 'us' and 'them'. If the boundary is unclear or does not exclude many others, it may lead to numerous claims by fellow countrymen for assistance, especially if one is successful. Granovetter (1992, 1995) describes why Chinese businessmen are not swamped by claims by their fellow countrymen. They have clear-cut cultural boundaries indicating who is family and who, by that criterion, has a legitimate claim for help. The most important unit within their culture, the family clan, comprises about one to two hundred people, which is usually enough to amass all kinds of help.

The culture of the small Turkish entrepreneur does not provide such a clear criterion as the descent rule among the Chinese. Turks are obliged to help each other, yet not indiscriminately. There are several secondary rules that specify who should help, who should be helped first and foremost, and how much help should be provided. Only those who have the means to do so are obliged to help, starting with those closest to them; if there is anything left, however, other, should also be helped. Finally, as much help should be provided as means allow. It is conceivable that such rules are partly responsible for the difficulties Turkish entrepreneurs have in handling claims by their fellow countrymen.

However we suggest another, more plausible version of the cultural interpretation. In the case of Turkish entrepreneurs, their culture of honour and shame, in which honour and reputation are of the utmost importance, could act as a brake on more rationalised economic relations. Honour and reputation are important to them not because of religion, but because they are used to the situation in their country of origin, where the state provides few opportunities to redress wrongs by invoking the law via its official representatives. People must ensure that they can trust the people they deal with by making it a point of honour to be trustworthy themselves and not to tolerate betrayal by others.

An instrumental interpretation

A more instrumental interpretation of the adverse effects of having too much social capital is also possible. In fact our interpretation in the previous section was more or less instrumental. In the literature on job seekers one sometimes finds the opposite side of the coin of social capital. Grieco (1987), in a critique of the microeconomic job-search theory, emphasises reciprocity costs for help. People help with an eye to the future – somebody who is helped could be successful later on. Such outstanding debts are sometimes a burden. There is an Arabic saying: 'I don't understand why he is mad at me, I never gave him any help.'

The notion of social capital also implies an investment theory of social relations. People will invest in others according to perceived future returns. While making investment decisions, future returns are part of their considerations on the value of alternatives. Portes and Sensenbrenner (1993, pp. 1327–32) point to situationally determined solidarity. If one has no alternative but to invest in others who find themselves in the same situation, this can make a real group out of a number of individuals who originally only belonged to a common category, for example according to a tax rule. The example of bounded solidarity given long ago by a Scottish moral philosopher is also enlightening: two businessmen from Birmingham who hardly greet each other in the street of their home town will engage in friendly conversation if they meet in London, but will throw themselves into each other's arms if they meet in a faraway place abroad.

Li (1977) describes how immigrants from China to Chicago receive help from relatives in finding a job, but these jobs are in the family business, where they do not develop qualifications for the general labour market. Such dead-end jobs are detrimental to their long-term career chances. People cannot escape from these jobs because of the debt incurred by accepting help. Is the situation of Turkish employers and employees in the garment industry and the restaurant and green-grocery businesses somewhat akin to that of the Chinese immigrants in Chicago? Is their business success hampered by reciprocity costs that have to be paid? Is their entry into business the result of negative choices by both the entrepreneur and his or her employees, as other trades are more or less sealed off for them?

It is our contention that these conditions hold for most entrepreneurs among immigrant minorities. Not knowing the native language, deprived of information on financial, business and legal regulations, unhelpful banks and outside discrimination, the logic of their situation causes them to search for opportunities, status and help within their own community.

Conclusions

The budding research programme of social capital theory has been gaining momentum in recent years, and its potential for the study of ethnic entrepreneurship is beginning to be recognised. The basic assumption is that those who dispose of more social capital are more likely to succeed in starting and maintaining a business.

Empirical research indeed underscores that social capital is a key factor in the success of small ethnic firms. However empirical research on social capital as a major cause for the differential success in small enterprises in general and small ethnic enterprises in particular does not yet abound. Aldrich and Reese (1993), using crude and global measures of networks and network activities, have found that neither the survival nor the general economic performance of newly established small firms are significantly related to networking activity. Other large-scale, quantitative studies of native and immigrant ethnic entrepreneurs do indicate that social capital probably stimulates the venture into life and subsequent success. Brüderl *et al.* (1996), employing more refined measures of network features and business success, demonstrate quite convincingly the significant contribution of social capital as a source of emotional support and business information, as provided by both strong and weak ties. In a representative sample of different groups of immigrants in the United States, and controlling for age, education, years in the United States and proficiency in English, Sanders and Nee (1996) report positive effects on self-employment of being married and living with one's spouse, of having a number of teenage relatives, and of having other adults in the household, as they support the business.

However Bates (1994), in a large-scale study of Asian small businesses in the United States, shows that heavy use of social support networks typifies the less successful, more failure-prone. Those serving a minority clientele are more likely to go out of business than those serving a non-minority public. The purchase of existing firms is also more likely to lead to business failure, probably because former owners adjust their books to make the business look better than it is – it is frequently the case that firms are sold when well on their way to failure (ibid., p. 685).

Until now, social capital has mainly been regarded as positive. Furthermore it is often treated as an undifferentiated lubricant that eases the acquisition of most of the things an entrepreneur might need. However there are arguments and research findings that have led us to reconsider this simple and optimistic view. Portes has already hinted at this and some empirical indications came to light during our own research. Bates' findings, however, are the first 'hard evidence' that something is wrong with the perceived positive view of social capital.

Not only is the successful use of social capital by a particular ethnic entrepreneur or group of entrepreneurs often detrimental to the business chances of other ethnic entrepreneurs or groups of entrepreneurs with less or less effective social capital, there is another consideration. One can also have social capital of a kind that does not work. Finally, one can have too much social capital, leading to adverse effects.

The major questions arising from our discussion of social capital and ethnic entrepreneurship are as follows: under what conditions will social capital be helpful in starting and operating a business, and under what conditions will adverse effects occur?

Concerning the wrong kind of social capital, social capital is not undifferentiated, but it is goal-specific. Different people are required for different goals. For transactions that require considerable trust, for example borrowing a large sum of money, one has to appeal to strong ties, that is, to close family and friends. For business information and the supply of labour, weaker ties to colleagues and other acquaintances are more effective since such ties bring better information on a wider range of alternatives. As people differ in the number of strong and weak ties they have, it is obvious that ethnic entrepreneurs will often have the wrong kind of social capital to be successful. An important explanation that has not been discussed until now, but which might explain why turning to others for a particular type of help does not always prove fruitful, is that these others lack their own resources and thus cannot provide 'second-order resources' (cf. de Graaf and Flap, 1988).

What about a specific case of an adverse effect involving social capital? Everybody wants to help and it still goes wrong! What are the essentials of an explanation of these adverse effects of having too much social capital? First, a strong status drive to become a successful business person, perhaps culturally instilled but more probably born out of a lack of alternatives. Second, the presence of many fellow countrymen who are prepared – stimulated by the locally circumscribed status drive – to provide the necessary capital to start a business, thus adding the necessary acid to the mixture. Finally, misleading or false information on what it takes to run a business in general and on the prospects of the particular business site – a product of the same status drive, coupled with misinformation on the often sad state of someone's business. Together they close the vicious circle.

Our preliminary answers leave other issues open for discussion. A somewhat unconventional reading of Williamson's (1985, p. 26) transaction costs theory would predict that misinformation is advantageous to an entrepreneur in his or her transactions with others and hence close relations are given no insight into his or her dealings, thus creating a misinformation market. But why do prospective entrepreneurs go along with these stories, even if they know the reality from examples in their own close family. We need to know more about local circumscription of the status drive. Do would-be entrepreneurs substitute economic well-being for social approval in such circumstances (cf. Lindenberg, 1996)?

There is other unfinished work in the research area of social capital and ethnic entrepreneurship; for instance even if a positive effect of social capital can be demonstrated, what is the mechanism that produces these results? Is it imitation of successful others, providing legitimation of choices made in an insecure world, giving useful information and instrumental help, or what? (see also Flap, 1996).

Yet another question is how various institutions influence the instrumental value of the social capital of ethnic entrepreneurs. The instrumental value of social capital depends on conditions such as the extent to which the community is the sole or principal source of reward, approval and business opportunities. Yet another starting point is whether closure or autonomy within the network is profitable or whether interests are better served by competition or cooperation. That success in some kinds of business requires not competition but high levels of trust – as in the diamond trade – and that in such a situation a high premium is placed on having social capital of a community type, is only the beginning of an answer.

Note

1 An earlier version of this chapter was presented at the Fourth International Social Network Conference, London, 6–10 July 1995.

9
Globalisation and Migration Networks

Ivan Light[1]

Introduction

Large informal sectors have existed in Third World cities since at least 1945 (Light, 1983). However until about 1973 urban informal sectors existed *only* in the cities of the Third World (Castells and Portes, 1989, pp. 18–25), not in cities of the developed world. Times have changed. Since the early 1970s immigrant-dominated informal sectors have developed in large cities in North America and Western Europe.[2] True, these informal sectors are only a fraction of the size of those in the Third World and they have not expanded into squatter suburbs, as happened in the Third World – but they do now exist. Although the informal sectors of the developed world contain both immigrants and non-immigrants, immigrants are drastically overrepresented and constitute the majority (Waldinger, 1996b). Therefore if all the immigrants were repatriated tomorrow, the informal sectors of the developed countries would drastically shrink, but they would continue to exist.

Sassen (1991b, p. 79) defines the informal economy as 'income-generating activities that take place outside the framework of public regulation where similar activities are regulated'. Informal sector workers earn low wages that often fall below the statutory minimum. Working in substandard conditions, and sometimes at home, informal sector workers also receive few or negligible social insurance benefits that are grossly inferior to those received by non-immigrant employees in the formal sector. Most employees in the informal sector work off the books altogether, receiving their compensation in cash without any records being forwarded to tax collectors. They are non-union employees whose job tenure is insecure. Because industrial corners are cut, informal workers are cheap to hire and the goods they produce can be sold

162

more cheaply than goods produced in the formal sector (Sassen-Koob, 1989, pp. 62–72; Stepick, 1989, pp. 116–25).

Informal production occurs in many industries. The garment manufacturing industries of Los Angeles and Amsterdam are large and conspicuous informal industries.[3] In addition to garment manufacturing, informal firms and workers also participate in the construction, personal services and retail sectors of Amsterdam, Los Angeles and other large cities (Lopez-Garza, 1989; Soja *et al.*, 1987). Immigrants in garment manufacturing work long hours under dangerous and unhealthy conditions and their hourly wages are routinely below the legal minimum. Immigrants in construction build and repair houses for firms that have a shadowy legal existence, pay wages in cash and buck union requirements and standards. Immigrant service workers are generally domestic servants, gardeners and nannies. They work long hours, receive their wages in cash and kind, and rarely receive social security credit. Immigrant retailers hawk clothing, tools, cameras and utensils laid out on blankets on the pavement or curbside stands. Most of the employees of these industries are immigrants, without whom these informal sectors would virtually disappear (Waldinger, 1996a, pp. 64–5, 69–72, 153–5, 159–63, 204–5).

The evolution of immigrant-dominated informal sectors in developed countries is a perplexing problem. For a long time, globalisation theory has offered a demand-driven explanation (Petras, 1983). Demand-driven means that globalisation theory identifies demand as the motor of change that attracts immigrants to developed economies. Consumer demand is the effective agent of change.[4] Naturally, to reach consumer demand, globalisation theory starts with the impact of global restructuring upon income distribution in advanced countries. The growth of consumer services creates jobs for low-wage workers while the growth of producer services creates jobs for high-wage workers. These parallel trends polarise the income structures of advanced countries (Hamnett, 1994, p. 404; Kloosterman, 1996a, pp. 468–9). Globalisation theory then deduces from this increasingly unequal income distribution changes in consumer demand that encourage both informalisation in and immigration to advanced countries.

Weaker versions of globalisation theory parcel out the share of informalisation that is attributable to immigration and that which is attributable to restructuring, stressing that immigration cannot explain it all.[5] In view of the preponderance of immigrants in the informal sectors of developed countries, this division seems attractive. However the solution is not universal. Indeed the leading proponent of globalisation theory, Sassen, has rejected *any independent* role of immigration in the informalisation of the advanced economies. Asking rhetorically 'whether the expansion of low-wage jobs is a function of the large new Third World immigrant influx', her answer is 'no' (Sassen-Koob, 1989, p. 302). Elsewhere she declares that immigrants 'cannot be said to cause the informal economy' (Sassen, 1996). Rather in her formulation it is restructured consumer demand that causes immigration, which has no independent role in informalisation in developed countries. Taking an equally structural if less global starting point, Bailey and Waldinger echo Sassen's conclusion. Wanting to 'ground informalization within the basic properties of advanced urban economies', Bailey and Waldinger (1991, p. 80) declare that such an explanation is incompatible with 'the common notion that the growth of an informal economy in cities like New York and Los Angeles results from the survival strategies of Third World immigrants'. The strength of this argument depends on the temporal priority of demand for immigrant labour. In short, no demand for immigrant workers, no immigrants; and no immigrants, no informalisation.

However new findings and new ideas now permit a critique of globalisation theory from the point of view of migration networks. Since this limited critique overlooks the state's role in migration outcomes, it understates the restraints on globalisation.[6] The critique views the migration network as a codeterminant of both immigration and informalisation in developed countries. That is, contrary to extreme globalisation theorists, who attribute informalisation to demand pull, the networks approach claims that immigration contributes to informalisation with a push from the supply side.[7] On the empirical side of this debate, three findings encourage this conclusion. Firstly, in connection with the United States, Waldinger disputes the claim that global restructuring causes immigration from the Third World. After all, he reasons, unemployed African-Americans are available to take the informal sector jobs that go instead to Third World immigrants. Indeed African-Americans initially tried to get those jobs; but they failed and are now permanently locked out by referral networks (Waldinger, 1992, pp. 112). Waldinger attributes the success of Third World immigrants to the effective exploitation of their social capital and to employers' disparaging attitude towards the work ethic of native blacks (Waldinger, 1996a, pp. 16, 32, 56, 80–6, 255–7; see also Waldinger, 1996b, pp. 269–72, 274–7). His conclusion raises the possibility of informalisation without immigration, in which case, at least in the United States, Third World immigration would not be an inescapable consequence of global restructuring.

Secondly, several researchers have reported that immigrant-domi-nated informal sectors expand when formal sectors contract or become saturated. Rath (1998) observes that Turkish businesses in Amsterdam started to mushroom in the early 1980s when the formal sector ceased to produce new jobs for unskilled workers; that is, when the supply of jobs dried up immigrants turned to self-employment. Simon (1993, p. 130) makes the same point about immigrant-owned businesses in France in that period. This sequence implies a continuing immigration that pries open new doors when old ones close; in which case immi-grants are actively remaking the host economy, not just entering it. Similarly Tienda and Raijman (1996) find that the increased flow of immigrants to the United States caused 'a glut of potential workers in low-wage markets'. As a result the unemployment of immigrants increased and in the wake of this unemployment Mexican immigrants in Chicago turned increasingly to the informal economy, a result that 'challenges demand side explanations' of informalisation. Behind Tienda and Raijman's objection is the notion that employment demand, once satisfied, cannot explain why immigration continues. This idea exposes an empirical limitation of globalisation theory, which assumes that initial demand explains all the immigration that ensues thereafter, even after the demand has been satisfied.

Thirdly, in a comparison of Australia, Canada and the United States, Reitz (1995) finds that in the United States low-skilled immigrants clus-ter in metropolitan areas where the average educational level is much above the national average. Reitz calls these 'education cities'. Of course this finding is exactly what restructuring theorists have observed, and on the strength of this they have offered their globalisation interpreta-tion. However, Reitz continues, the clustering of immigrants in 'educa-tion cities' is much less marked in Canada than in the United States, and in Australia this clustering is negligible. Since global restructuring must have the same effects everywhere, global restructuring alone can-not explain these international differences in immigrant settlement. Instead the clustering of immigrants with a low level of education in US cities with a high level of education, which Sassen has 'erroneously attributed to restructuring', Reitz attributes instead to 'processes of dif-ferentially-selective recruitment', suggesting that these international differences 'could be a policy effect' related to chain migration.[8]

Building on these observations, recent development of migration net-work theory now makes possible a conceptual critique of globalisation theory. Network theory is supply driven; that is, once mobilised the social capital of the immigrants becomes the motor of immigration.

Indeed, as critics allege, migration network theory proposes that survival strategies imported from the Third World engender informalisation in developed countries.[9] However, important as they are, culturally derived strategies are not the only source of informalisation in developed countries. Rather migration network theory stresses the social networks of the immigrants themselves and deduces from the cost-cutting capabilities of those networks the relentless immigration of Third World people into developed countries. The end product of this relentless immigration is the reproduction of Third World informalisation in the developed economies, but the causes of this reproduction are as much structural as cultural.[10]

The debate between globalisation theory and migration network theory need not involve a forced choice between one or the other. Indeed, as is very well known, in the social sciences forced choices between opposites usually mask fallacies. Therefore instead of boarding the bandwagon of globalisation or migration networks, this chapter examines the logic of both positions with an eye to ascertaining whether a synthesis is possible. Accordingly the first task of this review is to compare critically the two approaches in order to expose the comparative strengths and weaknesses of each. That done, the second task is to suggest a synthetic explanation of informalisation in developed countries that integrates the strengths of both and the weaknesses of neither.

Globalisation theory

In its broadest sense globalisation refers to all the processes that incorporate the peoples of the world into a single world society (Nederveen Pieterse, 1994, p. 161). These processes are economic, social and political. However in the narrower economic sense, globalisation means the attainment of a globally integrated market for labour and capital, especially the latter. This attainment requires many painful disjunctures in all the countries of the world. Global restructuring is economic globalisation in action (Dicken, 1992, pp. 207–27). Global restructuring calls attention to local economic changes produced by resource and factor shifts in the world market. In that unitary world market, capital flows freely across international boundaries in response to profit incentives, and labour, which is more inhibited, flows more freely than before (Petras, 1983, pp. 48–9; see also Zolberg, 1991). The agents of global restructuring are transnational corporations, which, spanning continents, reallocate jobs and industrial functions among them in response to profit incentives and are indifferent to political or cultural loyalties or boundaries (Bornschier and Stamm, 1990). In this new international division of labour, jobs in producer services, finance and top-level administration remain in the developed world, where they are very well-paid indeed. Manufacturing jobs are exported to low-wage countries. The exportation of manufacturing jobs occurs when transnational corporations close factories in high-wage regions of Europe and North America and open new ones in newly industrialised countries or the Third World. In either overseas setting, labour is much cheaper than in the developed countries.

Driven by profit incentives, global restructuring has created an international urban hierarchy centred upon a handful of world cities. From these organising nodes – London, Tokyo and New York in Sassen's influential account – transnational business corporations reach out to control the local economies they penetrate. As a result the local economies operate more and more as players in an international play whose script has been written by distant financiers. Once again international bankers control the world's destiny.[11]

The transnationals' decisions have relocated blue-collar manufacturing to low-wage countries, leaving Western Europe, Canada and the United States increasingly dependent for employment upon a growing service sector and high-level information technology and finance sectors (Savitch, 1990, p. 151; Scott and Storper, 1992, pp. 3–4, 11). The growing personal service sector offers low-wage jobs that attract immigrants from Third World countries. Still concentrated in the big cities of the developed world, the growing technology and financial sectors provide well-paid jobs for elite managers. As formerly secure and well-remunerated manufacturing jobs are exported to new industrial countries, the argument continues, the stable working class and lower middle class of the developed countries disintegrate, and the income pyramid of the developed countries becomes hour-glass shaped (Bluestone and Harrison, 1987; Kloosterman, 1996a, pp. 468–9; Nazario and Shutt, 1995). There are more rich people, more poor people and fewer middle-class people. The income share of the top fifth of the population increases and the share of the bottom fifth declines. Income inequality increases for this reason, but also because the managerial elite increases its relative income advantage over the dwindling middle class, while the informal sector's distressed workers undercut what used to be the bottom end of income distribution (Hiltzik, 1996).

Moore and Pinderhughes (1993, p. xxvii) declare that the 'growth of an informal economy is part and parcel of late twentieth-century economic restructuring'. This judgement epitomises restructuring theory, which explains the growth of informal economies in developed countries as a by-product of newly polarised income distribution arising from restructuring (Sassen, 1986, pp. 114–5; Sassen-Koob, 1989, p. 70; see also Sassen-Koob, 1985, p. 255). Restructuring theorists explain immigration in terms of a growing demand for the products of cheap immigrant labour.[12] At the top of the income distribution league, newly rich, dual-income households need servants to keep their house, wash their cars, tend their gardens and mind their children (Wrigley, 1997). Immigrants from poor countries will accept these low-wage jobs; unemployed native workers will not.[13] These immigrant workers receive no social security benefits, no employer-paid health care, their wages are not reported to tax officials and their job tenure is insecure. The underpaid employees of rich households cannot afford mainstream products and services that require a mainstream income. Like the newly impoverished natives of the former middle class, they look for discounted goods produced and sold in the informal sector. Like the rich, the immigrant poor buy clothing manufactured in the informal sector. Unlike the rich, who buy their clothes in fancy boutiques, the workers of the informal sector and distressed former middle-class natives buy cheap garments manufactured in the informal sector from informal sector vendors on street corners and swap meets. Figure 9.1 is a flow-chart diagram that shows how globalisation begets informalisation.

The garment industries of Amsterdam and Los Angeles epitomise this informalisation in manufacturing. In both cities the now thriving garment manufacturing industry relies upon immigrant workers whose low wages typically do not include social security or medical coverage.[14] In both cities garment manufacturing takes place in unsanitary and unsafe conditions that are formally illegal.[15] A 1996 survey of employment conditions in the garment industry of Los Angeles found hazardous conditions in 75 per cent and minimum-wage violations in 43 per cent of workplaces, and one third of garment manufacturing firms had failed to register with the state in an attempt to evade supervision (Silverstein and White, 1996). Whether due to corruption, indifference or political interest, public authorities routinely tolerate these substandard and illegal conditions.[16] In Amsterdam, however,

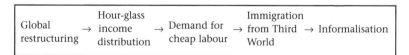

Figure 9.1   Globalisation and informalisation

since 1994 the public authorities have embarked on a comprehensive project to improve conditions in garment industry. This intervention has resulted in a serious decrease in immigrant workplaces.

Globalisation theory effectively links economic processes in the advanced and developing countries, thus creating a coherent vision of a master process of which immigration and informalisation are by-products. No wonder globalisation theory has enjoyed wide popularity. However globalisation theory has provoked criticism because of its overemphasis on global structure at the expense of local agency.[17] For example, as shown in Figure 9.1, once global restructuring has occurred the other linked changes fall mechanically into place. This claim has encouraged criticism of restructuring theory's economism and linear determinism.[18] Economism means overemphasis on market forces to the neglect of cultural, social and political responses (Fernández Kelly and Garcia, 1989, p. 250). Determinism means the utter elimination of political choice and immigrant agency. Thus Logan and Swanstrom (1990) observe that the global restructuring literature represents markets as natural forces separate from and superior to national and local states.[19] However they insist that 'a great deal more [political] discretion exists to shape economic and urban restructuring than is commonly believed' (ibid., pp. 5–6). Kloosterman (1996a, p. 468) declares that interregional differences prove that restructuring does not determine urban outcomes. Marxist critics have taken a similar view. Gottdiener and Komninos (1989, p. 8) wish to escape 'one-dimensional, deterministic explanations' in order to forge 'approaches that consider political and cultural as well as economic dimensions'.

Migration network theory

To respond fully to this critique would require an examination of the relative autonomy of state and migration networks in shaping migration outcomes. However a full response would be a big job, so this chapter limits itself to an examination of migration networks, over-looking for now the state's autonomous role (see also the Chapter 6 of this volume). Migration network theory offers a supply-driven explanation of the link between immigration and informalisation. This version avoids the linearity, determinism and economism of globalisation theory. Massey (1998, p. 396) defines migration networks as 'sets of inter-personal ties that link migrants, former migrants, and nonmigrants in origin and destination areas through the bonds of kinship, friendship, and shared community origin'. Once formed, networks promote the semi-independence of migratory flows from global restructuring. Firstly, once network connections reach a certain threshold level they amount to an autonomous social structure that supports immigration. This support arises from the reduced social, economic and emotional costs of immigration that networks permit[20] – that is, network-supported migrants have important help in arranging transportation, finding housing and jobs in their place of destination, and adjusting personally and emotionally to cultural marginality. These benefits make migration easier and cheaper, thus encouraging migration by those who would otherwise have stayed at home. Unless migrants are refugees, for whom migration may afford the only hope of survival, potential migrants always have the option of staying home (Bozorgmehr and Sabagh, 1991). Given that choice, the reduced cost of migration increases the volume of migration.

Secondly, families allocate their labour within the constraint of their own needs and aspirations in a cost-efficient and risk-minimising way (Massey, 1990, p. 8) Many Third World households are economically precarious and may face high risks if they choose not to migrate. Moreover modernisation and development create social and economic dislocations that intensify the unstable and unpredictable economic environment. In the absence of other ways to control such risks, diversification of the family members' location minimises overall family income risk (Massey, 1988, p. 398, 1990, pp. 9–11). Migration is sometimes a risk-diversification strategy for households in this situation. International migration is especially effective because international borders create discontinuities that promote independence of earnings at home and abroad. Good times abroad can match hard times at home, and *vice versa*. Migration networks reduce the economic risks of immigration, thus rendering the strategy more attractive from a risk-diversification perspective (Massey, 1988, p. 398; Massey and Espana, 1987, p. 734).

In great cities of the Third World such as Lagos and Rio de Janeiro, 30–70 per cent of the labour force works in the urban informal sector (Castells and Portes, 1989, pp. 17–19). As these statistics indicate, migration networks are not dependent on or limited by the employment capacity of the formal sector. If they were, a majority of Rio's labour force would have been unable to reside in that city due to their inability to earn a living there. Nonetheless saturated conditions in the formal sector do compel migration networks to adapt in order to release additional migrants for whom the target economy now provides no waiting employment niche. Migration networks utilise immigrant entrepreneurship to access emergent latent demand that native employers have not organised as jobs (Light *et al.*, 1993). Immigrant entrepreneurship in the informal sector renders the migration network semi-independent of formal sector jobs.[21] As the formal and informal labour markets reach saturation point in destination localities, and as network participants' job search times and unemployment increase, network participants have three realistic and productive alternatives to begging, theft or return migration. The first is entrepreneurship, defined here as owning and operating firms that employ paid labour in the informal sector (Portes and Rumbaut, 1990, p. 88).[22] Wealthy immigrants who employ poor immigrants in the informal sector have selected this option. The second alternative is waged employment in immigrant-owned firms in the formal and informal sectors. Immigrants who work for wages in informal garment manufacturing plants have selected this option, but obviously this option would only have been open to them if other immigrants had previously started employer firms. The third option is self-employment in the informal sector without employees of one's own. In a low-income Mexican community in Chicago, Tienda and Raijman (1996, p. 63) found that 'almost 19 per cent of the total family income, and 23 per cent of labour income is generated by informal self-employment activities'. This self-employment can supplement a low-wage job or represent full-time work (Sirola, 1992). In Los Angeles the quintessential self-employed immigrant in the informal sector peddles bags of oranges at freeway entrances.

Restructuring theorists implausibly explain immigration in terms of labour demand, as if immigrants were independent calculators endowed with instant access to accurate information about real wages in distant labour markets while lacking either the desire or the ability to help or inform one another. This unrealistic assumption quite overlooks self-propelling migration networks. Migrations forge social networks, which then feed the very migrations that produced them (Massey, 1988, 1990; Massey and Espana, 1987; Massey *et al.*, 1987). Therefore, whatever global conditions may have initially caused migration, the originating pushes and pulls, the expanding migratory process becomes semi-independent of globalisation's job supply. It achieves this independence as the self-employment of the immigrants releases latent demand that the native employers have not organised as jobs. Unlike taking a job offered by a native employer, immigrant self-employment mobilises resources that originated in the sending country to fulfil a latent demand in the destination economy.

Spillover immigration

Our problem now is to reconcile the structuralism and economism of globalisation theory with the agency of network theory. In this intellectual situation, the concept of spillover immigration reconciles the theoretical conflict between globalisation theory and network theory. Spillover immigrations occur when the motor of continuing immigration switches from the demand to the supply side in midstream. In immigration spillovers, demand conditions trigger migration, but immigrant social networks thereafter expand it beyond what the initial demand can support. What began because of novel demand conditions continues or expands past some threshold because social networks lower the social, economic and emotional cost of taking distant jobs. As the migration network grows the expanding immigrant labour force in the target destination becomes surplus to the new demand, causing a decline in incomes and conditions in the informal sector. The informal sector then expands *despite* the declining conditions because the migration networks partially or wholly compensate the decline in income.

To illustrate this, consider a town with a new factory in the suburbs and poor public transport. The workers live in the core; the new jobs are on the periphery. When the factory opens its high wages attract enough workers to fill the available jobs despite the high cost of travel. Later the transportation authority reduces the bus fares. This reduction permits additional workers to seek jobs at the factory, which promptly lowers its wages and then stops hiring altogether. In this example the first wave of workers went to the new factory because the high wages offset the high travel costs. The second wave went because the cost of the bus journey declined. So the factory's workforce consisted of some workers who responded to its initially high wage offer and others who accepted a lower wage when reduced bus fares made this economical. These are two separate causes (high wages plus reduced bus fares), not one. Thanks to the reduced bus fares the welfare of the later workers, who earned lower wages, was comparable to the welfare of the early workers, whose high wages had to defray high bus fares.[23] Moreover, even though the factory had stopped hiring, thanks to the immigrant network self-employed workers travelled from the inner city to sell goods and services around the factory to employees and to suburban housewives. At that point the immigrant network broke free of the factory's labour demand, although without this, it must be added, the network would never have formed.

In this illustration the initially high factory wages represented a globalisation-induced surge in the locality's demand for labour. The pioneer workers lacked the support of a migration network. The initially high wages compensated the pioneers for the expense and hardships that pioneering imposed. This was one cause. However once these pioneers were firmly in place a migration network formed around them. This was a second cause. As it matured, the migration network progressively lowered the social, emotional and economic costs of migration, rendering immigration attractive, even at lower incomes than those which initially prevailed. The network-driven influx of workers drove down wages and working conditions in the target destination when the immigrant influx outstripped the initial demand for their labour. Nonetheless immigration continued because immigrants turned to self-employment in the general economy, creating work for themselves and other immigrants. Immigrant entrepreneurship and informalisation are the names we give to these linked processes. By the time the scenario had played itself out the migration network had saturated the initial job supply, driving down wages; and it spilled over into augmented self-employment in a vastly expanded informal sector in which immigrant employers supplied jobs to immigrant workers. Labour demand initiated the migration; but the migration network pushed it beyond the initial labour demand by means of immigrant entrepreneurship and progressive informalisation.

What are the signs of spillover immigration? Spillovers are signalled when immigrants' real wages and working conditions in the destination decline but their migration continues at the same level or even increases in volume. If the immigrants' wages and working conditions do not decline as the immigration continues, then the destination's demand for immigrant labour is presumably expanding at the same pace as the immigrant influx. Those who arrive later receive work on terms as attractive as those offered to the earliest arrivals because unsaturated demand is still driving this immigration. However, when initial wages and working conditions decline but immigration continues or even increases, the network-driven influx has presumably outstripped labour demand, causing wage decline but permitting newcomers to survive anyway. Indeed even when working conditions decline and wages outstrip the ability of the informal sector to compensate, the migration network can continue to supply workers to the target destination, recruiting them, if necessary, from groups of lesser social status in the country of origin. When immigration networks are in operation, there is virtually no demand-side limit to the capacity of rich countries to attract Third World immigrants.

This discussion does not imply that informalisation can only occur in the wake of globalisation. In fact globalisation is not a necessary prerequisite for spillover. When new labour demand begins in the formal sector and an informal sector subsequently develops in the destination labour markets, as indeed occurred in Western Europe between 1949 and 1974, this sequence indicates a deterioration of the wages and working conditions in the destination labour markets. Many immigrant workers first entered European economies as guest workers in manufacturing industries. Later, global restructuring reassigned those manufacturing jobs to Third World countries, reducing the formal sector job supply, especially for immigrant workers. Network-driven migration then created an informal sector to catch the newly redundant immigrant workers and permit a continuing influx. In the beginning, before an informal sector existed, immigrant workers in Western Europe enjoyed the advantageous conditions of the formal sector; later there were still immigrants in the formal sector but others were working in the new informal sector where conditions were much worse. The average earnings of immigrants declined during the two periods. Therefore, the emergence of an informal sector in the wake of the saturation of the formal sector is a sign of spillover migration that began before global restructuring. In North America the actual historical sequence was more complex than in Western Europe because the migration of the mid 1960s was already dualistic. Unlike Europe, neither the United States nor Canada underwent a postwar reconstruction that required immigrant labour in the manufacturing sector. Right from the start, one section of North America's postwar immigrants consisted of skilled and professional workers who moved into high-wage professional and technical jobs in the formal sector (Portes and Rumbaut, 1990, pp. 18–23, 57–79). Medical professionals were an important component. The other section consisted of low-skilled workers, at least some of whom moved directly into informal sector jobs provided by native employers. These people became gardeners, nannies and domestic servants. Interestingly the ability of the low-wage group to migrate was assisted in the United States by continuing migration networks left over from earlier migrations (ibid., pp. 30–1). Such networks were initially absent in Western Europe and only came into existence when the new migrants built them *de novo*. Nonetheless, as in Western Europe, the United States has witnessed declining skill levels among newer immigrants (Borjas, 1990), expanding immigrant entrepreneurship and continuous and accelerating informalisation since that initial influx (Castles and Miller, 1993, pp. 75–84). In both continents, thanks to migration networks, the extent of immigration and informalisation outstripped what global restructuring could have accomplished by itself.[24]

All these factors have come together in the garment industries of Los Angeles and Amsterdam. Granted, these industries principally produce clothing for domestic consumption,[25] and therefore depend on consumer demand profiles that reflect global restructuring in the destination economy. Nonetheless global restructuring alone could not have produced the informal garment industries without support from the migration networks. Take away the supporting networks and the immigrant entrepreneurs of the garment industry would not have the key resource that lowers recruitment costs in the immigrant and ethnic economies.[26] Cheap labour would become more expensive. The price of garments would rise, fewer garments would be purchased, fewer immigrant-owned shops would operate and fewer immigrants would find employment in the garment industry. Take away the supporting networks and fewer low-skilled immigrants could survive the inferior working conditions and low wages that prevail in the garment factories. Their wages would have to rise to compensate them for the expense and personal hardship of doing without network resources. Consequently the price of immigrant-made garments would have to rise, fewer would be sold, fewer immigrant-owned factories would operate and fewer Third World immigrants could live in Los Angeles or Amsterdam.

In fact immigrants are the only workers and the only entrepreneurs in the garment manufacturing industry of Los Angeles, and garment manufacturing is now the metropolitan area's second largest industry (Light *et al.*, 1996). All the human, social and financial capital invested in garment manufacturing belongs to immigrants. In Amsterdam a comparable situation exists with regard to the production (but not the design and marketing) of fashionable outerwear. In Amsterdam most of the garment industry's entrepreneurs and virtually all the workers are Turkish (see Chapter 1 of this volume). In some cases immigrant employers hire coethnic immigrant workers. In other cases they hire non-coethnic immigrant workers. Either way the immigrants have created from their own resources a social structure that permits them to extract a livelihood from a recalcitrant opportunity structure. From the point of view of economic demand, we can distinguish this entire informal industry from the situation of domestic servants, another informal industry. Domestic servants have native employers who organise the demand for their cheap labour into jobs in their household. In other words the native population makes this demand easily accessible to immigrant workers. In contrast the public demand for sweatshop-produced clothing only becomes accessible to immigrants when immigrant entrepreneurs first perceive that demand and then exploit it, usually evading the law to accomplish the feat. This latent demand is not easy to access. The immigrants' ability to break into this concealed and inaccessible demand depends on the mobilisation of network resources that originated in their country of origin. Therefore informalisation requires immigrant agency, which in turn also contributes to informalisation.

Conclusion

Globalisation theory claims that global restructuring provides a complete explanation of immigration and informalisation in advanced countries. As an explanation of immigration and informalisation, globalisation theory is demand-driven. It proposes that global restructuring has reshaped incomes in the advanced countries such that the share of the wealthy and the poor has increased relative to the share of the middle class. In response to this shift in consumer demand, it is argued, Third World immigrants have poured into advanced countries, taking jobs in expanding informal sectors whose products are sold to the new rich and the new poor. Some of the informal sector's products are consumed by the new rich; others by the new poor. Either way the change in consumer demand came first, followed by the immigrants, who satisfied the demand, and informalisation came last. Given the globally restructured consumer demand, the rest followed.

This chapter has offerred a conceptual critique of globalisation theory from the point of view of migration network theory. The intention has been to show that global restructuring cannot have caused all the migration to advanced countries even if, for the sake of argument, we assume that global restructuring works as its proponents claim. To a substantial extent, immigration has caused itself and also the economic informalisation that is a condition of its self-production. This view explains immigration and informalisation by reference to the mature migration network's capacity to lower the economic, social and emotional costs and hardships of migration. This cost-cutting capacity increases the degrees of informalisation in and migration to developed countries by permitting the economic exploitation of unorganised and covert demand that would otherwise have remained inaccessible. It does this in two ways. Firstly, the networks reduce the hardship and costs of low-wage work, thus permitting many more immigrants to find employment in the destination economy and many more informal firms to exist. Secondly, networks permit immigrant entrepreneurs to exploit ethnic social capital in the recruitment, training and retention of workers, thus lowering the costs incurred by immigrant-owned firms. Globalisation theory credits demand in the advanced countries with too much determinism and immigrants with too little agency. In general, demand simply cannot explain supply (Light, 1977, p. 475). Consumer demand is passive and incomplete. It is passive because, like a girl in an old-fashioned dancing school, demand has to wait for someone to notice her and then to initiate action. It is incomplete because, like wallflowers who never attract a dancing partner, many consumer demands are never noticed. These demands are the 'spinsters' of the economy; they exist without issue for want of suitors. If we credit restructured consumer demand with all the immigration and informalisation that have occurred, we have to explain why consumer demand did not produce more or less immigration and informalisation than it actually did. We claim, in effect, that demand had to produce exactly what it did, neither more nor less. In this immigrant entrepreneurs and migration networks are the two principal forms of immigrant agency. The immigrant entrepreneurs actively perceive and respond to latent demand, exploiting their social capital to organise firms in the informal sector. The migration networks provide resources that permit immigrants to survive in informal industries. Together the migration networks and the immigrant entrepreneurs represent an immigrant agency that releases a latent demand that would not otherwise be accessible. Without that agency, demand would have supported fewer immigrants and informalisation would have been less extensive.

To reconcile globalisation theory and migration network theory, this chapter has proposed the concept of spillover migration. Spillover migrations start as demand-driven, but in midstream they become network-driven because migration networks reduce the costs and hardships of migration, expanding the supply of migrants and lowering their reservation wages. Informalisation also progresses because immigrant entrepreneurs tap the social capital of migration networks, thus permitting them to access hitherto inaccessible demand. The concept of spillover migration links globalisation theory and migration network theory into a plausible but not necessarily inevitable sequence. Since states can regulate the economic conditions and immigration within their borders, they can impede or possibly even disconnect this linkage. States disconnect the linkage when they regulate economic informality out of existence, successfully exclude immigrant self-employment and prohibit chain migration. To the extent that they succeed in these objectives, they partially disconnect the linkage. Although European states have been – and remain – more successful in disconnecting this linkage than has the United States, no state has completely achieved any of these three goals, nor is it easy to see how they could. Therefore, given their own social momentum and in the absence of fully effective political restraints, demand-induced migrations spill over into supply-driven migration as migration networks mature. An interesting but unanswered question is how much of total immigration and total informalisation can be traced to initial changes in consumer demand and how much is caused by spillover migration. Conceivably the shares are equal; but it is more likely that, thanks to spillover migration, small initial changes in demand for cheap labour trigger vast, self-sustaining migrations from Third World countries.

Notes

1 The author acknowledges with thanks a small grant from the Center for German and European Studies at the University of California. Thanks are also extended to David Lopez, Jan Rath and Georges Sabagh for critical suggestions on an earlier draft.

2 'Informal work seems to have grown since the early 1970s. Department of Labor Violations, raids by the Immigration and Naturalization Service, union organizers, interviews with homeworkers, and other sources all point to an increase of production workers in unregistered work situations, notably sweatshops and industrial homework' (Bailey and Waldinger, 1991, p. 89; see also Sassen-Koob, 1989, p. 61).

3 'Wherever the garment industry has taken root in the US, unlicensed, sub-standard sewing shops have sprung up by the hundreds. They are illegal, off-the-books, pay no minimum wages, unemployment insurance, or health benefits and ignore child-labor laws or overtime pay regulations. In New York or Philadelphia, Asian or Latina women may be working 12 and 14 hours a day or 7 days a week, without overtime pay, to make the Arrow shirts or Liz Claiborne blouses we buy at the mall' (Petras, 1992, p. 77; see also Fernández Kelly and Garcia, 1989).

4 'Linking the informalization and casualization of work to growth trends takes the analysis beyond the notion that the emergence of informal "sectors" in such cities as New York and London is due to the large presence of immigrants and their supposed propensity to replicate survival strategies typical of Third World countries. It suggests, rather, that basic traits of advanced capitalism may promote conditions for informalization. The presence of large immigrant communities then can be seen as mediating in the process of informalization rather than directly generating it. The demand side of the process of informalization is therewith brought to the fore' (Sassen, 1991a, p. 282; see also Harrison and Bluestone, 1988, p. 70).

5 Thus Castells and Portes (1989, p. 25) conclude that the 'underlying causes for the expansion of the informal economy go well beyond the availability of a tractable foreign labor supply'.

6 In this sense, this exposition is conservative. If the role of the state is taken into account, a project reserved for a future effort, one could certainly reduce still further the plausibility of extreme globalisation theories. The author has elsewhere argued that state policies can boost or hamper the entrepreneurship of immigrants, thus encouraging or discouraging immigration (see Light and Karageorgis, 1997).

7 Hamnett (1994, p. 408) first raised the possibility that immigration is the cause rather than an effect of income polarisation.

8 That is, US immigration law prioritises family reunification, thus encouraging chain migration. However Canada and Australia tend to select immigrants on the basis of the skills they possess, thus reducing chain migration.

9 'Since much of the expansion of the informal economy in developed countries has been located in immigrant communities, this has led to an explanation as being due to the large influx of Third World immigrants and their assumed propensities to replicate survival strategies typical of their home countries. Related to this view is the notion that backward sectors of the economy are kept backward, or even kept alive, because of the availability of a large supply of cheap immigrant workers. Both of these views posit or imply that if there is an informal sector in advanced industrialized countries, the sources are to be found in Third World immigration and in the backward sectors of the economy – a Third World import or a remnant from an earlier phase of industrialization' (Sassen, 1988, p. 285).

10 'Migration is a network-driven process, and the operation of kin and friendship ties is nowhere more effective than in guiding new arrivals toward pre-established ethnic communities. This process may continue indefinitely and accounts for the high concentration of most foreign groups in certain regions of the country and their near absence from others' (Portes and Rumbaut, 1990, p. 32).

11 'Again' because the world conspiracy of bankers was a stock in trade of the Nazi and Marxist ideologies of the 1930s (see Sassen, 1988, pp. 22–3, 136, 145, 160, 185; see also Solomon, 1995).

12 'The expansion of the high-income work force, in conjunction with the emergence of new cultural forms in everyday living, has led to a process of high-income gentrification, which rests, in the last analysis, on the availability of a vast supply of low-wage workers' (Sassen, 1991a, p. 279; see also ibid., pp. 281–2).

13 Waldinger (1996a, pp. 12–29) points out that the emergent demand for low-wage labour in American cities did not require impoverished immigrants as globalisation theory maintains. After all, unlike European cities, American cities already had an existing labour reserve of impoverished, unemployed and underemployed native-born blacks. These blacks were available to take the low-wage service and manufacturing jobs that globalisation created. Instead the Latino, Caribbean and Asian immigrants got these jobs, monopolising the entire informal sector, and the native-born blacks remained impoverished and unemployed. The causes of this perplexing outcome, Waldinger declares, must be sought first in the folklore of

American labour markets that disparage the desirability of black American employees. This is a cultural issue. Second, in Waldinger's view the social networks of the immigrants permitted them to outcompete native blacks for initial access to the growing informal sector, and then to exclude native blacks from their newly acquired industrial niches.

14   In 1989 more than 20 per cent of California's adults had no paid health coverage, and 80 per cent of these unprotected adults held jobs (Beck, 1989).

15   Even slavery has come back. In Los Angeles a Thai employer held 70 immigrant Thai women as slaves, working them seven days a week in garment sweatshops under the supervision of her adult sons (Krikorian, 1996).

16   Elizabeth Petras (1992, p. 102) claims that Mafia families control the garment industry in New York City and Philadelphia. The Mafia's influence constrains those politicians and district attorneys who are officially responsible for overseeing labour conditions (see also Bonacich, 1994, pp. 152–3).

17   'Larger translocal economic forces have far more weight than local policies in shaping urban economies' (Sassen, 1990, p. 237). 'Global forces and transnational flows are becoming more and more dominant at the national and local levels' (Knight, 1989, p. 25).

18   'Another shortcoming of world systems theorists who have built upon Wallerstein has been their tendency to view migrants as essentially units of labor' (Schiller *et al.*, 1992, p. 8).

19   For someone who says exactly this, see Peterson (1981).

20   We must not overlook the emotional hardships of immigration. 'Long-distance journeys entail a set of engulfing life events (losses, changes, conflicts, and demands) that, although varying widely in kind and degree, severely tests the immigrant's emotional resilience. Migration can produce profound psychological distress, even among the best prepared and most motivated and even under the most receptive of circumstances' (Portes and Rumbaut, 1990, p. 144).

21   'In the face of more limited employment opportunities in low-wage markets, immigrants will turn to self-employment and stimulate the formation of new businesses' (Tienda and Raijman, 1996, p. 23).

22   If immigrant employers enter the formal sector, the jobs they create stave off the saturation of formal sector labour markets. If entrepreneurs can create employer firms in the formal sector, the formal sector is not yet saturated. This discussion concerns only the scenario that unfolds when the formal sector is saturated.

23   Suppose the initial wage is $5 a day and the bus fare is $4. Workers net $1 for every day they work. If, in response to an influx of workers, the factory drops the wage to $3, but the bus fare drops to $2, the workers still net $1 for every day they work.

24   'However, the secondary sector appears to be only one mode of immigrant labour market incorporation in the US; increasingly immigrants enter the labour market through the portals of immigrant-owned firms' (Waldinger, 1985, p. 214).

25   Actually that assumption is truer in Los Angeles than in Amsterdam, where a substantial proportion of garment production is exported. The exportation of garments weakens the globalisation argument because products

derive no competitive advantage from geographical proximity to ultimate markets, and could have been produced elsewhere with that advantage.

26 Immigrant economies arise when entrepreneurs in one immigrant group hire workers from another immigrant group. The immigrant economy of any locality consists of all the immigrant entrepreneurs plus all of their non-coethnic immigrant employees (see Light and Karageorgis, 1994).

10
International Migration, Undocumented Immigrants and Immigrant Entrepreneurship

Richard Staring[1]

Introduction

At first sight it seems difficult to find similarities between unauthorised taxi driver in New York City and a rose seller in Amsterdam.[2] However if one takes a closer look at the two they resemble each other in various ways. Both are engaged in entrepreneurial activities, often practised informally and within an urban context, and both are often classified as undocumented immigrants (Lemann, 1991).[3]

Globalisation – the process whereby people are increasingly engaged in world-wide dependency networks – has many manifestations, of which world-wide flows of capital, technology, goods, ideas and people are among the most important. The transnational movement of people, for instance as tourists, migrants or exiles, can be seen as one of the central and most apparent expressions of this global process (cf. Appadurai, 1990). Ever more countries as well as people are involved in and affected by international migration. Contemporary migration flows can consequently be characterised as more complex and increasingly diverse, and this holds in particular for the economic, cultural and social background of the persons involved (Campani, 1995, p. 547; Castles and Miller, 1993, p. 8; cf. Champion, 1994; Pugliese, 1993). Different types of immigrant – such as refugees, asylum seekers, illegals, family reunificationers, professionals, entrepreneurs and labour immigrants – can be distinguished and are often simultaneously present in many immigration countries (Champion, 1994; Cohen, 1995, p. 3). Within all this diversity, undocumented immigrants are becoming a more prominent and growing category world-wide (Champion, 1994; Miller, 1995).

Traditional immigration countries such as the United States, Canada and Australia, but also Western European countries such as Germany, the Netherlands and France, are all increasingly confronted with the presence of undocumented immigrants. Experts estimate that there are between three and five million undocumented immigrants living in the United States (cf. Migration News, 1997). In Southern Europe, traditional labour-exporting countries such as Italy, Greece and Spain have become new immigration countries and are also dealing with the presence of undocumented immigrants (Hugo, 1995, p. 401; Migration News, 1997). For Europe as a whole the number of undocumented immigrants is estimated to be somewhere around 2.6 million (Castles and Miller, 1993, p. 79), at least 60 000 of whom live in the Netherlands (Burgers, 1995, p. 34). Although it is difficult to determine the accuracy of these figures – quite a number of estimates hardly go beyond the realms of an 'educated guess' (cf. Larson and Sullivan, 1987) – it is predicted that in the future there will be more rather than less illegal migration (Miller, 1995, p. 539; cf. Castles and Miller, 1993, p. 92).

The economic restructuring of Third World countries and economically advanced countries alike is another important element of the globalisation process. Advanced economies are characterised by a decline in manufacturing industries and a rise in service industries, and also by an increase in informal economic practices, especially at the lower end of the market. Immigrants represent a cheap and motivated workforce for firms at the bottom end (and often informal segments) of the service industry. They are willing to take on the poorly paid, menial, dead-end jobs – often referred to as 3D jobs: dirty, dangerous and difficult – that most natives eschew (Kearney, 1995, p. 554; Portes and Rumbaut, 1990, p. 232). As Mahler (1995, p. 10) writes in her ethnography on Middle and South-American immigrants in New York City, 'immigrants with their minimal skills serve as the perfect labour supply for these dead-end jobs'. However not all immigrants find a job in these sectors of the labour market as some start a business of their own. Many scholars have pointed to the importance of ethnic minority self-employment, and some authors speak of these immigrant businesses as 'a standard feature of advanced urban economies' (Barrett *et al.*, 1996, p. 783). There are indications that this holds not only for documented immigrants but also for undocumented ones.

The international movement of people across borders can to some extent be understood as a response to the economic restructuring of Western countries. In turn, however, such flows of people have an impact on the economic restructuring process as they help to reshape Western cities and regions. Sassen (1991a, p. 315), for instance, suggests that the existence of these different immigrants 'creates a captive market for ethnic shopkeepers'. Fielding (1993, p. 16) also alludes to this when he states that immigrants not only respond to economic restructuring but also alter the social and cultural composition, thereby enhancing the growth of small firms within the city or region. This last observation resembles the findings of Light *et al.* (1993), who comment on the labour-creating potential of immigrant entrepreneurs. The demand for labour by immigrant firms can lead to the arrival of further immigrants from their home country. Within these small immigrant firms informal activities are part and parcel of their strategy to survive their harsh economic circumstances. At the crossroads of the process of economic restructuring, international migration and immigrant firms stands the undocumented immigrant. In this chapter I shall elaborate on this issue.

My theoretical argument is basically as follows. Scholars have increasingly appreciated the relevance of personal networks in explaining the complex process of international migration. Also, within the field of immigrant entrepreneurship attention is directed towards the personal network. When describing these networks the legal status of the immigrants involved is usually not taken into account. Illegal migrants therefore seem to be not only obscured in the statistics but also excluded from theories of international migration. In reality, however, legal status matters. The difference between documented and undocumented immigrants is significant not only for the actual migration process but also for the process of settlement. Especially in the labour market and within the immigrant economy, the legal status of immigrants is of importance for the entrepreneur as well as for the immigrants involved.

Three different 'P-roles' will be described, as undocumented immigrants promote, produce and participate in immigrant business in a very specific way that sets them apart from their legal conationals. In short it is hard to imagine that one could theoretically understand immigrant entrepreneurship without examining international migration in general and the role of undocumented immigrants in particular. Before elaborating on this, the characteristics of those who are classified as 'illegal' will briefly be discussed.

Characterising undocumented immigrants

In general, an undocumented immigrant is often defined as someone residing in a country without an official residence permit (Miller, 1995; Muus, 1995, pp. 96–7). However the concept of an illegal or undocumented immigrant, although frequently and easily used, is problematic as both 'residence' and 'relevant residence permits' are themselves concepts that are difficult to delineate. Undocumented immigrants are first and foremost a legal construct, and as such they are products of (restrictive) migration policies. Undocumented immigrants came into existence when states tried 'to fence off their countries from unwanted foreign immigrants' (Cohen, 1995, p. 5). One of the first examples presented in literature concerns Chinese migrants to the United States. Under the Chinese Exclusion Act, which was implemented in 1882, Chinese could not apply for naturalisation and could not enter the country as regular immigrants until 1943. This, however, did not stop them from entering the country during this period (Siu, 1987, p. 195).

Illegal migration and undocumented immigrants, therefore, are not a relatively new phenomenon that started in Europe in the post-industrial context after the recruitment phase and the family reunification phase were over. In his review of recent literature, Champion (1994) identifies three major types of post-industrial migrant: highly skilled workers, asylum seekers and undocumented immigrants. They are, in his view, 'similar only in that they have all grown substantially in importance during the 1980s' (ibid., p. 658). However during the period of active labour recruitment in Western Europe, starting in the mid 1950s, a substantial number of immigrants were already 'spontaneous workers' and their arrival was encouraged by governments.[4] Furthermore, due to restrictions on family reunification an unknown number of family members entered clandestinely (Castles and Kosack, 1973, pp. 209–10). Another indication of the presence of undocumented immigrants some decades ago are the regularisation and amnesty programmes that started in the mid 1970s in various European countries, such as the Netherlands, France, Italy and Spain (cf. Calavita, 1994a; Cornelius, 1994; Hollifield, 1994; Tinnemans, 1994). However the shift from the term 'spontaneous workers' to the use of 'undocumented immigrants' reflects some of the changes in attitude towards these immigrants. In most Western countries undocumented immigrants are increasingly perceived as a problem and a threat to the arrangements of the welfare state. Nowadays it is hardly possible to imagine the use of the term 'spontaneous worker' as it has been replaced by such terms as 'illegals', 'clandestine workers' and 'irregular immigrants'.

Undocumented immigrants do not constitute an homogeneous category. Their diversity expresses itself in three general domains. First, there is variety in the social backgrounds of the immigrants involved.

It is not just the poor with a rural background or the highly skilled who migrate, but also, as Margolis (1994) describes for Brazil, people with a middle-class background are increasingly involved in illegal migration to the United States.

Secondly, undocumented immigrants come from many different countries. In our own research, among 169 illegal aliens in the Dutch harbour city of Rotterdam we encountered 18 different nationalities.[5] Among the most prominent countries represented were Turkey, Morocco and the Cape Verde Islands, which accounted for 66.7 per cent of our research group. We have also spoken with undocumented immigrants from Surinam, a former Dutch colony located between French and British Guyana (4.7 per cent). Among the remaining countries, a significant group of illegal immigrants originate from former Eastern European countries such as Poland, Czechoslovakia, Bulgaria, Romania, Russia, Moldavia, Georgia and the former republic of Yugoslavia (together 14.8 per cent). Other undocumented immigrants are from countries as diverse as Algeria, Togo, Jamaica, Palestine, Cameroon and India (14.2 per cent). Rotterdam police records of apprehended undocumented immigrants show an even greater diversity: during the period 1989–93 the police apprehended undocumented immigrants from 43 different countries.

A third component of the diversity of the undocumented immigrant population is their migration motive. A common perspective on undocumented immigrants is expressed by Miller (1995), who states that most undocumented immigrants work in specific industries. However it is important to note that undocumented immigrants are not precisely the same as illegal foreign workers. There are many different routes that can lead to illegal residence. For instance asylum seekers who are not admitted or recognised as such by governments can go into hiding, and as such become illegal (Koser, 1997). Female immigrants come as workers (cf. Hillman, 1996) and for reasons of family reunification or family formation, but due to restrictive migration policies they can end up illegal (cf. Veraart, 1996).

Besides the abovementioned, an important characteristic of undocumented immigrants relates to the means by which they enter their new country of residence. All too often it is assumed that undocumented immigrants enter the country of residence illegally. However studies show that this is not always the case, and that to a large extent these immigrants do enter legally, on a tourist visa or some other kind of temporary visa that subsequently expires (Hollifield, 1994, p. 162). In Japan, one of the new immigration countries, women from Thailand

and the Philippines enter the country under the provisions of the Immigration Control Act on a one-year visa as entertainers, but often end up staying on illegally and working as prostitutes (Hugo, 1995, p. 399; Loiskandle, 1995, pp. 371–3). In the case of Japan it has been observed that once immigrants have entered the country legally as tourists they have surmounted the biggest obstacle. Due to the weak control on illegal stay and labour, these women can work with relative ease. In our own research in the city of Rotterdam, approximately two thirds of the undocumented immigrants interviewed had entered the Netherlands on a visa, mainly a tourist one, but this had since expired. Other respondents had a tourist visa that allowed them entry to another European country. About one third of our sample had entered the Netherlands illegally as they either lacked official documents or were in the possession of false papers.

Undocumented immigrants and immigration policies

For the overwhelming majority of undocumented immigrants, their illegal status is a temporary one. Most of them are illegal only for a limited period as they are legalised via marriage to a legal inhabitant of the country in question on by virtue of a loophole in the immigration maze (work, false papers), or in the end they return to their home country. It has been 15 years since the last regularisation was enforced in the United States, and several European countries have implemented general amnesty programmes (Cornelius *et al.*, 1994b; Meissner *et al.*, 1993). However it is hard to imagine that new legalisation programmes will be proclaimed as governments are increasingly fearful that this would attract even more immigrants. Other opportunities to legalise their status are increasingly slim as the governments of most Western countries have adopted restrictive migration policies (Cornelius *et al.*, 1994b).

In the Netherlands for instance, several restrictive laws have been implemented that have had serious consequences for the daily lives of illegal immigrants. Before November 1991 everyone – undocumented migrants included – could acquire a social security number: one only had to register as a resident in a city and it was not necessary to produce a residence permit. Nowadays receipt of a social security number – which is essential when applying for a formal job – is conditional on having a residence permit. As a consequence it is almost impossible for undocumented migrants to apply for a legal job in a regular way. At the same time the Dutch government has clamped down on illegal workers. Employers, for instance, have been penalised for hiring undocumented workers. In this context the introduction of the Compulsory Identification Act in June 1994 can also be seen as an instrument to prevent illegal labour as it directly limits the chance of undocumented workers obtaining work in the formal sector (Burgers and Engbersen, 1995).

These kinds of restrictive legislation not only limit the possibility of undocumented immigrants becoming legalised, but also directly limit the number of jobs available to them. Our research in Rotterdam illustrates this: almost 40 per cent of our sample were unemployed at the time we interviewed them, and half of those who were employed only worked on a temporary, often irregular basis. Although not every undocumented immigrant wanted to work, many of those who were unemployed just could not find a job.

All this puts some employers in a powerful position. The abundance of unemployed, undocumented immigrants with poor access to formal jobs gives a special meaning to employment opportunities within the community. As undocumented immigrants are being marginalised in several respects by restrictive immigration policies, they are becoming increasingly dependent on conational employers. As jobs are scarce for these immigrants, immigrant businesses provide the possibility of a job and for the entrepreneur it means cheap labour. In the Netherlands at least, the fall in traditional industrial jobs has coincided with an increase in immigrant businesses (Kloosterman *et al.*, 1997b), from which undocumented immigrants can profit.

Before turning to this topic it is important to focus our attention on theories of international migration and personal networks. Social scientists are increasingly pointing to the relevance of these networks (which are often the same networks that render assistance during the stay) for the process of international migration. These issues are the subject of the next section.

Theories of international migration and personal networks

Since Ravenstein (1885) wrote his 'Laws of Migration', scholars of international migration have dealt with such central issues as the origin, direction, volume and persistence of large-scale movements of individuals and the settlement process of the immigrants involved (Borjas, 1989; Massey *et al.*, 1993). Ravenstein was one of the first scientists to attribute central importance to the economic motive in migration. As he states, 'nothing can compare with the desire inherent in most men to better themselves in material respects' (Ravenstein, quoted in Lee, 1969). Since then, within most theories of international migration, economic motives play the most important role in explaining and interpreting the movement of people.

The point of departure of most economic theories – whether on a micro or a macro level – is the demand for labour, which prompts the migration of people. This demand can be due to a real shortage of labour, as was the case in the early 1960s when some West European countries recruited labourers from Mediterranean countries. It can, however, also be created because certain types of work are shunned by native labourers (cf. Portes, 1995c). However once economical circumstances, such as the demand for labour in industry or the low-wage secondary sector, change or no longer exist, the expectation that international migration will keep track with demand is not realised.

Several authors argue that international migration cannot be sufficiently explained by solely or mainly economical factors. For instance Hondagneu-Sotelo (1994, p. 187) states that although 'political and economic transformations may set the stage for migration, ... they do not write the script'. Massey *et al.* (1993, p. 448) have also convincingly argued that 'new conditions that arise in the course of migration come to function as independent causes themselves'. These authors describe a whole range of conditions, such as the growth of institutions and organisations that are set up to arrange the entry of immigrants. They also point to several socioeconomic factors that could be influenced by migration, such as the distribution of land and income, which in turn have a cumulative effect on migration (ibid., pp. 450–3). In migration system theories, where migration is regarded as the outcome of interacting macro and micro structures, authors also point to other important sociological elements to explain the continuation of migration, even in times when employment opportunities in traditional immigrant industries are disappearing (Castles and Miller, 1993, p. 22; Mahler, 1995, pp. 7–8).

One example of such a migration systems approach is the 'promigration cycle', which Portes and Rumbaut (1990) developed because of their dissatisfaction with push–pull theories. The promigration cycle is also one of the few theories to explicitly claim to deal with the forces behind illegal border crossing in search of employment. According to this model, macro as well as micro structures play an important role in the migration of undocumented immigrants. At the macro level, colonial or other historical linkages of political or economic intervention between countries are seen as important. These linkages have resulted in a restructuring of the economy of the country of emigration, whereby traditional lifestyles have slowly disappeared and new, more modern life patterns have evolved. Formal labour recruitment, accompanied by the establishment of social networks between countries, make it easier for people to migrate. According to the authors, people in the countries of emigration increasingly perceive migration as a means to satisfy new consumption ambitions. Instead of migration being the outcome of individual choice, following 'the push and pull of economic conditions', migration should be seen as the outcome of 'progressive network building' (ibid., pp. 232–3). The promigration cycle is an attractive model explaining the movement of people across political borders. It accommodates (global) economic restructuring processes and links them to the individual level by highlighting the importance of social networks. Within the promigration cycle, the authors also attribute a central role to the personal network as this gives the process its self-sustaining and cumulative character (ibid., p. 234; see also Chapter 9 of this volume). Of the various non-economic forces that stimulate and perpetuate international migration, the personal network seems to be one of the most important (cf. Boyd, 1989; Massey *et al.*, 1993). These issues, as they relate to undocumented immigrants and immigrant businesses, will be dealt with in the following section.

Immigrant entrepreneurship, personal networks and undocumented immigrants

Several types of immigrant or ethnic entrepreneurs are distinguished in the literature (cf. Portes, 1995a). First of all there are the middlemen minorities (Bonacich, 1973; see also Chapter 7 of this volume). Secondly there are the entrepreneurs who operate within so-called 'ethnic enclaves', which are defined as spatially clustered networks of businesses owned by members of the same minority that in the first instance serve the needs of coethnics. According to Zhou (1992, p. 4), who perceives the enclave economy as an alternative method of incorporation into mainstream society, entrepreneurs within these enclaves lean heavily on the ethnic solidarity displayed within the extended family or other ethnic institutions. Lastly there are immigrant entrepreneurs who act within ethnic occupational niches. According to Portes (1995a, p. 28), occupational niches are gradually transformed into ethnic occupational niches as employed individuals bring conationals from their network into the (not necessarily immigrant-owned) workplace.

This gradual transformation of an occupational niche bears some resemblance to the process of chain migration (Price, 1963), in which networks also play an essential role. Bovenkerk and Ruland (1992) describe several characteristics of ethnic firms. In their view these firms are mostly small urban enterprises that to a large extent are active in the informal sector. Bovenkerk and Ruland emphasise that these enterprises often start as family enterprises and flourish on the solidarity and trust within the network.

Portes and Sensenbrenner (1993; Portes, 1995a) have elaborated on these sources of social capital. In their search for mechanisms through which social structures affect economic action, these authors have introduced the concepts of 'solidarity' and 'enforceable trust'. Bounded solidarity, as defined by Portes (1995a) originates from the 'situational reaction of a class of people faced with common adversities', which can lead to internal solidarity and mutual support. The authors mention several factors that are important in activating this situational solidarity: cultural and linguistic differences, outside discrimination, exit opportunities and the presence of a cultural repertoire. Enforceable trust, on the other hand, can be seen as a source of social capital whereby individuals behave in certain predictable ways by anticipating and expecting rewards and sanctions linked to their group membership. The extent to which enforceable trust is present depends on the existence of valuable opportunities outside and inside the ethnic community, and on the possibility of sanctioning those members who disregard these unwritten laws (Portes and Sensenbrenner, 1993, pp. 1327–44).

If one takes a closer look at undocumented immigrants, their migration motives, their method of travel and their work, the *Leitmotif* in the lives of these immigrants is the personal network. Due to their illegal status in the host country these immigrants are highly dependent on the assistance of supportive family members, friends or locals. These networks are not only significant as a resource when travelling abroad, but also for the opportunities open to the undocumented immigrant in his or her new country of residence. The central importance of networks in the field of international migration is not new (Boyd, 1989, p. 639; Massey *et al.*, 1987, p. 5), but it appears that illegal immigrants are much more dependent on their network than is the case with legal immigrants. As Yücel (1987, p. 124) states, for undocumented immigrants 'all the stages of migration, from taking the decision to migrate to finding a job abroad, are performed within the actor's social network'. The importance of supportive immigrant networks for immigrant entrepreneurship has also been emphasised by Light *et al.* (1993, pp. 36–8), who describe three different functions of immigrant networks for immigrant entrepreneurship. Firstly, the network supplies low-cost coethnic labour to immigrant entrepreneurs. Secondly, migration networks feed economic information both to established immigrant entrepreneurs and to aspiring ones. Finally, migration networks provide various kinds of mutual aid and assistance in addition to information on credit and training.

However the solidarity that undocumented immigrants encounter from members of their community also has a negative side that has recently received the attention of researchers (see Chapter 8 of this volume). Mahler (1995, p. 225), for instance, minces no words in her 'narrative of disillusionment' on undocumented immigrants from Central and South America in New York when she states that within ethnic communities 'portrayals of solidarity may reflect a romanticization of the immigrant experience'. Undocumented immigrants not only enjoy the help and solidarity of members of their ethnic community, but also encounter disloyalty and are sometimes betrayed by 'friends' or even relatives to the authorities (cf. Böcker, 1994; Mahler, 1995; Staring, 1998). Seen in this perspective, social networks not only facilitate the migration and settlement of undocumented immigrants but can also impede or prevent the same processes. In this case, hospitality, solidarity and trust are accompanied by or substituted for hostility, disjunction and mistrust. In the next section the main focus will be on the different roles of undocumented immigrants in relation to immigrant businesses. When describing these different roles, some attention will be paid to the negative sides of the personal network and the consequences they may have for undocumented immigrants.

Undocumented immigrants as participants, promoters and producers of immigrant businesses

One can think of several possible roles that interlink international migration, undocumented immigrants and immigrant entrepreneurship. I shall distinguish three different 'P-roles' of undocumented immigrants in relation to immigrant businesses, namely those of participant, promoter or producer. In most of these examples it is not that clear whether it is the presence of undocumented immigrants that contributes to the start-up, growth or even survival of these immigrant firms, or whether it is the existence of these firms that encourages further international migration. As mentioned earlier, international migration often continues independently of the original reasons for migrations.

Firstly, the undocumented immigrant can be characterised as a *participant* in immigrant businesses, and this role is perhaps the best documented. As is often stated in the literature on ethnic entrepreneurship, these firms are – in addition to the possible use of strategies such as minimal investment, tax evasion and the use of cheap raw materials – highly dependent on the availability and effective use of cheap labour (Kloosterman *et al.*, 1997b; Zhou, 1992, p. 102). According to Waldinger, immigrant firm owners are often highly dependent on kin and coethnics. These employers frequently recruit premigration friends and acquaintances, or newly arrived immigrants who are recommended by relatives and friends already at work. They are loyal and relatively cheap workers (Waldinger, 1986, p. 158). Furthermore employers frequently have to deceive the authorities. Due to the restrictive immigration policies of most Western countries, new workers may arrive with a tourist visa but ultimately overstay and end up as undocumented immigrants. Recruitment in the home country can take place for several reasons. For instance there may be a lack of qualified workers (belonging to the same ethnic group) in the host country. The garment industry, with its highly specialised jobs, is well known for recruiting experienced workers in the home country (cf. Snowden, 1990). However employers more often look for undocumented workers in the vicinity, thereby further reducing their costs.

For employers, the advantage of using undocumented immigrants rather than legal immigrants working informally is not only restricted to the cheap labour they represent. These immigrants are easily accessible via the personal network, speak the same language and – because of their weak legal position – motivated. During my research among Turkish undocumented immigrants working for conational employers in Rotterdam it became clear that they were in no position to complain about their working conditions. Due to their marginalised position they had to put up with extremely long working hours, low, postponed or even no payment at all, the absence of insurance and, maybe worst of all (social) humiliation during their work.

Beside these informal activities there are also criminal immigrant businesses in which undocumented immigrants, due to their legal status, can occupy a special position. Prostitution is one of the best known 'criminal' branches in which female undocumented immigrants in particular find employment. Undocumented immigrants can also flourish in the drugs trade due to their status. Our research in Rotterdam revealed that certain criminally active undocumented immigrants, whose identity was difficult to discover, could not be deported by the immigration authorities, or only with great difficulty, and could therefore continue their criminal activities without running too many risks (Engbersen *et al.*, 1995).

Secondly, the undocumented immigrant can be portrayed as a *promoter* of immigrant businesses. The presence of undocumented immigrants has a certain influence on further migration to cities in advanced economies. Although most estimates of the number of undocumented immigrants have to be treated with caution, their concentration in certain cities and certain neighbourhoods within those cities contributes to the specific character of inner-city neighbourhoods. The presence of undocumented immigrants in these areas – irrespective of their reasons for migration – gives rise to a demand for entrepreneurs who aim their business at their own ethnic group. This is in line with the theoretical argument by Sassen (1991a, p. 315), who suggests that immigrants not only seek their own economic transformation but also constitute a captive market for ethnic shopkeepers. Although she does not explicitly distinguish between immigrants on the basis of their legal status, it seems obvious that both legal and undocumented immigrants fuel this demand. In the Netherlands for instance, some ethnic restaurants largely owe their survival to the presence of undocumented immigrants, who visit these places after work or during the day.

One can also call to mind several other immigrant businesses that flourish at least partly because of the presence of undocumented immigrants, for instance special offices from where they can make relatively cheap phone calls to their home countries. Likewise lodging houses, cheap hotels and pensions often rely heavily on undocumented immigrants as customers (cf. Burgers, 1995; Spierings, 1996). Another example is that of (illegal) contractors, who sometimes employ undocumented conationals. In the agricultural sector in the Netherlands, for instance, it is well known that contractors actively mediate for undocumented immigrants (cf. Jonkman-Te Winkel, 1994, pp. 27–9).

Undocumented immigrants may also contribute to the growing demand for the services of hustlers, racketeers, traffickers and counterfeiters of official documents. Such criminal entrepreneurs are flourishing thanks to increasingly restrictive immigration regimes and the great difficulties faced by many would-be immigrants, or even the impossibility of entering Western countries legally (cf. Massey *et al.*,

1993, p. 451). Although little research has been conducted on this kind of entrepreneurial activity, its importance must not be underestimated as experts estimate that such business is as lucrative as organised drug-related crime but with relatively shorter prison sentences (*NRC Handelsblad*, 8 March 1997).

Sometimes these enterprises operate at the individual level, but a huge and lucrative network also exists to transport migrants illegally to their chosen countries of destination.[6] In Japan, for instance, migrants are being smuggled in by the Japanese crime syndicate *Yakuza*, which is involved in many cases of organised illegal entry (Loiskandle, 1995). Recently Albanian smugglers asked up to US$1500 for a one-way trip from an Albanian coastal town to the port of Brindisi in Italy (*NRC Handelsblad*, 17 March 1997). Koser (1997), writing about Iranian asylum seekers, describes the extensive involvement of traffickers at all stages of the migration process. Traffickers have not only facilitated an exodus from Iran, but have also played a central role in planning escape routes across Europe to destinations chosen by them. In the case of the United States, much has been written about migrants who cross the Mexican–American border illegally and their dependence on the so-called 'coyotes'. Those who travel illegally to their country of destination are not only exposed to great physical danger but also incur high travel costs (cf. Mahler, 1995). Networks also flourish to accompany migrants across borders. The availability of entrepreneurs who offer illegal migration services to conationals or coethnics has give rise to a growing influx of undocumented immigrants. Sometimes round trips are offered that include a job in a European country, as is the case with Chinese immigrants, who usually ended up working in a Chinese restaurant (*NRC Handelsblad*, 8 March 1997). The presence of such traffickers and forgers has contributed to the continuation of international migration even where restrictive immigration laws apply.

In their third and most academically neglected role, undocumented immigrants can be depicted as *producers* of immigrant businesses. Undocumented immigrants may start a business of their own, thereby increasing the number of immigrant enterprises. At the beginning of this chapter two examples were given of undocumented immigrants who have started their own business: the rose sellers and the unauthorised taxi drivers. Among numerous other examples are barbers who give haircuts in coffeeshops, and the shoeshine boys and soft drink sellers found on the streets of many Western countries. The activities of all these entrepreneurs constitute what Mahler has called 'parallel institutions', defined as entrepreneurial activities initiated by immigrants so that they can fulfil their goals despite their marginalisation from mainstream institutions (Mahler, 1995, p. 29). In most cases such immigrant entrepreneurs act informally, although this is not always the case. The existence of these institutions caused some of the undocumented immigrants in our study to feel that the differences between living in Turkey and in the Netherlands were not that great. This in fact makes it even more attractive for would-be immigrants to take a chance, as no severe problems of adaptation are to be expected, thereby illustrating the cumulative causes described by Massey *et al.* (1993, pp. 451–4).

Conclusions

Explaining the migration and settlement of undocumented immigrants by looking solely or mainly at economic or labour-market factors takes too little account of the origin and motivations of the (undocumented) immigrants involved. Once the initial (economic) motives are triggered, other independent causes take over that result in international migration even in times when there is no economic demand for labourers. Consequently undocumented immigration and the presence of undocumented immigrants can only be partially explained by studying the labour market in general and immigrant entrepreneurship in particular. Although it is possible to identify some direct relationships between undocumented immigrants and immigrant business, in general these linkages are more indirect. In this chapter, when describing the three roles of undocumented immigrants in immigrant businesses – the 'P-roles' – these connections were unfolded.

The first and best documented role of such immigrants is as *participants* in immigrant businesses. Immigrant entrepreneurs often depend on undocumented employees as they are loyal, hard working and cheap. For their part the latter earn at least some kind of income, but they are not in a position to complain about bad working conditions. Nonetheless, due to increasingly restrictive immigration policies such jobs within the immigrant community are gaining in importance for undocumented immigrants.

Undocumented immigrants can also be characterised as *promoters* of immigrant businesses. By their number alone they boost the demand for the specific products provided by these businesses. Undocumented immigrants not only promote legal coethnic businesses, they also stimulate criminal activities such as forgery and trafficking. The presence and availability of criminal entrepreneurs in turn encourages and facilitates further migration.

In their third role, undocumented immigrants are *producers* of immigrant businesses as some start their own business, often small and to a large extent informal. These largely neglected entrepreneurial activities of undocumented immigrants, which deserve more systematic attention, highlight the lack of opportunities in the formal labour market.

Undocumented immigrants are participators, promoters and producers of immigrant businesses in a specific way that to some extent sets them apart from their legal coethnics. This is mainly the result of their legally weak and increasingly marginalised position in society. Unlike legal immigrants they cannot rely on the welfare state or claim social rights, so in many ways they are dependent on the solidarity and loyalty of their own ethnic community. However this puts them at risk being exploited by coethnics. The presence of unemployed undocumented immigrants indicates to some extent that the informal labour market is unable to provide sufficient jobs. This situation worsens the already vulnerable position of illegal immigrants as there are always others in their number who are willing and motivated to do the job.

This brings us to another important difference between legal and illegal immigrants, namely that of the personal network. Both groups have personal networks, but illegal immigrants depend heavily on a personal network, that is mostly restricted to members of their ethnic community, while legal immigrants can also turn to state or other institutions for help. Although many of the support structures within the community are typified by solidarity and trust, from the perspective of undocumented immigrants there can also be distrust, hostility, exploitation and even humiliation. These two opposite characteristics of personal networks may occur simultaneously, such that the solidarity displayed by legal conationals towards undocumented immigrants can smooth the path for their exploitation.

The significance of the distinction between undocumented and legal immigrants and its consequences for daily life also seems to depend on the local context. Legal status matters all the more in countries with extensive welfare provisions. In countries such as the United States, where these provisions are minimal and benefit payments are low, the distinction between the two types of immigrant blurs as they become competitors. In advanced welfare states such as the Netherlands, however, there is less competition between the two and few legal immigrants are forced into activities such as polishing shoes or selling roses to drunken lovers.

Notes

1   I would like to thank Leo Chavez, Godfried Engbersen, Robert Kloosterman
    and especially Jan Rath for their useful and stimulating comments on earlier
    versions of this article.
2   According to Marosi (1997), unauthorised taxi drivers use unmarked cars and
    go anywhere for a fare, including those city neighbourhoods where regular
    yellow cabs are hard to find.
3   I use the concepts of illegal immigrants and undocumented immigrants
    interchangeably.
4   Wentholt (1967, p. 189), for instance, writes that the majority of work per-
    mits in the Netherlands were handed out to these 'spontaneous workers'. In
    Germany it is estimated that during the 1960s about one third of Turkish
    immigrants originally came as 'tourists' (Martin, 1994a, p. 200).
5   In summer 1993 a research project was initiated at Utrecht University titled
    'The Unknown City: Life and Work of Undocumented Migrants in the City
    of Rotterdam'. An interdisciplinary team of researchers conducted fieldwork
    in Rotterdam – a harbour city of approximately 650 000 inhabitants – and
    interviewed 169 undocumented immigrants from several countries. I partici-
    pated in this research for my doctoral thesis and focused in particular on
    Turkish undocumented immigrants.
6   A large trade has also been developed around the deportation of undocu-
    mented immigrants (de Stoop, 1996).

References

Albert, M. (1991) *Capitalisme Contre Capitalisme* (Paris: Éditions du Seuil).

Aldrich, H. E. (1991) 'Methods in our madness?: Trends in entrepreneurship research', in D. Sexton and J. D. Kasarda (eds), *The State of the Art of Entrepreneurship* (Boston: PWS-Kent Publishing).

Aldrich, H., J. Cater, T. Jones and D. McEvoy (1981) 'Business development and self-segregation: Asian enterprise in three British cities', in C. Peach, V. Robinson and S. Smith (eds), *Ethnic Segregation in Cities* (London: Croom Helm).

Aldrich, H., J. Cater, T. Jones, D. McEvoy and P. Velleman (1985) 'Ethnic residential concentration and the protected market hypothesis', *Social Forces*, vol. 63, no. 4, pp. 996–1009.

Aldrich, H., T. Jones and D. McEvoy (1984) 'Ethnic advantage and minority business development', in R. Ward and R. Jenkins (eds), *Ethnic Communities in Business: Strategies for Economic Survival* (Cambridge: Cambridge University Press).

Aldrich, H. E. and P. R. Reese (1993) 'Does networking pay off? A panel study of entrepreneurs in the research triangle', *Frontiers of Entrepreneurship Research*, vol. 7, pp. 325–39.

Aldrich, H. and R. Waldinger (1990) 'Ethnicity and entrepreneurship', *Annual Review of Sociology*, vol. 16, pp. 111–35.

Aldrich, H., C. Zimmer and T. Jones (1986) 'Small business still speaks with the same voice: A replication of the voice of small business and the politics of survival', *Sociological Review*, vol. 34, pp. 335–56.

Aldrich, H., C. Zimmer and D. McEvoy (1989) 'Continuities in the study of ecological succession: Asian businesses in three British cities', *Social Forces*, vol. 67, no. 4, pp. 920–43.

Althauser, R. (1989) 'Internal labor markets', *Annual Review of Sociology*, vol. 15, pp. 143–61.

Ang, J. (1991) 'The theory of small business uniqueness and financial management', *Journal of Small Business Finance*, vol. 1, pp. 1–13.

Anthias, F. (1992) *Ethnicity, Class, Gender and Migration: Greek-Cypriots in Britain* (Aldershot: Avebury).

Appadurai, A. (1990) 'Disjuncture and difference in the global cultural economy', *Public Culture*, vol. 2, no. 2, pp. 1–24.

Appelbaum, R. P. and G. Gereffi (1994) 'Power and profits in the apparel commodity chain', in E. Bonacich, L. Cheng, N. Chinchilla, N. Hamilton and P. Ong (eds), *Global Production: The Apparel Industry in the Pacific Rim* (Philadelphia: Temple University Press).

Aris, S. (1970) *The Jews in Business* (London: Jonathan Cape).

Audretsch, D. (1993) 'New firm formation activity in US manufacturing', in B. Johannesson, C. Karlsson and D. Storey (eds), *Small Business Dynamics: International, National and Regional Perspectives* (London: Routledge).

Auster, E. and H. E. Aldrich (1984) 'Small business vulnerability, ethnic enclaves and ethnic enterprise', in R. Ward and R. Jenkins (eds), *Ethnic Communities in Business: Strategies for Economic Survival* (Cambridge: Cambridge University Press).

Bach, R. (1992) 'Settlement policies in the United States', in G. Freeman and J. Jupp (eds), *Nations of Immigrants: Australia, the United States, and International Migration* (Melbourne and New York: Oxford University Press).

Bagnasco, A. and C. Sabel (eds) (1995) *Small and Medium-size Enterprises* (London: Pinter).

Bailey, N., A. Bowes and D. Sim (1995) 'The Chinese community in Scotland', *Scottish Geographical Magazine*, vol. 110, pp. 66–75.

Bailey, T. (1987) *Immigrant and Native Workers: Contrasts and Competition* (Boulder, CO: Westview).

Bailey, T. and R. Waldinger (1991) 'The changing ethnic/racial division of labor', in J. H. Mollenkopf and M. Castells (eds), *Dual City: Restructuring of New York* (New York: Russell Sage Foundation).

Bakker, E. S. J. and L. J. Tap (1987) *Etnische Ondernemers in Rotterdam en Utrecht* (Den Haag: Hoofdbedrijfschap Ambachten).

Barrett, G. A. (1997) 'Multiple Disadvantage and Black Enterprise: Aspects of South Asian and African-Caribbean Business', unpublished PhD thesis, Liverpool, John Moores University.

Barrett, G. A., T. P. Jones and D. McEvoy (1996) 'Ethnic minority business: Theoretical discourse in Britain and North America', *Urban Studies*, vol. 33, nos 4/5, pp. 783–809.

Basu, A. (1995) *Asian Small Businesses in Britain: An Exploration of Entrepreneurial Activity*, University of Reading discussion paper 303, series A, volume VII.

Bates, T. (1994) 'Social resources generated by group support may not be beneficial to Asian immigrant-owned small businesses', *Social Forces*, vol. 72, pp. 671–89.

Bauböck, R. (1994) *Transnational Citizenship: Membership and Rights in International Migration* (Aldershot: Edward Elgar).

Beblawi, H. and G. Luciani (1987) *The Rentier State* (London: Croom Helm).

Bechhofer, F. and B. Elliott (eds) (1981) *The Petite Bourgeoisie: Comparative Studies of the Uneasy Stratum* (London: Macmillan).

Beck, V. (1989) 'An unhealthy lack of insurance', *UCLA Magazine*, vol. 1, p. 19.

Berghe, P. van den (1978) *Race and Racism: A Comparative Perspective* (New York: Wiley).

Bertaux, D. and I. Bertaux-Wiame (1981) 'Artisanal bakery in France: How it lives and why it survives', in F. Bechhofer and B. Elliott (eds), *The Petite Bourgeoisie: Comparative Studies of the Uneasy Stratum* (London: Macmillan).

Bester, H. (1987) 'The role of collateral in credit markets with imperfect information', *European Economic Review*, vol. 31, pp. 887–99.

Betts, K. (1988) *Ideology and Immigration: Australia 1976 to 1987* (Melbourne: Melbourne University Press).

Binks, M., C. Ennew and G. Reed (1992) 'Small businesses and their banks 1992', Forum of Private Business Report.

Birch, D. (1987) *Job Creation in America: How Our Smallest Corporations Put the Most People to Work* (New York: Free Press).

Birrell, R. (1992) 'Problems of immigration control in liberal democracies: The Australian experience', in G. Freeman and J. Jupp (eds), *Nations of Immigrants: Australia, the United States, and International Migration* (Melbourne and New York: Oxford University Press).

Birrell, R. (1994) 'Immigration control in Australia', *The Annals*, no. 534, pp. 106–17.

Blanchflower, D. and A. Oswald (1990) *What Makes a Young Entrepreneur?*, working paper no. 3252 (Cambridge, Mass.: National Bureau of Economic Research).

Blaschke, J., J. Boissevain, H. Grotenbreg, I. Joseph, M. Morokvasic and R. Ward (1990) 'European trends in ethnic business', in R. Waldinger, H. Aldrich, R. Ward and Associates (eds), *Ethnic Entrepreneurs: Immigrant Business in Industrial Societies* (London: Sage).

Bloeme, L. and R. van Geuns (1987) *Ongeregeld Ondernemen: Een Onderzoek naar Informele Bedrijvigheid* (Den Haag: Ministerie van Sociale Zaken en Werkgelegenheid).

Bluestone, B. and B. Harrison (1987) 'The impact of private disinvestment on workers and their communities', in R. Peet (ed.), *International Capitalism and Industrial Restructuring* (Boston: Allen and Unwin).

Böcker, A. (1994) *Turkse Migranten en Sociale Zekerheid: Van Onderlinge Zorg naar Overheidszorg?* (Amsterdam: Amsterdam University Press).

Bodnar, J. (1985) *The Transplanted: A History of Immigrants in Urban America* (Bloomington: University of Indiana Press).

Bodnar, J., R. Simon and M. Weber (1982) *Lives of Their Own: Blacks, Italians, and Poles in Pittsburgh, 1900–1960* (Urbana: University of Illinois Press).

Body-Gendrot, S. and E. Ma Mung (1992) 'Entrepreneurs entre deux mondes', *Revue Européenne des Migrations Internationales, Special issue*, vol. 8, no. 1.

Böhning, W. R. and D. Maillat (1974) *The Effects of the Employment of Foreign Workers* (Paris: OECD).

Boissevain, J. F. (1974) *Friends of Friends: Networks, Manipulators, and Coalitions* (New York: St Martin's Press).

Boissevain, J. F. (1984) 'Small entrepreneurs in contemporary Europe', in R. Ward and R. Jenkins (eds), *Ethnic Communities in Business: Strategies for Economic Survival* (Cambridge: Cambridge University Press).

Boissevain, J. F. (1992) 'Les entreprises ethniques aux Pays-Bas', *Revue Européenne des Migrations Internationales*, vol. 8, no. 1, pp. 97–106.

Boissevain, J. and H. Grotenbreg (1986) 'Culture, structure, and ethnic enterprise: The Surinamese in Amsterdam', *Ethnic and Racial Studies*, vol. 9, no. 1, pp. 1–23.

Bonacich, E. (1972) 'A theory of ethnic antagonism: The split labor market', *American Sociological Review*, vol. 37, pp. 549–59.

Bonacich, E. (1973) 'A theory of middleman minorities', *American Sociological Review*, vol. 38, pp. 583–94.

Bonacich, E. (1975) 'Abolition, the extension of slavery, and the position of free blacks: A study of split labor markets in the United States, 1830–1865', *American Journal of Sociology*, vol. 81, pp. 601–28.

Bonacich, E. (1976) 'Advanced capitalism and black/white relations in the United States: A split labor market analysis', *American Sociological Review*, vol. 41, pp. 34–51.

Bonacich, E. (1979) 'The past, present and future of split labor market theory', *Research in Race and Ethnic Relations*, vol. 1, pp. 17–64.

Bonacich, E. (1981a) 'Capitalism and race relations in South Africa: A split labor market analysis', in M. Zeitlin (ed.), *Political Power and Social Theory*, vol. 2 (Greenwich, CT: JAI Press).

Bonacich, E. (1981b) 'Reply to burawoy', in M. Zeitlin (ed.), *Political Power and Social Theory*, vol. 2 (Greenwich, CT: JAI Press).

Bonacich, E. (1993) 'The other side of ethnic entrepreneurship: A dialogue with Waldinger, Aldrich, Ward and associates', *International Migration Review*, vol. 27, no. 3, pp. 685–92.

Bonacich, E. (1994) 'Asians in the Los Angeles garment industry', in P. Ong, E. Bonacich and L. Cheng (eds), *The New Asian Immigration in Los Angeles and Global Restructuring* (Philadelphia: Temple University).

Bonacich, E. and J. Modell (1980) *The Economic Basis of Ethnic Solidarity* (Berkeley: University of California Press).

Borjas, G. J. (1987) 'Self-selection and the earnings of immigrants', *American Economic Review*, vol. 77, pp. 551–3.

Borjas, G. J. (1988) *International Differences in the Labor Market Performance of Immigrants* (Kalamazoo, MI: W. E. Upjohn Institute).

Borjas, G. J. (1989) 'Economic theory and international migration', *International Migration Review*, vol. 23, 457–85.

Borjas, G. J. (1990) *Friends or Strangers? The Impact of Immigrants on the Economy* (New York: Basic Books).

Bornschier, V. and H. Stamm, (1990) 'Transnational corporations', in A. Martinelli and N. J. Smelser (eds), *Economy and Society* (Newbury Park: Sage).

Borowski, A. and A. Nash (1994) 'Business migration', in H. Adelman *et al.* (eds), *Immigration and Refugee Policy: Australia and Canada Compared*, vol. I (Melbourne: Melbourne University Press).

Bourdieu, P. (1973) 'Cultural reproduction and social reproduction', in R. Brown (ed.), *Knowledge, Education and Cultural Change* (London: Tavistock).

Bourdieu, P. (1981) 'Le capital social: Notes provisoires', *Actes de la Recherche en Sciences Sociales*, vol. 3, pp. 2–3.

Bourdieu, P. and M. de Saint Martin, (1978) 'Le patronat', *Actes de la Recherche en Sciences Sociales*, vol. 1, pp. 3–82.

Bovenkerk, F. (1982) 'Op eigen kracht omhoog: Etnisch ondernemerschap en de oogkleppen van het minderhedencircuit', *Intermediair*, vol. 18, pp. 1–11.

Bovenkerk, F., A. Eijken and W. Bovenkerk-Teerink (1983) *Italiaans IJs. De Opmerkelijke Historie van de Italiaanse IJsbereiders in Nederland* (Meppel/ Amsterdam: Boom).

Bovenkerk, F., R. Miles and G. Verbunt (1990) 'Racism, migration and the state in Western Europe: A case for comparative analysis', *International Sociology*, vol. 5, no. 4, pp. 475–90.

Bovenkerk, F. and L. Ruland (1992) 'Artisan entrepreneurs: Two centuries of Italian immigration to the Netherlands', *International Migration Review*, vol. XXVI, no. 3, pp. 927–39.

Boxman, E., P. de Graaf and H. Flap (1991) 'Social capital, human capital, and income attainment: The impact of social capital and human capital on the income attainment of Dutch managers', *Social Networks*, vol. 13, pp. 51–73.

Boyd, M. (1989) 'Family and personal networks in international migration: Recent developments and new agendas', *International Migration Review*, vol. 23, no. 3, pp. 638–71.

Bozorgmehr, M. and G. Sabagh (1991) 'Iranian exiles and immigrants in Los Angeles', in A. Fathi (ed.), *Iranian Refugees and Exiles since Khomeini* (Costa Mesa, CA: Mazda).

Brah, A. (1996) *Cartographies of Diaspora: Contesting Identities* (London: Routledge).

Brenner, R. and M. Glick (1991) 'The regulation approach: Theory and history', *New Left Review*, no. 188, pp. 45–119.

Brody, D. (1960) *Steelworkers in America: The Non-Union Era* (Cambridge, MA: Harvard University Press).

Brüderl, J., P. Preisendörfer and R. Ziegler (1992) 'Survival chances of newly founded business organizations', *American Sociological Review*, vol. 57, pp. 227–42.

Brüderl, J., P. Preisendörfer and R. Ziegler (1996) *Der Erfolg Neugegründeter Betriebe: Eine Empirische Studie zu den Chancen und Risiken von Unternehmensgründungen* (Berlin: Duncker and Humblot).

Brusco, S. (1982) 'The Emilian model: Productive decentralisation and social integration', *Cambridge Journal of Economics*, vol. 6, pp. 167–84.

Buckland, R. and E. Davis (eds) (1995) *Finance for Growing Enterprises* (London: Routledge).

Bull, A., M. Pitt and J. Szarka (1993) *Entrepreneurial Textile Communities. A Comparative Study of Small Textile and Clothing Firms* (London: Chapman & Hall).

Burgers, J. (1995) *Niet Thuis: De Woonsituatie van Illegale Vreemdelingen in Rotterdam* (Utrecht: Onderzoekschool AWSB).

Burgers, J. and G. Engbersen (1995) 'Mondialisering, migratie en illegale vreemdelingen', *Amsterdams Sociologisch Tijdschrift*, vol. 22, pp. 225–49.

Burstein, M., L. Hardcastle and A. Parkin (1994) 'Immigration management control and its policy implications', in H. Adelman *et al.* (eds), *Immigration and Refugee Policy: Australia and Canada Compared*, vol. I (Melbourne: Melbourne University Press).

Burt, R. S. (1992) *Structural Holes: The Social Structure of Competition* (Cambridge: Harvard University Press).

Calavita, K. (1994a) 'Italy and the new immigration', in W. Cornelius, P. Martin and J. Hollifield (eds), *Controlling Immigration: A Global Perspective* (Stanford, CA: Stanford University Press).

Calavita, K. (1994b) 'US immigration and policy responses: The limits of legislation', in W. Cornelius, P. Martin and J. Hollifield (eds), *Controlling Immigration: A Global Perspective* (Stanford, CA: Stanford University Press).

Campani, G. (1995) 'Women migrants: From marginal subjects to social actors', in R. Cohen (ed.), *The Cambridge Survey of World Migration* (Cambridge: Cambridge University Press).

Carroll, G. R. (1984) 'Organizational ecology', *Annual Review of Sociology*, vol. 10, pp. 71–93.

Cassarino, J. P. (1997) *The Theories of Ethnic Entrepreneurship, and the Alternative Arguments of Social Action and Network Analysis*, EUI working paper SPS no. 97/1 (Badia Fiesolana, San Domenico, FI: European University Institute, Department of Political and Social Sciences).

Casson, M. (1982) *The Entrepreneur: An Economic Theory* (Oxford: Martin Robertson).

Castells, M. (1993) 'European cities, the informational society, and the global economy', *Tijdschrift voor Economische en Sociale Geografie*, vol. 84, pp. 247–57.

Castells, M. and A. Portes (1989) 'World underneath: The origins, dynamics and effects of the informal economy', in A. Portes, M. Castells and L. A. Benton (eds), *The Informal Economy: Studies in Advanced and Less Developed Countries* (Baltimore, MD: Johns Hopkins University Press).

Castles, S. and G. Kosack (1973) *Immigrant Workers and Class Structure in Western Europe* (London, New York and Toronto: Oxford University Press).

Castles, S. and G. Kosack (1985) *Immigrant Workers and Class Structure in Western Europe*, 2nd edn (Oxford: Oxford University Press).

Castles, S. and M. J. Miller, (1993) *The Age of Migration: International Population Movements in the Modern World* (London: Macmillan).

Castles, F. and D. Mitchell (1993) 'Worlds of welfare and families of nations', in F. Castles (ed.), *Families of Nations: Patterns of Public Policy in Western Democracies* (Aldershot: Dartmouth).

Castles, S. *et al.* (1989) *The Recognition of Overseas Trade Qualifications* (Canberra: Bureau of Immigration Research).

Cater, J. and T. Jones (1979) 'Ethnic, residential space: The case of Asians in Bradford', *Tijdschrift voor Economische en Sociale Geografie*, vol. 70, pp. 86–97.

CBS (Central Bureau of Statistics) (several years) *Statistiek van de Aan-, Af-en Doorvoer* (The Hague: CBS).

Champion, A. G. (1994) 'International migration and demographic change in the developed world', *Urban Studies*, vol. 31, nos 4/5, pp. 653–77.

Chapman, B. and R. Iredale (1993) 'Immigrant qualifications: Recognition and relative wage outcomes', *International Migration Review*, vol. 27, no. 2, pp. 359–87.

Cheng, L. and G. Gereffi (1994) 'US retailers and Asian garment production', in E. Bonacich, L. Cheng, N. Chinchilla, N. Hamilton and P. Ong (eds), *Global Production: The Apparal Industry in the Pacific Rim* (Philadelphia: Temple University Press).

Chesire, P. (1995) 'A new phase of urban development in Western Europe?: The evidence for the 1980s', *Urban Studies*, vol. 32, pp. 1045–63.

Clark, P. and M. Rughani (1983) 'Asian entrepreneurs in wholesaling and manufacturing in Leicester', *New Community*, vol. 11, pp. 23–33.

Clark, W. A. V. (1998) 'Mass migration and local outcomes: Is international migration to the United States creating a new urban underclass?', *Urban Studies*, vol. 35, no. 3, 371–83.

Clarke, R. and T. McGuinness (eds) (1987) *The Economics of the Firm* (Oxford: Blackwell).

Coffey, W. J. (1996) 'The "newer" international division of labour', in P. W. Daniels and W. F. Lever (eds), *The Global Economy in Transition* (Harlow: Addison Wesley Longman).

Cohen, R. (1987) *The New Helots: Migrants in the International Division of Labour* (Aldershot: Gower).

Cohen, R. (1995) 'Prologue', in R. Cohen (ed.), *The Cambridge Survey of World Migration* (Cambridge: Cambridge University Press).

Cohen, R. and J. Henderson (1982) 'The International Restructuring of Capital and Labor: Britain and Hong Kong', paper presented to ISA Tenth World Congress of Sociology, August.

Cohen, S. (1983) *American Modernity and Jewish Identity* (New York: Tavistock).

Coleman, J. S. (1987) 'Norms as social capital', in G. Radnitzky and P. Bernholz (eds), *Economic Imperialism* (New York: Paragon House).

Coleman, J. S. (1988) 'Social capital in the creation of human capital', *American Journal of Sociology*, vol. 94 (supplement), pp. 95–120.

Coleman, J. S. (1990) *Foundations of Social Theory* (Cambridge: Belknapp Press).

Commission for the Study of International Migration and Cooperative Economic Development (1990) *Unauthorized Migration: An Economic Development Response* (Washington, DC: USGPO).

Cornelius, W. (1994) 'Spain: The uneasy transition from labor exporter to labor importer', in W. Cornelius, P. Martin and J. Hollifield (eds), *Controlling Immigration: A Global Perspective* (Stanford, CA: Stanford University Press).

Cornelius, W., P. Martin and J. Hollifield (eds) (1994a) *Controlling Immigration: A Global Perspective* (Stanford, CA: Stanford University Press).

Cornelius, W., P. Martin and J. Hollifield (1994b) 'Introduction: The ambivalent quest for immigration control', in W. Cornelius, P. Martin and J. Hollifield (eds), *Controlling Immigration: A Global Perspective* (Stanford CA: Stanford University Press).

Cox, D. and P. Glenn (1994) 'Illegal immigration and refugee claims', in. H. Adelman *et al.* (eds), *Immigration and Refugee Policy: Australia and Canada Compared*, vol. I (Melbourne: Melbourne University Press).

Craig, J. (1994) *The Face of Fashion* (London: Routledge).

Creed, R. and R. Ward (1987) *Black Business Enterprise in Wales* (South Glamorgan: CRE).

Cross, M. and R. Waldinger (1992) 'Migrant minorities and the ethnic division of labour', in S. Fainstein, D. Gordon and M. Harloe (eds), *Divided Cities: New York and London in the Contemporary World* (Cambridge, MA: Blackwell), pp. 151–74.

Curran, J., R. Blackburn and A. Woods (1991) 'Profiles of the Small Business in the Service Sector', paper to 'ESRC Small Business Initiative', University of Warwick, 18 April.

Davis, F. (1992) *Fashion, Culture and Identity* (Chicago, Ill.: University of Chicago Press).

Dhaliwal, S. and V. Amin (1995) *Profiles of Five Asian Entrepreneurs* (London: Asian Business Institute).

Dicken, P. (1992) *Global Shift: The Internationalization of Economic Activity*, 2nd edn (London: Paul Chapman).

Dijst, M. J., M. Hessels, R. van Kempen *et al.* (1984) *Onder de Markt: Een Onderzoek naar Marokkaanse, Surinaamse en Turkse Ondernemers in de Oude Pijp* (Amsterdam: Instituut voor Sociale Geografie, Universiteit van Amsterdam).

Dijst, M. J. and R. van Kempen (1991) 'Minority business and the hidden dimension: The influence of urban contexts on the development of ethnic enterprise', *Tijdschrift voor Economische en Sociale Geografie*, vol. 82, no. 2, pp. 128–38.

Dirks, G. (1995) *Controversy and Complexity: Canadian Immigration Policy during the 1980s* (Montreal: McGill-Queen's University Press).

Doeringer, P. and M. J. Piore (1971) *Internal Labor Markets and Manpower Analysis* (Lexington: Heath).

Eccles, R. G. and H. C. White (1988) 'Price and authority in inter-profit center transactions', *American Journal of Sociology*, vol. 94 (supplement), pp. 17–51.

Economic Council of Canada (1991) *Economical and Social Impacts of Immigration* (Ottawa: Minister of Supply and Services Canada).

EIM (Economic Institute for Middle and Small-sized Firms) (1995) *The European Observatory for Small and Middle-Sized Enterprises* (Zoetermeer: EIM).

Elbaum, B. (1984) 'The making and shaping of job and pay structures in the iron and steel industry', in P. Osterman (ed.), *Internal Labor Markets* (Cambridge: MIT Press).

Engbersen, G., J. van der Leun and P. Willems (1995) *Over de Verwevenheid van Criminaliteit en Illegaliteit* (Utrecht: Vakgroep Algemene Sociale Wetenschappen, Rijksuniversiteit Utrecht).

Epstein, R. A. (1994) 'The moral and practical dilemmas of an underground economy', *Yale Law Journal*, vol. 103, no. 8, pp. 2157–78.

Erickson, B. H. (1996) 'Culture, class, and connections', *American Journal of Sociology*, vol. 102, pp. 217–51.

Eskinasi, M. and T. Kleine (1995) 'Commotie in het Amsterdamse Chinatown', *Rooilijn*, vol. 2, pp. 77–81.

Esping-Andersen, G. (1990) *The Three Worlds of Welfare Capitalism* (Cambridge: Polity Press).

Esping-Andersen, G. (ed.) (1993) *Changing Classes* (London, Thousand Oaks and New Delhi: Sage).

Esping-Andersen, G. (1996a) 'After the golden age?: Welfare state dilemmas in a global economy', in G. Esping-Andersen (ed.), *Welfare States in Transition: National Adaptations in Global Economies* (London, Thousand Oaks and New Delhi: Sage).

Esping-Andersen, G. (ed.) (1996b) *Welfare States in Transition: National Adaptations in Global Economies* (London, Thousand Oaks and New Delhi: Sage).

Esping-Andersen, G. (1996c) 'Welfare states without work: The impasse of labour shedding and familialism in continental European social policy' in G. Esping-Andersen (ed.), *Welfare States in Transition: National Adaptations in Global Economies* (London, Thousand Oaks and New Delhi: Sage).

Evans, D. and B. Jovanovic (1989) 'Estimates of a model of entrepreneurial choice under liquidity constraints', *Journal of Political Economy*, vol. 95, pp. 657–74.

Fainstein, S. S., I. Gordon and M. Harloe (1992) *Divided Cities: New York and London in the Contemporary World* (Oxford: Blackwell).

Fassmann, H. and R. Münz (eds) (1994) *European Migration in the Late Twentieth Century: Historical Patterns, Actual Trends, and Social Implications* (Laxenburg: International Institute for Applied Systems Analysis).

Feige, E. (1990) 'Defining and estimating underground and informal economies: The new institutional economics approach', *World Development*, vol. 18, no. 7, pp. 989–1002.

Fernández Kelly, M. P. (1994) 'Social and cultural capital in the urban ghetto', in A. Portes (ed.), *The Economic Sociology of Immigration: Essays on Networks, Ethnicity, and Entrepreneurship* (New York: Russell Sage).

Fernández Kelly, M. P. and A. M. Garcia (1989) 'Informalization at the core: Hispanic women, homework, and the advanced capitalist state', in A. Portes, M. Castells and L. A. Benton (eds), *The Informal Economy: Studies in Advanced and Less Developed Countries* (Baltimore, MD: Johns Hopkins University Press).

Fielding, A. (1993) 'Mass migration and economic restructuring', in R. King (ed.), *Mass Migration in Europe: The Legacy and the Future* (Chichester: John Wiley and Sons).

Fischer, C. (1982) *To Dwell among Friends* (Chicago, Ill.: University of Chicago Press).

Fix, M. (ed.) (1991) *The Paper Curtain: Employer Sanctions' Implementation, Impact and Reform* (Washington, DC: The Urban Institute).

Flap, H. (1988) 'The research program of a social capital theory', in H. Flap (ed.), *Conflict, Loyalty and Violence* (Bern: Peter Lang).

Flap, H. (1991) 'Social capital in the reproduction of inequality, a review', *Comparative Sociology of Family, Health and Education*, vol. 20, pp. 6179–202.

Flap, H. (1996) ' "No Man is an Island": The Research Program of a Social Capital Theory', unpublished manuscript, University of Utrecht.

Florax, R. J. G. M. and V. A. J. M. Schutjens (1996) 'The Spatial Dynamics of Firm Formation and Close Down', paper presented at the 36th European Congress of the Regional Science Association, Zurich, 26–30 August.

Freeman, G. (1992) 'Migration policy and politics in the receiving states', *International Migration Review*, vol. 26, pp. 1144–67.

Freeman, G. (1994a) 'Can liberal states control unwanted migration?', *The Annals*, no. 534, pp. 17–30.

Freeman, G. (1994b) 'The Quest for Skill: A Comparative analysis', paper presented at a conference at the MIT, Cambridge, MA.

Freeman, G. (1995) 'Modes of immigration politics in liberal democratic states', *International Migration Review*, vol. 29, pp. 881–902.

Freeman, G. and J. Jupp (eds) (1992) *Nations of Immigrants: Australia, the United States, and International Migration* (Melbourne and New York: Oxford University Press).

Fröbel, F., J. Heinrichs and O. Kreye (1980) *The New International Division of Labor: Structural Unemployment in Industrial Countries and Industrialisation in Developing Countries* (Cambridge: Cambridge University Press).

Fröbel, F., J. Heinrichs and O. Kreye (1986) *Umbruch in der Weltwirtschaft: Die Globale Strategie: Verbilligung der Arbeitskraft/Flexibilisierung der Arbeid/Neue Technologien* (Hamburg: Rowohlt).

Ganguly, P. (1985) 'Life span analysis of business in the UK 1973–1982', *British Business*, vol. 12, pp. 838–45.

Garcia y Griego, M. (1994) 'Canada: Flexibility and control in immigration and refugee policy', in W. Cornelius, P. Martin and J. Hollifield (eds), *Controlling Immigraion: A Global Perspective* (Stanford, CA: Stanford University Press).

Gasperz, J. B. R. and W. van Voorden (1987) 'Spatial aspects of internal labour markets', *Tijdschrift voor Economische en Sociale Geografie*, vol. 78, no. 5, pp. 359–65.

Geertz, C. (1963) *Peddlers and Princes: Social Change and Modernization in Two Indonesian Towns* (Chicago, Ill.: University of Chicago Press).

Glazer, N. and D. P. Moynihan (1962) *Beyond the Melting Pot* (Cambridge, MA: MIT Press).

Goldscheider, C. and A. Zuckerman (1984) *The Transformation of the Jews* (Chicago, Ill.: Chicago University Press).

Gordon, D. (1988) 'The global economy: New edifice or crumbling foundations', *New Left Review*, vol. 168, pp. 24–64.

Gottdiener, M. and N. Komninos (1989) 'Introduction', in M. Gottdiener and N. Komninos (eds), *Capitalist Development and Crisis Theory: Accumulation, Regulation, and Spatial Restructuring* (New York: St Martins Press).

Gottlieb, P. (1987) *Making Their Own Way* (Urbana: University of Illinois Press).

Gould, W. B. (1977) *Black Workers in White Unions* (Ithaca, NY: Cornell University Press).

Graaf, N.-D. de and H. Flap (1988) 'With a little help from my friends: Social resources as an explanation of occupational status and income in the

Netherlands, the United States and West Germany', *Social Forces*, vol. 67, pp. 453–72.

Granovetter, M. (1973) 'The strength of weak ties', *American Journal of Sociology*, vol. 78, pp. 1360–81.

Granovetter, M. (1984) 'Small is bountiful: Labour market and establishment size', *American Sociological Review*, vol. 49, pp. 323–34.

Granovetter, M. (1985), 'Economic action and social structure: The problem of embeddedness', *American Journal of Sociology*, vol. 91, no. 3, pp. 481–510.

Granovetter, M. (1992) 'Economic institutions as social constructions: A framework for analysis', *Acta Sociologica*, vol. 35, pp. 3–11.

Granovetter, M. (1995) 'The economic sociology of firms and entrepreneurs', in A. Portes (ed.), *The Economic Sociology of Immigration: Essays on Networks, Ethnicity, and Entrepreneurship* (New York: Russell Sage).

Green, N. (1985) *Les Travailleurs Immigres Juifs à la Belle Epoque* (Paris: Fayard).

Greenberg, S. B. (1980) *Race and Class in Capitalist Development* (New Haven, CT: Yale University Press).

Grieco, M. S. (1987) *Keeping It in the Family: Social Networks and Employment Chance* (Oxford: Oxford University Press).

Gross, N. (ed.) (1975) *The Economic History of the Jews* (New York: Schocken).

Grossman, J. P. (1989) *Land of Hope* (Chicago, Ill.: University of Chicago Press).

Hall, P. (1993) 'Forces shaping Europe', *Urban Studies*, vol. 30, pp. 883–98.

Hammar, T. (1985) 'Sweden', in T. Hammar (ed.), *European Immigration Policy: A Comparative Perspective* (Cambridge: Cambridge University Press).

Hamnett, C. (1994) 'Social polarisation in global cities: Theory and evidence', *Urban Studies*, vol. 31, pp. 401–24.

Hamnett, C. (1996) 'Why Sassen is wrong: A response to Burgers', *Urban Studies*, vol. 33, no. 1, pp. 107–11.

Hannerz, U. (1980) *Exploring the City: Inquires toward an Urban Anthropology* (New York: Columbia University Press).

Harrison, B. and B. Bluestone (1988) *The Great U-Turn: Corporate Restructuring and the Polarizing of America* (New York: Basic Books).

Harvey, D. (1989) *The Condition of Postmodernity* (Oxford: Basil Blackwell).

Haugen, R. (1995) *Modern Investment Theory*, 2nd edn (Englewood Cliffs, NJ: Prentice-Hall).

Häussermann, H. and I. Oswald (eds) (1997) *Zuwanderung und Stadtentwicklung*, Leviathan, special issue, 17.

Hawkins, F. (1989) *Critical Years in Immigration: Canada and Australia Compared* (Montreal: McGill-Queen's University Press).

Hawthorne, L. (1994) *Labour Market Barriers for Immigrant Engineers in Australia* (Canberra: Bureau of Immigration and Population Research).

Hillmann, F. (1996) 'Immigrants in Milan: Gender and household strategies', in C. C. Roseman, H. D. Laux and G. Thieme (eds), *Ethnicity: Geographic Perspectives on Ethnic Change in Modern Cities* (London: Rowman and Littlefield).

Hiltzik, M. A. (1996) 'Taking stock of CEO Pay', *Los Angeles Times*, 10 May, section 1, p. 1.

Hiro, D. (1971) *Black British: White British* (London: Eyre and Spottiswood).

Hollifield, J. (1992) *Immigrants, Markets, and States* (Cambridge: Harvard University Press).

Hollifield, J. (1994) 'Immigration and republicanism in France: The hidden consensus, in W. Cornelius, P. Martin and J. Hollifield (eds), *Controlling Immigration: A Global Perspective* (Stanford, CA: Stanford University Press).

Hondagneu-Sotelo, P. (1994) *Gendered Transitions: Mexican Experiences of Immigration* (Berkeley: University of California Press).

Hoover, E. M. and R. Vernon (1962) *Anatomy of a Metropolis: The Changing Distribution of People and Jobs within the New York Metropolitan Region* (Garden City, NY: Doubleday).

Hugo, G. (1995) 'Illegal international migration in Asia', in R. Cohen (ed.), *The Cambridge Survey of World Migration* (Cambridge: Cambridge University Press).

Huygen, F. (1989) *De Kwalitatieve Struktuur van de Werkgelegenheid in Nederland*, vol. III (Den Haag: OSA Werkdocumenten).

Illeris, S. (1986) 'New firm creation in Denmark: The importance of cultural background', in D. Keeble and E. Wever (eds), *New Firms and Regional Development* (London: Croom Helm).

INS (Immigration and Naturalization Service) (1993) *INS Factbook* (Washington, DC: Department of Justice).

Jacoby, S. (1985) *Employing Bureaucracy: Managers, Unions, and the Transformation of Work in American Industry, 1900–1945* (New York: Columbia University Press).

Jenkins, R. (1984) 'Divisions over the international division of labour', *Capital and Class*, vol. 22, pp. 28–57.

Jenks, R. (1992) *Immigration and Nationality Policies of Leading Migration Nations* (Washington, DC: Center for Immigration Studies).

Jobse, R. B. and S. Musterd (1994) *De Stad in het Informatietijdperk: Dynamiek, Problemen en Potenties* (Assen: Van Gorcum).

Johannesson, B., C. Karlsson and D. Storey (eds) (1993) *Small Business Dynamics: International, National and Regional Perspectives* (London: Routledge).

Jones, T. (1981) 'Small business development and the Asian community in Britain', *New Community*, vol. 9, pp. 467–77.

Jones, T. (1989) 'Ethnic Minority Business and the Post-Fordist Entrepreneurial Renaissance', paper presented at the Conference on Industrial Restructuring and Social Change in Western Europe, University of Durham, 26–28 September.

Jones, T. (1993) *Britain's Ethnic Minorities* (London: Policy Studies Institute).

Jones, T.J. Cater, P. de Silva and D. McEvoy (1989) 'Ethnic Business and Community Need', report to the Commission for Racial Equality, Liverpool, Liverpool Polytechnic.

Jones, T. and D. McEvoy (1992) 'Ressources ethniques et egalites des chances: Les entreprises, indo-pakistanaises en Grande-Bretagne et au Canada', *Revue Européenne des Migrations Internationales*, vol. 8, pp. 107–25.

Jones, T., D. McEvoy and G. Barrett (1992) 'Small Business Initiative: Ethnic Minority Business Component', end of award report to the Economic and Social Research Council.

Jones, T., D. McEvoy and G. Barrett (1993) 'Labour intensive practices in the ethnic minority firm', in J. Atkinson and D. Storey (eds), *Employment, the Small Firm and the Labour Market* (London: Routledge).

Jones, T., D. McEvoy and G. Barrett (1994) 'Raising capital for the ethnic minority firm', in A. Hughes and D. Storey (eds), *Finance and the Small Firm* (London: Routledge).

Jong, M. W. de (ed.) (1987) *Ruimte voor Detail: De Ontwikkelingen van de Distributieve Verzorgingsstructuur in Nederland*, EGI paper no. 33 (Amsterdam: Universiteit van Amsterdam, Economisch Geografisch Instituut).

Jonkman-te Winkel, M. E. (ed.) (1994) *Illegalen aan het Werk: Over Ontmoediging en Solidariteit* (Den Haag: Stichting Maatschappij en Onderneming).

Joppke, C. (forthcoming) 'Asylum and state sovereignty: A comparison of the United States, Germany, and Britain', *Comparative Political Studies*.

Junne, G. (1985) 'Terug naar de regio?: Kansen voor een regionale herintegratie van productie en konsumptie ten gevolge van de ontwikkeling van nieuwe technologie', *Tijdschrift voor Politieke Ekonomie*, vol. 8, no. 4, pp. 58–67.

Junne, G. (1987) 'Automation in the North: Consequences for developing countries', in J. Caporaso (ed.), *A Changing International Division of Labour* (Boulder, CO: Lynne Rienner).

Jupp, J. (1992) 'Immigrant settlement policy in Australia', in G. Freeman and J. Jupp (eds), *Nations of Immigrants: Australia, the United States, and International Migration* (Melbourne and New York: Oxford University Press).

Jupp, J. and M. Kebala (eds) (1993) *The Politics of Australian Immigration* (Canberra: Australian Government Publishing Service).

Kasarda, J. D. (1989) 'Urban industrial transition and the underclass', *The Annals of the American Academy*, no. 501, pp. 26–47.

Kearney, M. (1995) 'The local and the global: The anthropology of globalization and transnationalism', *Annual Revue of Anthropology*, vol. 24, pp. 547–65.

Keasey, K. and R. Watson (1993) *Small Firm Management: Ownership, Finance and Performance* (Oxford: Basil Blackwell).

Keasey, K. and R. Watson (1996) 'Owner-manager drawings, firm performance and financial structure', *Journal of Business Finance and Accounting*, vol. 23, pp. 753–78.

Keeble, D. and E. Wever (eds) (1986) *New Firms and Regional Development* (London: Croom Helm).

Kessner, T. (1981) 'New Yorkers in prosperity and depression: A preliminary reconnaissance', in D. Ravitch and R. Goodenow (eds), *Educating an Urban People* (New York: Teachers College Press).

Killingsworth, M. (1983) *Labor Supply* (Cambridge: Cambridge University Press).

Kirzner, I. M. (1997) 'Entrepreneurial discovery and the competitive market process: An Austrian approach', *Journal of Economic Literature*, vol. XXXV, pp. 60–85.

Klerk, L. de and J. Vijgen (1992) 'Inner Cities as a Cultural and Public Arena: Plans and People in Amsterdam and Rotterdam', paper presented at the conference on 'European Cities: Growth and Decline', the Hague, 13–16 April.

Kloosterman, R. (1994) 'Amsterdamned: The rise of unemployment in Amsterdam in the 1980s', *Urban Studies*, vol. 31, pp. 1325–44.

Kloosterman, R. (1996a) 'Double Dutch: Trends of polarisation in Amsterdam and Rotterdam after 1980', *Regional Studies*, vol. 30, no. 5, pp. 467–76.

Kloosterman, R. (1996b) 'Mixed experiences: Post-industrial transition and ethnic minorities on the Amsterdam labour market', *New Community*, vol. 22, no. 4, pp. 637–53.

Kloosterman, R. and J. Burgers (1996) *Informele Activiteiten en de Rol van Migranten in de Postindustriële Stad* (Den Haag: Rijksplanologische Dienst).

Kloosterman, R. and J. van der Leun (forthcoming) 'Just for starters: The emergence of ethnic economies in Amsterdam and Rotterdam', *Housing Studies*.

Kloosterman, R., J. van der Leun and J. Rath (1997a) *De Economische Potenties van het Immigrantenondernemerschap in Amsterdam: Een inventariserende en explorerende studie in het kader van 'Ethnic Minorities Participation (or Involvement in Urban Market-Economies (EMPORIUM)* (Amsterdam: Municipality of Amsterdam, Dept. of Economic Affairs/University of Amsterdam, IMES).

Kloosterman, R., J. van der Leun and J. Rath (1997b) *Over Grenzen: Immigranten en de Informele Economie* (Amsterdam: Het Spinhuis).

Kloosterman, R., J. van der Leun and J. Rath (1998) 'Across the border: Economic opportunities, social capital and informal business activities of immigrants', *Journal of Ethnic and Migration Studies*, vol. 24, no. 2, pp. 239–58.

Kloosterman, R., J. van der Leun and J. Rath (forthcoming) 'Economic opportunities, social capital and informal business activities of immigrants', *International Journal of Urban and Regional Research*, vol. 24.

Knight, R. (1989) 'The emergent global society', in R. V. Knight and G. Gappert (eds), *Cities in a Global Society* (Newbury Park: Sage).

Koot, W. and J. Rath (1987) 'Ethnicity and emancipation', *International Migration*, vol. 25, no. 4, pp. 427–40.

Koser, K. (1997) 'Het toelatingsbeleid: Ervaringen van Iraanse asielzoekers in Nederland', *Migrantenstudies*, vol. 13, no. 1, pp. 42–55.

Krikorian, M. (1996) 'Woman, 66, gets 7-year sentence for running sweatshop', *Los Angeles Times*, 7 May, part B, p. 3.

Kumcu, A., H. Flap and B. Bulder (forthcoming) 'Perverse effects of social capital on the business success of Turkish entrepreneurs in Amsterdam and Utrecht'.

Lanphier, M. and O. Lukomskyj (1994) 'Settlement policy in Australia and Canada', in H. Adelman *et al.* (eds), *Immigration and Refugee Policy: Australia and Canada Compared*, vol. II (Melbourne: Melbourne University Press).

Larson, E. M. and T. A. Sullivan (1987) ' "Conventional numbers" in immigration research: The case of the missing Dominicans', *International Migration Review*, vol. XXI, no. 4, pp. 1474–97.

Lee, E. S. (1969) 'A theory of migration', in J. A. Jackson (ed.), *Migration* (Cambridge: Cambridge University Press).

Lehmbruch, G. (1984) 'Concertation and the structure of corporatist networks', in J. Goldthorpe (ed.), *Order and Conflict in Contemporary Capitalism: Studies in the Political Economy of Western European Nations* (Oxford: Clarendon Press).

Lemann, N. (1991) 'The other underclass', *The Atlantic Monthly*, vol. 268, no. 6, pp. 96–110.

Leonard, K. and C. Tibrewal (1993) 'Asian Indians in Southern California', in I. Light and P. Bhachu (eds), *Immigration and Entrepreneurship: Culture, Capital and Ethnic Networks* (New Brunswick, NJ: Transaction Publishers).

Li, P. S. (1977) 'Occupational achievement and kinship assistance among Chinese immigrants in Chicago', *Sociological Quarterly*, vol. 18, pp. 478–89.

Liao, Y. (1993) 'The geography of the Chinese catering trade in Greater Manchester', *Manchester Geographer*, vol. 14, pp. 54–82.

Lieberson, S. (1961) 'A societal theory of race and ethnic relations', *American Sociological Review*, vol. 26, no. 2, pp. 902–10.

Light, I. (1972) *Ethnic Enterprise in America* (Berkeley: University of California Press).

Light, I. (1977) 'The ethnic vice industry, 1880–1944', *American Sociological Review*, vol. 42, pp. 464–79.

Light, I. (1979) 'Disadvantaged minorities in self-employment', *The International Journal of Comparative Sociology*, vol. 20, pp. 31–45.

Light, I. (1983) *Cities in World Perspective* (New York: Macmillan).

Light, I. (1984) 'Immigrant and ethnic enterprise in North America', *Ethnic and Racial Studies*, vol. 7, pp. 195–216.

Light, I., P. Bhachu and S. Karageorgis (1993) 'Migration networks and immigrant entrepreneurship', in I. Light and P. Bhachu (eds), *Immigration and Entrepreneurship: Culture, Capital, and Ethnic Networks* (New Brunswick, NJ: Transaction Publishers).

Light, I. and E. Bonacich (1988) *Immigrant Entrepreneurs: Koreans in Los Angeles, 1965–1982* (Berkeley, CA: University of California Press).

Light, I. and S. Karageorgis (1994) 'The ethnic economy', in N. J. Smelser and R. Swedberg (eds), *The Handbook of Economic Sociology* (Princeton and New York: Princeton University Press and Russell Sage Foundation).

Light, I. and S. Karageorgis (1997) 'Economic saturation and immigrant entrepreneurship', in I. Light and R. Isralowitz (eds), *Immigrant Entrepreneurs and Immigration Absorption in the United States and Israel* (Aldershot: Ashgate).

Light, I. and E. Roach (1996) 'Self-employment: Mobility ladder or economic lifeboat?', in R. Waldinger and M. Bozorgmehr (eds), *Ethnic Los Angeles* (New York: Russell Sage Foundation), pp. 193–213.

Light, I., E. Roach and K. Kan (1996) 'The Immigrant Economy in the Garment Industry of Los Angeles', paper presented at the 1996 Annual Meeting of the American Sociological Association, New York City.

Light, I. and C. Rosenstein (1995a) 'Expanding the interaction theory of entrepreneurship', in A. Portes (ed.), *The Economic Sociology of Immigration: Essays on Networks, Ethnicity, and Entrepreneurship* (New York: Russell Sage Foundation).

Light, I. and C. Rosenstein (1995b) *Race, Ethnicity, and Entrepreneurs in Urban America* (New York: Aldine de Gruyter).

Lindenberg, S. (1988) 'Contractual relations and weak solidarity: The behavioral basis of restraints on gain-maximization', *Journal of Institutional and Theoretical Economics*, vol. 144, pp. 39–58.

Lindenberg, S. (1992) 'An extended theory of institutions and contractual discipline', *Journal of Institutional and Theoretical Economics*, vol. 148, pp. 125–54.

Lindenberg, S. (1996) 'Continuities in the theory of social production functions', in H. Ganzeboom and S. Lindenberg (eds), *Verklarende Sociologie: Opstellen voor Reinhard Wippler* (Amsterdam: Thesis).

Lipietz, A. (1986) 'New tendencies in the international division of labor: Regimes of accumulation and modes of regulation', in A. J. Scott and M. Storper (eds), *Production, Work, Territory: The Geographical Anatomy of Industrial Capitalism* (London: Allen & Unwin).

Logan, J. and T. Swanstrom (1990) 'Urban restructuring: A critical view', in J. Logan and T. Swanstrom (eds), *Beyond the City Limits* (Philadelphia: Temple University).

Loiskandle, H. (1995) 'Illegal migrant workers in Japan', in R. Cohen (ed.), *The Cambridge Survey of World Migration* (Cambridge: Cambridge University Press).

Lopez-Garza, M. (1989) 'Immigration and economic restructuring: The metamorphosis of Southern California', *California Sociologist*, vol. 12, pp. 93–110.

Loury, G. C. (1977) 'A dynamic theory of racial income differences', in P. Wallace and A. LaMond (eds), *Women: Minorities, and Employment Discrimination* (Lexington: Lexington Books).

Loveman, G. and W. Sengenberger (1991) 'The re-emergence of small-scale production: An international comparison', *Small Business Economics*, vol. 1, pp. 1–38.

Machielse, C. and P. A. de Ruijter (1988) *Economisch-technologische Vernieuwing en Ruimtelijke Organisatie* (Delft: Instituut voor Ruimtelijke Organisatie/ Nederlandse Organisatie voor Toegepast Natuurwetenschappelijk Onderzoek).

Mahler, S. J. (1995) *American Dreaming: Immigrant Life on the Margins* (Princeton: Princeton University Press).

Ma Mung, E. (1992) 'L'expansion du commerce ethnique: Asiathiques et Mahrébins dans la région parisienne', *Revue Européenne des Migrations Internationales*, vol. 8, no. 1, pp. 39–59.

Ma Mung, E. and M. Guillon (1986) 'Les commercants etrangers dans l'agglomeration Parisienne', *Revue Européene des Migrations Internationales*, vol. 2, no. 3, pp. 105–34.

Margolis, M. L. (1994) *Little Brazil: An Ethnography of Brazilian Immigrants in New York City* (Princeton, NJ: Princeton University Press).

Marie, C.-V. (1994) 'From the campaign against illegal migration to the campaign against illegal work', *The Annals*, no. 534, pp. 118–32.

Marks, C. (1989) *Farewell – We're Good and Gone* (Bloomington: University of Indiana Press).

Marosi, R. (1997) 'One of the most dangerous jobs in New York: Gypsy cab driver', Colombia News Service Webmaster, Colombia University Graduate School of Journalism, Colombia University New York.

Mars, G. and R. Ward (1984) 'Ethnic business development in Britain: Opportunities and resources', in R. Ward and R. Jenkins (eds), *Ethnic Communities in Business: Strategies for Economic Survival* (Cambridge: Cambridge University Press).

Martin, P. (1994a) 'Germany: Reluctant land of immigration', in W. Cornelius, P. Martin and J. Hollifield (eds), *Controlling Immigration: A Global Perspective* (Stanford, CA: Stanford University Press).

Martin, P. (1994b) 'Good intentions gone awry: IRCA and US agriculture', *The Annals*, no. 534, pp. 44–57.

Massey, D. (1984) *Spatial Division of Labour: Social Structures and the Geography of Production* (London: Macmillan).

Massey, D. (1988) 'Economic development and international migration in comparative perspective', *Population and Development Review*, vol. 14, pp. 383–413.

Massey, D. (1990) 'Social structure, household strategies, and the cumulative causation of migration', *Population Index*, vol. 56, pp. 3–26

Massey, D., R. Alarcón, J. Durand and H. González (1987) *Return to Aztlan: The Social Process of International Migration from Western Mexico* (Berkeley, Los Angeles and London: University of California Press).

Massey, D., J. Arango, G. Hugo, A. Kouaouci, A. Pellegrino and J. Taylor (1993) 'Theories of international migration: A review and appraisal', *Population and Development Review*, vol. 19, no. 3, pp. 431–66.

Massey, D. and G. Espana (1987) 'The social process of international migration', *Science*, vol. 237, pp. 733–7.

Mayer, N. (1987) 'Small business and social mobility in France', in R. Goffee and R. Scase (eds), *Entrepreneurship in Europe* (London: Croom Helm).

McEvoy, D. and H. Aldrich (1986) 'Survival rates of Asian and white retailers', *International Small Business Journal*, vol. 4, no. 3, pp. 28–37.

McEvoy, D. and T. P. Jones (1993) 'Relative economic welcomes: South Asian retailing in Britain and Canada', in H. Rudolph and M. Morokvasic (eds), *Bridging States and Markets* (Berlin: Edition Sigma).

Meissner, D. *et al.* (eds) (1993) *International Migration Challenges in a New Era* (New York: The Trilateral Commission).

Mendelsohn, E. (1970) *Class Struggle in the Pale* (Cambridge: Cambridge University Press).

Metcalf, H., T. Modood and S. Virdee (n.d.) *Asian Self-Employment: The Interaction of Culture and Economics in England* (London: Policy Studies Institute).

Meza, D. de and D. C. Webb (1987) 'Too much investment: A problem of asymmetric information', *Quarterly Journal of Economics*, vol. 102, pp. 281–92.

Meza, D. de and D. C. Webb (1990) 'Risk, adverse selection and capital market failure', *Economic Journal*, vol. 100, pp. 206–14.

Migration News (1997) 'Five million illegal aliens in US', http://migration.ucdavis.edu, March.

Miles, R. (1982) *Racism and Migrant Labour* (London: Routledge and Kegan Paul).

Miles, R. and D. Thränhardt (eds) (1995) *Migration and European Integration: The Dynamics of International Exclusion* (London: Pinter).

Miller, M. (1987) *Employer Sanctions in Europe* (Staten Island, NY: Center for Migration Studies).

Miller, M. J. (1995) 'Illegal migration', in R. Cohen (ed.), *The Cambridge Survey of World Migration* (Cambridge: Cambridge University Press).

Min, P. G. (1989) 'Some Positive Functions of Ethnic Business for an Immigrant Community: Koreans in Los Angeles', final report submitted to the National Science Foundation, Washington, DC.

Min, P. G. (1996) *Caught in the Middle: Korean Communities in New York and Los Angeles* (Berkeley, Los Angeles and London: University of California Press).

Mitter, S. (1986) 'Industrial restructuring and manufacturing homework', *Capital and Class*, vol. 27, pp. 37–80.

Moore, J. and R. Pinderhughes (1993) 'Introduction', in J. Moore and R. Pinderhughes (eds), *The Barrios: Latinos and the Underclass Debate* (New York: Russell Sage Foundation).

Morokvasic, M. (1993) 'Immigrants in garment production in Paris and Berlin', in I. Light and P. Bhachu (eds), *Immigration and Entrepreneurship: Culture, Capital, and Ethnic Networks* (New Brunswick and London: Transaction Publishers).

Muus, P. (1995) *De Wereld in Beweging: Internationale Migratie, Mensenrechten en Ontwikkeling* (Utrecht: Jan van Arkel).

Nazario, S. and D. P. Shutt (1995) 'Many in middle class turn to county for medical help', *Los Angeles Times*, 30 October, section 1, p. 1.

Nederveen Pieterse, J. (1994) 'Globalization as hybridization', *International Sociology*, vol. 9, no. 2, pp. 161–84.

Nee, V., J. Sanders and S. Sernau (1993) 'Job transitions in an immigrant metropolis', *American Sociological Review*, vol. 59, pp. 849–72.

Nelson, D. (1975) *Managers and Workers* (Madison, WI: University of Wisconsin Press).

Niewyk, D. (1980) *The Jews in Weimar Germany* (Baton Rouge: Louisiana State University Press).

Noël, A. (1987) 'Accumulation, regulation and social change: An essay on French political economy', *International Organisation*, vol. 41, no. 2, pp. 303–33.

North, D. (1990) *Institutions, Institutional Change and Economic Performance* (Cambridge: Cambridge University Press).

North, D. (1994) 'Enforcing the minimum wage and employer sanctions', *The Annals*, no. 534, pp. 58–68.

OECD (1992) *Employment Outlook 1992* (Paris: OECD).

OECD (1993) *Employment Outlook* (Paris: OECD).

Ohri, S. and S. Faruqi (1988) 'Racism, employment and unemployment', in A. Bhat, R. Carr-Hill and S. Ohri (eds), *Britain's Black Population: A New Perspective* (Aldershot: Gower).

Olson, M. (1982) *The Rise and Decline of Nations: Economic Growth, Stagflation, and Social Rigidities* (New Haven: Yale University Press).

Orlick, A. (1987) 'The Soviet Jews: Life in Brighton Beach, Brooklyn', in N. Foner (ed.), *New Immigrants in New York City* (New York: Columbia University Press).

Ornbrandt, B. and M. Peura (1993) 'The Nordic Pact: An experiment in controlled stability', in D. Kubat (ed.), *The Politics of Migration Policies: Settlement and Integration* (New York: Center for Migration Studies).

Özüekren, A. S. and R. van Kempen (eds) (1996) *Housing Conditions of Turks in European Cities* (Utrecht: European Research Centre on Migration and Ethnic Relations).

Palmer, R. (1984) 'The rise of the Britalian culture entrepreneur', in R. Ward and R. Jenkins (eds), *Ethnic Communities in Business: Strategies for Economic Survival* (Cambridge: Cambridge University Press).

Panayiotopoulos, P. I. (1996) 'Challenging orthodoxies: Cypriot entrepreneurs in the London garment industry', *New Community*, vol. 22, no. 3, July, pp. 437–60.

Papademetriou, D. and K. Hamilton (1996) *Converging Paths to Restriction: French, Italian, and British Responses to Immigration* (Washington, DC: Carnegie Endowment for International Peace).

Parker, D. (1994) 'Encounters across the counter: Young Chinese people in Britain', *New Community*, vol. 20, pp. 621–34.

Patel, S. (1988) 'Insurance and ethnic minority business', *New Community*, vol. 15, pp. 78–89.

Perotti, R. (1994) 'Employer sanctions and the limits of negotiation', *The Annals*, no. 534, pp. 31–43.

Persky, J. and W. Wievel (1994) 'The growing localness of the global city', *Economic Geography*, vol. 70, no. 1, pp. 129–43.

Peterson, M. A. and R. G. Ragan (1994) 'The benefits of lending relationships: Evidence from small business data', *The Journal of Finance*, vol. 49, pp. 3–38.

Peterson, P. E. (1981) *City Limits* (Chicago, Ill: University of Chicago Press).

Petras, E. (1983) 'The global labor market in the modern world economy', in M. M. Kritz, C. B. Keely and S. M. Tomasi, *Global Trends in Migration* (New York: Center for Migration Studies).

Petras, E. (1992) 'The shirt on your back: Immigrant workers and the reorganization of the garment industry', *Social Justice*, vol. 19, pp. 76–114.

Phizacklea, A. (1990) *Unpacking the Fashion Industry: Gender, Racism, and Class in Production* (London: Routledge).

Phizacklea, A. (1992) 'Jobs for the girls: The productions of women's outerwear in the UK', in M. Cross (ed.), *Ethnic Minorities and Industrial Change in Europe and North America* (Cambridge: Cambridge University Press).

Phizacklea, A. and M. Ram (1996) 'Being your own boss: Ethnic minority entrepreneurs in comparative perspective', *Work, Employment and Society*, vol. 10, pp. 319–39.

Piore, M. (1979a) *Birds of Passage: Migrant Labor and Industrial Societies* (Cambridge: Cambridge University Press).

Piore, M. (1979b) 'Unemployment and inflation: An alternate view', in M. Piore (ed.), *Unemployment and Inflation: Institutionalist and Structuralist Views* (Armonk, NY: M. E. Sharpe).

Piore, M. (1980) 'The technological foundations of economic dualism', in S. Berger and M. Piore (eds), *Dualism and Discontinuity in Industrial Societies* (Cambridge: Cambridge University Press).

Piore, M. and C. Sabel (1984) *The Second Industrial Divide* (New York: Basic Books).

Polanyi, K. (1957) *The Great Transformation: The Political and Economic Origins of Our Time*, paperback edition (Boston: Beacon Press).

Pollins, H. (1982) *The Economic History of the Jews in England* (London: Associated University Presses).

Porter, M. E. (1990) *The Competitive Advantage of Nations* (New York: The Free Press).

Portes, A. (1994) 'The informal economy and its paradoxes', in N. J. Smelser and R. Swedberg (eds), *The Handbook of Economic Sociology* (Princeton and New York: Princeton University Press and Russell Sage Foundation).

Portes, A. (1995a) 'Economic sociology and the sociology of immigration: A conceptual overview', in A. Portes (ed.), *The Economic Sociology of Immigration: Essays on Networks, Ethnicity, and Entrepreneurship* (New York: Russell Sage Foundation).

Portes, A. (ed.) (1995b) *The Economic Sociology of Immigration: Essays on Networks, Ethnicity, and Entrepreneurship* (New York: Russell Sage Foundation).

Portes, A. (1995c) *Transnational Communities: Their Emergence and Significance in the Contemporary World System*, working paper series no. 16 (Baltimore, MD: Johns Hopkins University Press).

Portes, A. and L. E. Guarnizo (1990) *Tropical Capitalists: US-Bound Immigration and Small-Enterprise Development in the Dominican Republic*, working paper no. 457 (Washington, DC: Commission for the Study of International Migration and Cooperative Economic Development).

Portes, A. and R. Rumbaut (1990) *Immigrant America: A Portrait* (Berkeley, Los Angeles and Oxford: University of California Press).

Portes, A. and S. Sassen-Koob (1987) 'Making it underground: Comparative material on the informal sector in Western market economies', *American Journal of Sociology*, vol. 93, no. 1, pp. 30–61.

Portes, A. and J. Sensenbrenner (1993) 'Embeddedness and immigration: Notes on the social determinants of economic action', *American Journal of Sociology*, vol. 98, pp. 1320–50.

Portes, A. and A. Stepick (1993) *City on the Edge: The Transformation of Miami* (Berkely, CA: University of California Press).

Portes, A. and M. Zhou (1992) 'Gaining the upper hand: Economic mobility among immigrant and domestic minorities', *Ethnic and Racial Studies*, vol. 15, no. 4, pp. 491–522.

Portes, A. and M. Zhou (1996) 'Selfemployment and the earnings of immigrants', *American Sociological Review*, vol. 61, pp. 219–30.

Powell, W. W. (1990) 'Neither market nor hierarchy: Network forms of organization', *Research in Organizational Behavior*, vol. 12, pp. 295–336.

Preisendörfer, P. and J. Brüderl (1995) 'Network Support and Economic Success
of Newly Founded Business', paper presented to the conference on 'Immigrant
entrepreneurship in global cities', UvA/IMES, 31 August–2 September.

Price, C. A. (1963) *Southern Europeans in Australia* (Melbourne: Oxford University
Press).

Pugliese, E. (1993) 'Restructuring of the labour market and the role of Third
World migrations in Europe', *Environment and Planning D: Society and Space*,
vol. 11, pp. 513–22.

Putnam, R. (1993) *Making Democracy Work: Civic Traditions in Modern Italy*
(Princeton, NJ: Princeton University Press).

Ram, M. (1993) *Managing to Survive: Working Lives in Small Firms* (Oxford:
Blackwell).

Ram M. and D. Deakins (1996) 'African-Carribeans in business', *New Community*,
vol. 22, pp. 67–84.

Ram, M. and G. Hillin (1994) 'Achieving "break-out": Developing mainstream
ethnic minority business', *Small Business Enterprise and Development*, vol. 1,
pp. 15–21.

Ram, M. and T. P. Jones (forthcoming) *Ethnic Minority Business in Britain*
(London: Small Business Research Trust).

Rath, J. (1998) 'The informal economy as bastard sphere of social integration',
in E. Eichenhofer and P. Marschalck (eds), *Migration und Illegalität*, IMIS-
Schriften Bd. 7 (Osnabrück: Universitätsverlag Rasch).

Rath, J. (1999) 'A game of ethnic musical chairs? Immigrant businesses and the
formation and succession of niches in the Amsterdam economy', in S. Body-
Gendrot and M. Martiniello (eds), *Minorities in European Cities: The Dynamics
of Social Integration and Social Exclusion at the Neighbourhood Level* (London:
Macmillan).

Rath, J. and R. Kloosterman (eds) (1998) *Rijp en Groen: Het Zelfstandig
Ondernemerschap van Immigranten in Nederland* (Amsterdam: Het Spinhuis).

Rath, J. and R. Kloosterman (eds) (forthcoming) ' "Outsiders" business: Research
on immigrant entrepreneurs in the Netherlands', *International Migration Review*.

Razin, E. (1993) 'Immigrant entrepreneurs in Israel, Canada, and California', in
I. Light and P. Bhachu (eds), *Immigration and Entrepreneurship: Culture, Capital,
and Ethnic Networks* (New Brunswick, NJ: Transaction Publishers).

Razin, E. and A. Langlois (1996) 'Metropolitan characteristics and entrepreneurship among immigrants and ethnic groups in Canada', *International Migration
Review*, vol. xxx, no. 3, pp. 703–27.

Reeves, F. and R. Ward (1984) 'West Indian business in Britain', in R. Ward and
R. Jenkins (eds), *Ethnic Communities in Business: Strategies for Economic Survival*
(Cambridge: Cambridge University Press).

Reich, R. (1991) *The Work of Nations: Preparing Ourselves for the 21st Century
Capitalism* (New York: Alfred A. Knopf).

Reitz, J. G. (1995) 'Institutional Restructuring and the Impact of Non-European
Immigration on the Urban Areas of the US, Canada, and Australia', paper presented to the Association for Canadian Studies of Australia and New Zealand,
16 February.

Rekers, A. M. (1991) 'Arbeidsmarkt en etnisch ondernemerschap: Mogelijke
relaties in verschillende stedelijke contexten', in O.A.L.C. Atzema, M. Hessels

and H. Zondag (eds), *De Werkende Stad: Aspecten van de Grootstedelijke Arbeidsmarkt* (Utrecht: Stedelijke Netwerken).

Rekers, A. (1993) 'A tale of two cities: A comparison of Turkish enterprises in Amsterdam and Rotterdam', in D. Crommentuijn-Ondaatje (ed.), *Netherlands School of Housing and Urban Research* (Utrecht: Nethur).

Rekers, A., M. J. Dijst and R. van Kempen (forthcoming) *Turkish Entrepreneurs in Amsterdam and Rotterdam*.

Remy, P. (1991) *The Difficulties of Integrating Migrants into the Labour Market: Implicit or Explicit Discrimination?* (Paris: OECD).

Rex, J. (1970) *Race Relations in Sociological Theory* (London: Weidenfeld and Nicolson).

Reynolds, P. (1991) 'Sociology and entrepreneurship: Concepts and contributions', *Entrepreneurship: Theory and Practice*, vol. 16, no. 2.

Reynolds, P., D. J. Storey and P. Westhead (1994) 'Cross-national comparisons of the variation in new firm formation rates', *Regional Studies*, vol. 28, pp. 443–56.

Richmond, A. (1994) *Global Apartheid: Refugees, Racism, and the New World Order* (Toronto: Oxford University Press).

Rischin, M. (1962) *The Promised City* (Cambridge, MA: Harvard University Press).

Roberts, B. (1994) 'Informal economy and family strategies', *International Journal of Urban and Regional Research*, vol. 18, no. 1, pp. 6–23.

Robinson, V. (1986) *Transients, Settlers and Refugees* (Oxford: Clarendon).

Rogers, R. (ed.) (1985) *Guests Come to Stay* (Boulder, CO: Westview Press).

Ross, R. and K. Trachte (1990) *Global Capitalism: The New Leviathan* (New York: State University of New York Press).

Rozenblit, M. (1983) *The Jews of Vienna, 1867–1914: Assimilation and Identity* (Albany: SUNY Press).

Sanders, J. M. and V. Nee (1996) 'Immigrant self-employment: The family as social capital and the value of human capital', *American Sociological Review*, vol. 61, pp. 231–49.

Sassen, S. (1984) 'The new labour demand in global cities', in M. P. Smith (ed.), *Cities in Transformation: Class, Capital and the State* (Beverly Hills, CA: Sage).

Sassen, S. (1986) 'New York City: Economic restructuring and immigration', *Development and Change*, vol. 17, pp. 85–119.

Sassen, S. (1988) *The Mobility of Labor and Capital: A Study in International Investment and Labor Flow* (Cambridge: Cambridge University Press).

Sassen, S. (1990) 'Beyond the city limits: A commentary', in J. Logan and T. Swanstrom (eds), *Beyond the City Limits* (Philadelphia: Temple University).

Sassen, S. (1991a) *The Global City: New York, London, Tokyo* (Princeton, NJ: Princeton University Press).

Sassen, S. (1991b) 'The informal economy', in J. H. Mollenkopf and M. Castells (eds), *Dual City: Restructuring New York* (New York: Russell Sage Foundation).

Sassen, S. (1994) *Cities in a World Economy* (Thousand Oaks: Pine Forge Press).

Sassen, S. (1996) 'New employment regimes in cities: The impact of immigrant workers', *New Community*, vol. 22, pp. 579–94.

Sassen-Koob, S. (1985) 'Capital mobility and labor migration: Their expression in core cities', in M. Timberlake (ed.), *Urbanization in the World Economy* (Orlando, FA: Academic Press).

Sassen-Koob, S. (1989) 'New York City's informal economy', in A. Portes, M. Castells and L. A. Benton (eds), *The Informal Economy: Studies in Advanced and Less Developed Countries* (Baltimore, MD: Johns Hopkins University Press).

Savitch, H. V. (1990) 'Post-industrialism with a difference: Global capitalism in world-class cities', in J. Logan and T. Swanstrom (eds), *Beyond the City Limits* (Philadelphia: Temple University).

Scheffer, M. (1992) *Trading Places: Fashion Retailers and the Changing Geography of Clothing Production*, Nederlandse Geografische Studies no. 150 (Utrecht: Koninklijk Nederlands Aardrijkskundig Genootschap).

Schiller, N., L. Basch and C. Blanc-Szanton (1992) 'Transnationalism: A new analytic framework for understanding migration', *The Annals of the New York Academy of Sciences*, no. 634, pp. 1–24.

Schmiechen, J. G. (1984) *Sweated Industries and Sweated Labor: The London Clothing Trades, 1860–1914* (Urbana: University of Illinois Press).

Schoenberger, E. (1988) 'From Fordism to flexible accumulation: Technology, competitive strategies and international location', *Environment and Planning D: Society and Space*, vol. 6, pp. 245–62.

Schutjens, V. A. J. M. (1993) *Dynamiek in het Draagvlak: Huishoudensontwikkelingen en Winkelbestedingen in Oudere Naoorlogse Wijken* (Utrecht: Koninklijk Nederlands Aardrijkskundig Genootschap).

Scott, A. J. (1988) 'Flexible production systems and regional development: The rise of new industrial spaces in North America and Western Europe', *International Journal of Urban and Regional Research*, vol. 12, pp. 171–86.

Scott, A. J. (1990) *Metropolis: From the Division of Labor to the Urban Form* (Berkeley, Los Angeles and London: University of California Press).

Scott, A. J. and M. Storper (eds) (1986) *Production, Work, Territory: The Geographical Anatomy of Industrial Capitalism* (London: Allen & Unwin).

Scott, A. J. and M. Storper (1992) 'Industrialization and regional development', in M. Storper and A. J. Scott (eds), *Pathways to Industrialization and Regional Development* (London: Routledge).

Silverstein, S. and G. White (1996) 'Hazards found in nearly 75% of garment shops', *Los Angeles Times*, 8 May, section 1, p. 1.

Simon, G. (1993) 'Immigrant entrepreneurs in France', in I. Light and P. Bhachu (eds), *Immigration and Entrepreneurship: Culture, Capital, and Ethnic Networks* (New Brunswick, NJ: Transaction Publishers).

Simon, G. and E. Ma Mung (1987) 'Les Dynamiques des Commerces Maghrebin et Asiatiques et les Perspectives du Marche Interieur Europeen', paper presented to the Atelier Cultures Urbaines, University of Lyon II, November.

Simon, J. (1991) *The Economic Consequences of Immigration* (Oxford: Blackwell).

Sirola, P. (1992) 'Beyond Survival: Latino Immigrant Street Vendors in the Los Angeles Informal Sector', paper presented to the 17th International Congress of the Latin American Studies Association, Los Angeles, California, September.

Siu, P. C. P. (1987) *The Chinese Laundryman: A Study of Social Isolation* (New York and London: New York University Press).

Snowden, L. L. (1990) 'Collective versus mass behavior: A conceptual framework for temporary and permanent migration in Western Europe and the United States', *International Migration Review*, vol. XXIV, no. 3, pp. 577–90.

Soja, E., R. Morales and G. Wolff (1987) 'Industrial restructuring: An analysis of social and spatial change in Los Angeles', in R. Peet (ed.), *International Capitalism and Industrial Restructuring* (Boston, Mass.: Allen and Unwin).

Solomon, S. (1995) *The Confidence Game: How Unelected Central Bankers are Governing the Changed Global Economy* (New York: Simon and Schuster).

Soni, S., M. Tricker and R. Ward (1987) *Ethnic Minority Business in Leicester* (Birmingham: Aston University).

Sorkin, D. (1987) *The Transformation of German Jewry, 1780–1840* (London: Oxford University Press).

Soysal, Y. (1994) *Limits of Citizenship: Migrants and Postnational Membership in Europe* (Cambridge, Mass.: Harvard University Press).

Spierings, F. (1996) *Op Eigen Kracht: Een Onderzoek naar het Dagelijks Leven van Logementbewoners* (Utrecht: Uitgeverij SWP).

Srinavasan, S. (1995) *The South Asian Petty Bourgeoisie in Britain: An Oxford Case Study* (Aldershot: Avebury).

Stanworth, J. and C. Gray (eds) (1991) *Bolton 20 Years On: The Small Firm in the 1990s* (London: Paul Chapman).

Staring, R. (1998) ' "Scenes from a fake marriage": Notes on the flip side of embeddedness', in K. Koser and H. Lutz (eds), *New Migration in Europe: Social Constructions and Social Realities* (London: Macmillan).

Steinmetz, G. and E. O. Wright (1989) 'The fall and rise of the petty bourgeoisie: Changing patterns of self-employment in postwar United States', *American Journal of Sociology*, vol. 94, pp. 73–118.

Stepick, A. (1989) 'Miami's two informal sectors', in A. Portes, M. Castells and L. A. Benton (eds), *The Informal Economy: Studies in Advanced and Less Developed Countries* (Baltimore, MD: Johns Hopkins University Press).

Stiglitz, J. E. and A. Weiss (1981) 'Credit rationing in markets with imperfect information', *American Economic Review*, vol. 71, pp. 393–410.

Stiglitz, J. E. and A. Weiss (1987) 'Credit rationing with many borrowers', *American Economic Review*, vol. 77, pp. 228–31.

Stone, J. (1985) *Ethnic Conflict* (Cambridge, MA: Harvard University Press).

Stoop, C. de (1996) *Haal de Was maar Binnen: Aziza of een Verhaal van Deportatie in Europa* (Amsterdam: De Bezige Bij).

Storey, D. (1994) *Understanding the Small Business Sector* (London: Routledge).

Suarez-Orozco, M. (1994) 'Belgium and its immigrant minorities', in W. Cornelius, P. Martin and J. Hollifield (eds), *Controlling Immigration: A Global Perspective* (Stanford, CA: Stanford University Press).

Tanzi, V. (ed.) (1982) *The Underground Economy in the United States and Abroad* (Lexington, MA: Lexington Books).

Thistlethwaite, F. (1960) 'Migration from Europe overseas in the nineteenth and twentieth centuries', *Rapports, XIe Congres Internationale des Sciences Historiques* (Stockholm).

Thränhardt, D. (ed.) (1992) *Europe: A New Immigration Continent* (Hamburg: Lit).

Tienda, M. and R. Raijman (1996) 'Forging Mobility: Immigrants' Socioeconomic Progress in a Low-Wage Environment', paper presented to the conference on 'America Becoming/Becoming American: International Migration to the United States', Sanibel Island, Florida.

Tillaart, H. J. M. van den and T. J. M. Reubsaet (1988) *Etnische Ondernemers in Nederland* (Nijmegen: ITS).

Tinnemans, W. (1994) *Een Gouden Armband: Een Geschiedenis van Mediterane Immigranten in Nederland (1945–1994)* (Utrecht: Nederlands Centrum Buitenlanders).

Tokman, V. and E. Klein (eds) (1996) *Regulation and the Informal Economy: Microenterprises in Chile, Ecuador, and Jamaica* (Boulder, CO: Lynne Rienner).

Uzzi, B. (1996) 'The sources and consequences of embeddedness for the economic performance of organizations', *American Sociological Review*, vol. 61, pp. 674–98.

Veldkamp Marktonderzoek B. V. (1985) *Koop- en Bestedingsgedrag Etnische Groepen* (Diemen: Centraal Instituut Midden en Kleinbedrijf).

Veraart, J. (1996) *In Vaders Voetspoor: Jonge Turken op de Arbeidsmarkt* (Amsterdam: Thesis Publishers).

Verhorst, J. (1989) *Stadsvernieuwingsgebieden in de Stedelijke Economie* (Utrecht: Faculteit der Ruimtelijke Wetenschappen, Universiteit Utrecht).

Vijgen, J. and R. van Engelsdorp Gastelaars (1986) *Stedelijke Bevolkingscategorieën in Opkomst: Stijlen en Strategieën in het Alders Beats* (Amsterdam and Utrecht: Koninklijk Nederlands Aardrijkskundig Genootschap and the Instituut voor Sociale Geografie, Universiteit van Amsterdam).

Waldinger, R. (1985) 'Immigrant enterprise and the structure of the labour market', in B. Roberts, R. Finnegan and D. Gallie (eds), *New Approaches to Economic Life* (Manchester: Manchester University Press).

Waldinger, R. (1986) *Through the Eye of the Needle: Immigrants and Enterprise in New York's Garment Trade* (New York: New York University Press).

Waldinger, R. (1989) 'Structural opportunity or ethnic advantage? Immigrant business development in New York', *International Migration Review*, vol. XXIII, no. 1, pp. 48–72.

Waldinger, R. (1992) 'Taking care of the guests: The impact of immigrants on services – An industry case study', *International Journal of Urban and Regional Research*, vol. 16, no. 1, pp. 97–113.

Waldinger, R. (1993) 'The two sides of ethnic entrepreneurship: Reply to Bonacich', *International Migration Review*, vol. 27, no. 3, pp. 692–701.

Waldinger, R. (1995) 'The "other side" of embeddedness: A case-study of the interplay of economy and ethnicity', *Ethnic and Racial Studies*, vol. 18, pp. 555–79.

Waldinger, R. (1996a) *Still the Promised City: African-Americans and New Immigrants in Post-Industrial New York* (Cambridge, MA/London: Harvard University Press).

Waldinger, R. (1996b) 'Who makes the beds? Who washes the dishes? Black/immigrant competition reassessed', in H. Orcutt Duleep and P. Wunnava (eds), *Immigrants and Immigration Policy* (Greenwich, CT: JAI).

Waldinger, R., H. Aldrich and R. Ward (1990a) 'Opportunities, group characteristics, and strategies', in R. Waldinger, H. Aldrich, R. Ward and Associates (eds), *Ethnic Entrepreneurs: Immigrant Business in Industrial Societies* (London: Sage).

Waldinger, R., H. Aldrich, R. Ward and Associates (eds) (1990b) *Ethnic Entrepreneurs: Immigrant Business in Industrial Societies* (London: Sage).

Waldinger, R. and M. Bozorgmehr (eds) (1996) *Ethnic Los Angeles* (New York: Russell Sage Foundation).

Waldinger, R. and M. Lapp (1993) 'Back to the sweatshop or ahead to the informal sector?', *International Journal of Urban and Regional Research*, vol. 1, pp. 6–29.

Waldinger, R. and M. Lichter (1996) 'Anglos: Beyond ethnicity?', in R. Waldinger and M. Bozorgmehr (eds), *Ethnic Los Angeles* (New York: Russell Sage Foundation), pp. 413–41.

Waldinger, R., D. McEvoy and H. Aldrich (1990c) 'Spatial dimensions of opportunity structures', in R. Waldinger, H. Aldrich, R. Ward and Associates (eds), *Ethnic Entrepreneurs: Immigrant Business in Industrial Societies* (London: Sage).

Waldinger, R. and Y. Tseng (1992) 'Divergent diasporas: The Chinese communities of New York and Los Angeles compared', *Revue Européenne des Migrations Internationales*, vol. 8, no. 3, pp. 91–115.

Waldinger, R., R. Ward and H. Aldrich (1985) 'Ethnic business and occupational mobility in advanced society', *Sociology*, vol. 9, no. 4, pp. 586–97.

Ward, R. (1985) 'Minority settlement and the local economy', in B. Roberts, R. Finnegan and D. Gallie (eds), *New Approaches to Economic Life* (Manchester: Manchester University Press).

Ward, R. (1986) 'Ethnic business and economic change: An overview', *International Small Business Journal*, vol. 4, no. 3, pp. 10–12.

Ward, R. (1987a) 'Ethnic entrepreneurs in Britain and Europe', in R. Goffee and R. Scase (eds), *Entrepreneurship in Europe* (London: Croom Helm).

Ward, R. (1987b) 'Small retailers in urban areas', in G. Johnson (ed.), *Business Strategy and Retailing* (New York: Wiley).

Ward, R. (1991) 'Economic development and ethnic business', in J. Curran and R. Blackburn (eds), *Paths of Enterprise* (London: Routledge).

Watson, J. L. (1977) 'The Chinese: Hong Kong villagers in the British catering trade', in J. L. Watson (ed.), *Between Two Cultures: Migrants and Minorities in Britain* (Oxford: Blackwell).

Weaver, R. and B. Rockman (eds) (1993) *Do Institutions Matter? Government Capabilities in the United States and Abroad* (Washington, DC: The Brookings Institution).

Weber, M. (1923) *Wirtschafsgeschichte: Abriss der Universalen Sozial- und Wirtschafts-Geschichte* (München und Leipzig: Duncker und Humblot).

Weiner, M. (1995) *The Global Migration Crisis: Challenges to States and to Human Rights* (New York: Harper Collins).

Weiss, L. (1987) 'Explaining the underground economy: State and social structure', *The British Journal of Sociology*, vol. 38, no. 2, pp. 216–34.

Wentholt, R. (1967) 'Slotbeschouwing', in R. Wentholt (ed.), *Buitenlandse Arbeiders in Nederland* (Leiden: Spruyt, Van Mantgem & De Does).

Werbner, P. (1980) 'From rags to riches: Manchester Pakistanis in the textile trade', *New Community*, vol. 8, nos 1–2, pp. 84–95.

Werbner, P. (1984) 'Business on trust: Pakistani entrepreneurship in the Manchester garment trade', in R. Ward and R. Jenkins (eds), *Ethnic Communities in Business: Strategies for Economic Survival* (Cambridge: Cambridge University Press).

Werbner, P. (1990a) 'Renewing an industrial past: British Pakistani entrepreneurship in Manchester', *Migration*, vol. 8, pp. 17–41.

Werbner, P. (1990b) *The Migration Process: Capital, Gifts and Offerings among British Pakistanis* (New York: Berg).

Wertheimer, J. (1987) *Unwelcome Strangers: East European Jews in Imperial Germany* (New York: Oxford University Press).

Wever, E. (1984) *Nieuwe Bedrijven in Nederland* (Assen: Van Gorcum).

Wieczorek, J. (1995) 'Sectoral trends in world employment and the shift toward services', *International Labour Review*, vol. 134, no. 2, pp. 205–26.

Williams, A. (1984) *Southern Europe Transformed* (London: Harper & Row).

Williams, C. (1994) 'Spatial variations in the informal sector: A review of evidence from the European Union', *Regional Studies*, vol. 28, no. 8.

Williamson, O. E. (1985) *The Economic Institutions of Capitalism* (New York: The Free Press).

Wilson, E. (1985) *Adorned in Dreams: Fashion and Modernity* (London: Virago).

Wilson, P. and J. Stanworth (1987) 'The social and economic factors in the development of small black minority firms: Asian and Afro-Caribbean business in Brent, 1982 and 1984 compared', in K. O'Neill, R. Bhambri, T. Faulkner and T. Cannon (eds), *Small Business Development: Some Current Issues* (Aldershot: Avebury).

Wilson, W. J. (1987) *The Truly Disadvantaged: The Inner City, the Underclass, and Public Policy* (Chicago and London: University of Chicago Press).

Woldring, K. (1994) 'The Concrete Ceiling: A Sympathetic View of a Waste of Talent', paper presented to ANZAM '94, Annual Conference, Victory University, Wellington, NZ.

Wong, B. (1987) 'The role of ethnicity in enclave enterprises: A study of the Chinese garment factories in New York City', *Human Organization*, vol. 6, no. 2, pp. 120–30.

Wrigley, J. (1997) 'Immigrant women as childcare providers', in I. Light and R. Isralowitz (eds), *Immigrant Entrepreneurs and Immigration Absorption in the United States and Israel* (Aldershot: Ashgate).

Yücel, A. (1987) 'Turkish migrant workers in the Federal Republic of Germany: A case study', in H. C. Buechler and J. M. Buechler (eds), *Migrants in Europe: The Role of Family, Labor and Politics* (New York: Greenwood Press).

Zhou, M. (1992) *Chinatown: The Socioeconomic Potential of an Urban Enclave* (Philadelphia: Temple University Press).

Zimmer, C. and H. E. Aldrich (1987) 'Resource mobilization through ethnic networks: Kinship and friendship ties of shopkeepers in England', *Sociological Perspectives*, vol. 30, pp. 422–55.

Zolberg, A. R. (1991) 'Bounded state in a global market: The uses of international labor migrations', in P. Bourdieu and J. S. Coleman (eds), *Social Theory for a Changing Society* (Boulder, CO: Westview).

Index